THE DEVIL
IN BOOTLE

Published by The Bluecoat Press, Liverpool
Book design by March Graphic Design, Liverpool

ISBN 9781904438892

THE BLUECOAT PRESS
3 Brick Street
Liverpool L1 0BL

Telephone 0151 707 2390
Website www.bluecoatpress.co.uk

Cover picture, Teresa Higginson, aged 56.
Wearing mantilla and dressed for audience with Pope Leo XIII, in 1900.

ACKNOWLEDGMENTS

I owe, I feel, a primal debt to the late Mrs Margaret Farmer, who, then resident in the Lance Lane Convent, Wavertree, back in 1941, first brought the name and life of Teresa Higginson on to the horizon of my consciousness, and to the late Sister Albania, of the Covent of Notre Dame, Mount Pleasant, Liverpool, who, all those years ago, fostered my interest in the Cause.

To the dedication and hard work of those who have gone before me, signposting the way, Lady Anne Cecil Kerr, the Reverend A.M. O'Sullivan, O.S.B., Brian Honnor, and Bernadette F.G. Hurndall, I have every reason to be, and am, grateful.

I am further deeply indebted to Mrs Gladys Moreton; to Dr Meg Whittle, Archdiocesan Archivist, Liverpool; and to Sister Anne Cunningham, Archivist, at the Convent of the Sisters of Charity of St Paul of the Cross, Selly Park, Birmingham.

Among the illustrious pioneers the name of the late Miss Isabella Arkwright, of Aughton, shines forth incomparably lustrous. The notes and records that she left behind have been of immense value. And the Reverend Father Michael Hutchings, who has performed the mammoth task of setting Teresa Higginson's letters and papers in apple-pie order, and arranging for their conservation, safely embowered in the British Library, has been unstintingly helpful to me. I am extremely grateful to them both.

Stephanie Bilton provided positively heroic assistance in geaneaological and every other imaginable area of research. I cannot thank her sufficiently. And Nicholas Connell was a wonderfully reliable and admirably consistent producer of significant esoterica.

To my wife, Molly Whittington-Egan, I am, as always, indebted, not only for many sound criticisms and suggestions, but also for metaphysical discussions, which imported light to darkish places.

Richard Whittington-Egan

THE DEVIL
IN BOOTLE

THE LIFE AND AFTERLIFE OF
TERESA HIGGINSON

RICHARD WHITTINGTON-EGAN

THE BLUECOAT PRESS

CONTENTS

LIST OF ILLUSTRATIONS … … … … … … … … … … … … … … … 6

PREFACE … 8

PROLOGEMENA. A SMALL HOUSE IN ARIEL STREET … … 10

AD LECTOREM … … … … … … … … … … … … … … … … … 16

1. NATIVITY … … … … … … … … … … … … … … … … … … … 17

2. TEACHER … … … … … … … … … … … … … … … … … … … 40

3. MAGNIFICAT … … … … … … … … … … … … … … … … … 63

4. DIABOLUS … … … … … … … … … … … … … … … … … … 88

5. CHIMAERA … … … … … … … … … … … … … … … … … 114

6. EXODUS … … … … … … … … … … … … … … … … … … 132

7. BRIDAL … … … … … … … … … … … … … … … … … … 152

8. CONVENTUAL … … … … … … … … … … … … … … … 167

9. INTERREGNUM …   …   …   …   …   …   …   …   …   …   …   …   188

10. OBIT …   …   …   …   …   …   …   …   …   …   …   …   …   …   …   207

11. AFTERLIFE   …   …   …   …   …   …   …   …   …   …   …   …   …   241

12. SCRUTINY   …   …   …   …   …   …   …   …   …   …   …   …   …   257

13. MEMORIÆ   …   …   …   …   …   …   …   …   …   …   …   …   …   284

14. CAUSA …   …   …   …   …   …   …   …   …   …   …   …   …   …   302

15. SUMMARIUM   …   …   …   …   …   …   …   …   …   …   …   …   325

16. DILATA …   …   …   …   …   …   …   …   …   …   …   …   …   …   347

EPILOGEMENA. QUO?   …   …   …   …   …   …   …   …   …   …   …   365

BIBLIOGRAPHY …   …   …   …   …   …   …   …   …   …   …   …   …   368

INDEX   …   …   …   …   …   …   …   …   …   …   …   …   …   …   370

ILLUSTRATIONS

1. Robert Francis Higginson. Teresa's father.
2. Mary Bowness Higginson. Teresa's mother.
3. Convent of Our Lady of Mercy, Nottingham. Where Teresa was at school, 1854-1865.
4. The Chapel of the Convent of Our Lady of Mercy, Nottingham.
5. Interior of the Chapel of the Covent of Our Lady of Mercy, Nottingham.
6. Convent of Our Lady of Mercy, Nottingham. Our Lady's Cloister.
7. Convent of Our Lady of Mercy, Nottingham. Another view of Our Lady's Cloister.
8. Victorian Bootle. Litherland Road and Merton Road, Bootle Village.
9. St Alexander's Church, Bootle. The building to the right is the presbytery. The large building on the left is the school.
10. Father Ignatius Spencer.
11. St Mary's, Wigan.
12. Father Thomas Wells, Teresa's spiritual director at St Mary's, Wigan.
13. Susan Ryland – subsequently Sister Mary St Barbara. Teresa's greatest friend.
14. St Mary's Church, Sabden.
15. St Mary's School, Sabden.
16. Lamb's Lane, Sabden. Teresa lodged in the second house to the left.
17. Teresa used to walk over Pendle Hill, from Sabden to Clitheroe, to hear Mass. She told Miss Elizabeth Arkwright that once she was so severely buffeted by the wind that she felt she could go no further – when she suddenly found herself in the porch of Clitheroe church.
18. Ellen Nicholson on her wedding day, 1892, aged 25.

19. Mrs Helen Lonsdale (*née* Ellen Nicholson), who died in 1940, aged 73.
20. St Alexander's, the interior.
21. Edward Blackburn's trap in which Teresa was driven to Aughton by William Lonsdale.
22. St Alexander's in its heyday.
23. All that remained of St Alexander's after the May, 1941, Blitz.
24. Father Edward Powell. Teresa's spiritual director.
25. Father Alfred Snow. He succeeded Father Powell as Teresa's spiritual director.
26. Winter Scene. Bootle in the 1890s. Linacre Lane and Litherland Road.
27. No.15 Ariel Street, Bootle. Where the Devil came calling.
28. Teresa at the time she was fighting the Devil in Bootle, 1884. Aged 40.
29. Minnie Catterall. Teresa's friend and fellow-teacher. Taken with a group of teachers at Holy Cross School, Liverpool.
30. Father Thomas Smith. He blew hot and cold.
31. Higginson Family Group. Neston. 1884. Sitting: Louisa, Mother, Fanny, Teresa. Front: Minnie Matilda Jones and John Percy Jones.
32. Canon Snow and Jumbo, his Great Dane, outside the church and presbytery of St Mary's, Aughton.
33. St Winefride's Cottage, the School-house, Neston.
34. Louisa Higginson. Headmistress at Neston.
35. St Winefride's Church and presbytery, Neston.
36. The interior of St Winefride's Church, Neston.

37. The Church of St Michael and St John the Evangelist, Clitheroe.

38. No. 53 Lowergate, Clitheroe, where Teresa stayed with Lizzie Dawson.

39. The Room of the Mystical Marriage, at 53, Lowergate, Clitheroe.

40. Louise Lateau, the nineteenth-century Belgian stigmatic.

41. St Catherine's Convent, 4 Lauriston Gardens, Edinburgh. The place of Teresa's long retreat.

42. The Chapel at St Catherine's Convent, Edinburgh.

43. Father (later Canon) J. Constant Mussely.

44. Margaret Murphy. Father Mussely's housekeeper.

45. Kitty Deady. Aged 19.

46. Sister Mary Evangelist. The former Kitty Deady.

47. Margaret Garnett. The invalid in need.

48. Alfred Garnett.

49. William H. Smith, who took the portrait photograph of Teresa in the Mantilla.

50. Mrs Elizabeth Fleck. Teresa's benefactor.

51. The Garnetts' shop, at No.134 Mount Pleasant, Liverpool.

52, 53. Postcard written by Teresa to Alfred Garnett (in the author's posession).

54. The house and school-house at Chudleigh.

55. Teresa taken at Chudleigh in 1904, aged about sixty.

56. The last known photograph of Teresa (fifth from the left, back row) with some of her pupils at Chudleigh. 1904.

57. The room where Teresa died, at Chudleigh. The armchair is believed to have been there in Teresa's time.

58. Teresa's Grave. Pre-1930. No mention on the stone that she is buried there.

59. Close-up of the original inscription at Teresa's burial place. Note that little Freddie Hallifax's name is there.

60. Post-1930 additions to Teresa's grave.

61. Close-up of the newly affixed marble inscriptions on Teresa's grave.

62. Father Bertram Wilberforce, O.P.

63. Father Joseph Damien, the Leper priest.

64. Dom Adalbert M. O'Sullivan, Teresa's first biographer.

65. Anthony and Gladys Moreton, loyal workers in the Cause, tending Teresa's grave.

66. Miss Isabella Arkwright of Ormskirk. The Great Promoter of Teresa's cause for more than forty years.

67. Miss Elizabeth Arkwright, Isabella's sister and Canon Snow's housekeeper at St Mary's Church, Aughton.

68, 69. Louisa and Fanny share a burial place together with John Percy Jones in St Winefride's churchyard, Neston.

70. Canon Snow.

71. Miss Minnie Catterall in the time of her maturity.

72. Onkerzele. The chapel at the site of the Marian vision of 1933.

73. Monsignor John O'Brien, Vice-Postulator of the Cause of Teresa Higginson.

74. Margaret Murphy getting on in years.

75. Sister Albania of Mount Pleasant Training College, Liverpool.

PREFACE

Sixty-seven years ago, myself when young trod repeatedly the rain-washed cobbles, gleaming yellow in the reflected gaslight, of a scatter of remote Lancashire townships, delivering in Victorian church halls and the empty evening class rooms of Roman Catholic Elementary Schools, a painstakingly constructed lecture upon one whom many of the audience – and that to include the parish priest who invariably took the chair – had come to regard as a modern saint-in-the-making, Teresa Higginson.

The cause of her beatification and ultimate canonisation had been submitted to Rome in 1936. Two years later, the verdict of the College of Rites had been pronounced – *"Non expedire"*. Many were disappointed, but this was a postponement rather than a rejection. It left the doors of the Temple open, ajar.

The years have passed over our greying heads. No further echoes have, as yet, disturbed the silence that shrouds Teresa Higginson's modest tomb in the little country churchyard of St Winefride's, at Neston, on the Wirral peninsular. Many of those who listened so eagerly to what small tidings I brought to them have long ago left their pews for ever. Which thought reminds me of how, on one occasion, before being lead to the platform where I was to speak, I was taken to a nearby chamber to meet the priest who should have been my host. His name, a good old Lancashire one, was Father Catterall. Fully vestmented, he was lying in his coffin. He had been run over and killed. It was a shock. I remember to this day observing how his front teeth, obviously gritted in the agony of his end, had crumbled, all powdery along their edges.

The devotion to, the belief in, Teresa Higginson has never died. God's good time ticks on. Labourers still toil in the vineyard.

For me, time has wheeled its full circle. I have lived most of my life barely remembering Teresa Higginson and all those long-ago nights of my youth spent in publicly remembering hers. But now, as the twilight gathers, so has the memory of her come, suddenly and unbidden, back to me, fresh and vivid, and it was then that I realised that I would like to leave on record facts and fancies that weave about the enigma of her being.

PROLOGEMENA

A SMALL HOUSE IN ARIEL STREET

It was a wee, timorous household and the only one of the delicate young ladies who dwelt there who was unafraid was the one about whom the uncanny occurrences seemed to centre.

It is the autumn of the year 1883, and a small house in Ariel Street – Number 15 – a modest, two-up, two-down, brick-built, working-class dwelling, in a respectable working-class street in Bootle, had never known anything like the eruption which followed upon the heels of the entrance of a new young woman lodger into the household: a series of exceedingly strange events which, to many, remain to this day explicable only as the work of the Devil.

Bootle, a name whose comedic potentialities have been exploited, along with those of Wigan Pier, by generations of music-hall comedians, is in fact the geographic label of a 2,400-acre township stretching beyond the north-western edge of the adjoining city of Liverpool, and it is an unexpected terrain for the harbouring of such mysteries.

There have been, upon the settlement time-scale, two Bootles. The Bootle of the first half of the nineteenth century, which was "a species of watering-place", similar to New Brighton, over the water, on the opposite side of the river Mersey, where "tree-embowered cottages fringed the foreshore, dotted with a regiment of bathing-machines. The spot was visible from afar, thanks to the presence of two tall obelisks long since erected as landmarks." But the cottages, bathing-machines, and obelisks did not long survive the succession of Liverpool's gruff, Yorkshire-born Dock Engineer, Jesse Hartley, by George Lyster, and the acquirement of rights over the Bootle foreshore by the Mersey Docks and Harbour Board. By the 1880s, the first Bootle, where Gladstone had seen clambers of wild roses in the village centre, had vanished for ever, to be succeeded by the second Bootle, a kaleidoscopic progression of, briefly, rural retreat and merchant suburb, followed by the sweeping in of an irreversible tide of practical commercialism – docks, small factories and manufactuaries, and the inevitable attendant spread of artisan and near-slum properties.

"On Sunday night, the 19th August [1883]," wrote one of Bootle's residents, Miss Kate Catterall, a young schoolteacher who, along with her sister, Minnie, and a Miss Elizabeth Roberts, both of whom were also schoolteachers, rented rooms at No. 15 Ariel Street, "I noticed a knocking which seemed to come from the next house, but, remembering that no one was living there at the time, I thought it must be someone knocking at one of the houses near and took no more notice of it. Presently, the window opposite the bed was shaken, but not loudly, a noise was made on the landing, and rustling through our room, past the wall, and up to the second window, which was shaken so violently that I felt it would either fall out or be shaken to pieces: this seemed very singular to us as the night was as calm as it could be and there was no wind.

The following night I heard no sound of anything unusual, but Miss Roberts turned round towards me and asked me what I was laughing at. I was surprised at her asking me, as I had neither laughed myself, nor yet heard anyone else do it.

On Tuesday night, the 21st inst., shortly after eleven o'clock, I heard a terrible noise against the wall of Miss Higginson's room, nearest the landing, which sounded like a loud clap of thunder and seemed as if it would shake the wall down; then a loud knocking, as of furniture being broken to pieces on the floor

11

in one corner of her room. We were all three so terrified that I called out loudly for Miss Higginson, and after a short time she came to us looking deeply troubled. She told us not to be frightened, that it was the Devil who had terrified us, that he had told her he would let us know that he was there, but she did not think we should have heard him. We tried to persuade her to remain with us for the rest of the night, but could not succeed. I do not remember hearing any more noise during the night.

The next night (Wednesday),whilst kneeling saying my night prayers, I distinctly heard blows given with great force striking Miss Higginson, first on one side of the face and then on the other. I stood up and listened for a few seconds, when her head was knocked several times on the floor of her room. I thought it would be almost broken from the force of the knocks. Then most terrible and piercing screams and sounds of someone being dragged across the room towards the door, and struggling and pushing at it as if to get out, the screams continuing all the time, and ending with a fiendish yell. Then everything seemed quiet and settled.

One night, whilst staying in the house with Miss Higginson, I heard knocks given continually, but could not find anything or give any account of what caused it, or who did it. Just after getting into bed, I was quite frightened with one knock I heard, but did not speak for a bit until I saw Miss H. looking at me, and I asked her if she had heard it. She said yes, but told me not to mind anything, but to get to sleep soon. I heard nothing more after that. The night I heard these knocks was, I believe, the 2nd July, '83."

Kate's sister, Minnie, wrote: "On Sunday night, August 19th, after I had been in bed a few minutes, I heard a noise on the landing as if someone was shaking Miss Higginson's bedroom door very determinedly, then there was a slight rustling noise past the bed in our room, and both the windows shook very violently. I thought it very strange as the night was so calm.

Shortly after eleven o'clock on Tuesday night, August 21st, I was greatly alarmed by one knock at Miss Higginson's room door, then a confused noise almost like thunder. It seemed as if someone was kicking the door and flinging furniture about in her room. It was so terrible, and we were all so afraid, that my sister called at once for Miss Higginson, who came to us in a few minutes and told us not to be afraid, that it was the Devil who came to torment her. She tried to assure us that he could not harm us, that he was only frightening us in order to torment her the more, and to let us know he was there. But in spite of all she said, I was so frightened when I thought of the noise I had heard that I could not sleep at all during the night.

The next night, August 23rd, I was more terrified than ever. We had not been more than a few minutes in bed when I heard a noise in Miss Higginson's room as if someone gave her five heavy blows on the side of her head, then as if she was taken and banged violently against the room floor three or four times. Two or three minutes afterwards, I heard a terrible noise at her door, as if someone was kicking it and at the same time screeching and yelling most frightfully. This frightened me most of all. It seemed altogether so unearthly and so unnatural. I was again unable to sleep that night.

On Monday, August 20th, before I got to sleep, I noticed all at once an awful bad smell which seemed to come from the door. It was very disagreeable for a few minutes.

Again, on Wednesday night as I was passing through the kitchen, I noticed something like sulphur, it seemed to get in my throat and made me cough. I could not account for it in any way."

The third young teacher, Miss Elizabeth Roberts, wrote: "Sunday night, August 19th, '83. I was falling asleep when a loud shaking of the window near my bed awakened me. The night was calm.

August 20th. On Monday night I heard a laugh which seemed to be in the room. I thought it came from Miss Catterall, found no one in the room had laughed, and only Miss Flynn and myself had heard it.

August 21st. I heard loud knocking and shaking of furniture in Miss Higginson's room. The noise was so violent that it frightened us very much. We called Miss Higginson, who, in a short time, came to us. She told us not to fear as it was only the Devil who had tried to terrify us.

August 22nd. After being in bed for a short time I was disturbed by a loud noise, as of someone being slapped on the face. (The noise came from Miss Higginson's room). Then followed loud knocks, as if someone was being shaken and banged about the room; then Miss Higginson's door was shaken very violently and terrible unearthly screams were heard. The noises, and especially the screams, terrified us so much that we did not sleep at all during that night.:

Finally, Miss Joanna Flynn, the landlady of the Ariel Street lodgings, testified: "When sleeping with Miss Higginson one night during the last mid-summer holiday, I had just been talking with her and she had said goodnight, when I felt myself raised up from the bed and almost suffocated. As soon as I could, I called for Miss Higginson, and she asked me if I felt ill. I said 'Yes'. She told me to make the sign of the cross and say a 'Hail Mary', and I should be all right. I did so and fell asleep.

On the night of the 20th of August, I heard distinctly a scornful laugh which seemed to come from the door of the room in which I was at the time.

The next night [August 21st] I was disturbed in my sleep by a noise as of knocking, which awakened me, and then I heard someone call out. I was confused, and when my own name was called and someone knocked at my bedroom door, I thought something must be the matter. When I opened the door and saw

14

Miss Higginson standing and heard the other young ladies up, I was really frightened. She asked me if I was afraid and said the others wanted me to go into their room and stay with them they were so frightened.

The night after [August 22nd] there was a noise as of somebody being struck on the head and face, and soon a noise as if some person was talking, then loud screeching and yelling. We were all very much frightened, although we knew what it was."

It was scarcely to be expected that the alleged visitations of Lucifer himself would go unremarked in so normally mundane a world as that of nineteenth-century Bootle. And, indeed, they did not. The figure of the pale, retiring, shabbily-dressed, 38-year-old little teacher in the Roman Catholic Elementary School of St Alexander's, about whom the phenomena were said to be concentrated, was looked at askance. Local opinions regarding her rapidly polarised. There were those – a minority, but one which included in its ranks the parish priest – who regarded her as a woman of saintish sanctity: there were others who cried fraud, humbug, pretender, in her wake, as she toiled down the street bearing a wooden pail of soup in either hand for the nourishment of the poor and sick.

Her name was Teresa Higginson. Where did she come from? What manner of woman was she? In which direction did the path of her life wind? And where and how did it end? These are, among many more, questions which this book sets out to answer.

AD LECTOREM

This is the curious story of a very strange woman. Saint, fraud, self-deceiver, impostor, religious maniac, or insane? That is the question to be decided. To those who are not members of the Roman Catholic Faith and have no acquaintance with religious mysticism, there are passages in this book which will necessarily seem both incredible and offensive, unwholesome even. Much that to those who subscribe to little or no religious inclination makes nonsense takes on a different aspect if you are one of those who happens to think that Jesus was truly the son of God, for them, all things including miracles, become possible. The visions, the battles with the Devil, the reception of the stigmata, are no longer essentially subjectively hallucinatory, and none of these things are beyond the power of God to bring about today as surely as in ages past. Accept the existence of God, and everything is possible. But it *does* call for a heroic reorientation of one's mode of thinking. Each reader must give to it his or her own *nihil obstat*.

1

NATIVITY

It was at a ball at the Viceregal Lodge in the Dublin of the 1840s that Robert Higginson met the young woman whom he was to marry. Tall, slim, dignified, her name was Mary Bowness. They were both English. Robert Francis Higginson was a Lancashire man. He had been born in Preston, on August 12th, 1816. The blood of the old Catholic martyrs flowed through his veins. A man of high ideals, he came to play a zealous part in the Catholic revival of his time. He had crossed the Irish Sea to employment as Lord Dillon's agent at his estate at Loughglynn House, Roscommon.

Mary Bowness was also from Lancashire, having been born at Ulverston, although her family are said to have hailed from the Westmorland town on the eastern side of Lake Windermere whose name they bore. The exact year of her birth is fudged, but it is known to have been *circa* 1817, making her at least one year older than Robert. A cradle Catholic, Robert had been educated at the great Jesuit school, Stonyhurst. Mary was a zealous convert to Catholicism. She had been brought up a strict, old-fashioned Protestant in the bosom of a papist-hating family. Indeed, Jesuits were her father's particular *prêtres noirs*. He had, however, raised no objection, foreseen no danger, when his daughter proposed to travel on the Continent in company with some cousins.

When they came to Rome, she was enchanted by the beauties of the Holy City, its ancient churches and baldacchino'd basilicas. Exploring one day an especially magnificent church – most probably the *Gesù*, or *Santissima Nome di Gesù*, the main

17

1. Robert Francis Higginson. Teresa's father.

church of the Jesuit Order in Rome – she and her companion fell in with a kindly English priest, who seemed only too delighted to appoint himself guide to the two English ladies, showing them around, indicating with pride the treasures there preserved, and explaining to them the meanings and significances of things with which they were not familiar. Thoroughly charmed by their guide, impressed by his sagacity, and profoundly interested in all he had to tell them, they invited him to call upon them at their hotel. He did so, and that was when Mary confided to him her intense dislike of the Jesuits, and he, to her mortal embarrassment, quietly, and with some amusement, confessed that he himself was one. His tact and the persuasiveness of his theological argumentation having,

2. Mary Bowness Higginson. Teresa's mother.

however, successfully smothered her prejudices and won her over, she asked to be instructed in the Faith, and, proving a sincere and apt candidate for conversion, she was in due course received into the Latin Church.

When she made her confession to her father of her embrasure of Roman Catholicism, his anger at what he regarded as her religious treachery knew no bounds. In true Moulton Barrett mode, he turned her out of house and home, coldly informing her that he would rather see her dead at his feet than a Catholic.

And that is how she came to be, unabsolved, in Ireland, taking shelter with friends in Dublin, and it was in their company that she had gone to the Viceregal Lodge ball, where it was

19

ordained that she should meet her destiny. That destiny was consummated in matrimony on October 4th, 1841, at Roscommon.

The first offspring of the union was a daughter, born in 1842, in Ireland, who did not survive, but the couple welcomed the arrival of a second daughter, Mary Ann, also born in Ireland, in 1843. Their third child was again a daughter. By the time of her birth, the family had returned to England, and settled at Trent Port, Beckingham, a location beside the river Trent, close to the Nottinghamshire border, and some two or three miles west of Gainsborough, in Lincolnshire, the town, incidentally, about which, disguised as St Ogg, George Eliot would, in 1860, write, in *The Mill on the Floss*.

As the time of her confinement neared, Mary Higginson had not seemed too well, so, for the sake of her health, she made the cross-country trek to the holy and healing shrine of St Winifred, at Holywell, in North Wales – celebrated site of the legendary antics of the spoiled priest, Frederick William Serafino Austin Lewis Mary Rolfe, also known as Baron Corvo, and his joustings with Father Sidney de Vere Beauclerk, S.J. [*The Quest for Corvo*. A.J.A. Symons, Cassell, London, 1934.] – and it was there that, on Monday, May 27th, 1844, a leap-year, Teresa Ellen, that little flower of staunch Catholic stock, piously named after the great mystic, St Teresa of Avila, and her paternal grandmother, Ellen Tilberry, entered upon her earthly pilgrimage. Teresa's second baptismal name was, at some future undisclosed date, changed to Helena, which was that of the saint who is believed to have searched for, and discovered, the true cross of Christ, and who was the mother of the Roman emperor, Constantine.

Because of the fact that Catholic priests were at that period pretty thin on the ground and rather widely dispersed, it was not until the following June 22nd, that Teresa was baptised by a Father O'Carroll, at the church of St Winifred's Holywell, and even as late as 1848, when Teresa's brother, Robert Francis, was born, nearly two months elapsed before a priest came to officiate at his baptism. Things improved later, and the last three Higginson children – William Bowness (1849), Clara Elizabeth (1850), and John Edward (1851), were all baptised by Father J.B. Naughton, who appears to have been appointed about this time as the good Roman shepherd of the Catholic flock of the district. Louisa Agnes, the Higginsons' fourth surviving daughter, was born at Stone, in Staffordshire, in 1847.

Robert Higginson had now gone into profitable business as a wharfinger, the curiously obsolescent sounding title for one who is the owner or keeper of a wharf. Such a vocation made very sound business sense at that time, when a great deal of the country's traffic of commerce was being conveyed along the canals, and guaranteed an income that would yield a very agreeable standard of family living. He developed also an ancillary line as an agent for lime.

The Higginsons prospered. Their house provided comfort and space. And, since the recency of the Catholic Emancipation Act of 1829 meant that places of public worship for Catholics were still few and far between, it also provided a Catholic centre for the neighbourhood, boasting a small oratory, where Mass was celebrated, approximately, fortnightly. Many priests stayed with the Higginsons, and regular visitors included the Right Reverend Dr Richard Roskell, the Vicar Apostolic of the Northern District,[1] and such well-known priests as the Venerable Dominic Barberi, the celebrated Passionist (1792-1849), who brought Henry Newman into the Roman Church, and who baptised Teresa's sister, Louisa, and loved to carry little Teresa in his arms.

Father Ignatius Spencer,[2] another Passionist, who christened Teresa his "Little Apostle", in acknowledgement of her enthusiastic attempts to spread his league for the conversion of England back to the Old Faith; and Father Faber, poet and priest.[3] He it was, hazards Cecil Kerr[4] who said of Teresa that she would be "either a great saint or a great sinner." [*Teresa Helena Higginson: Servant of God, "The Spouse of the Crucified", 1844-1905.* Cecil Kerr. Sands, London, 1927, pp.17-18.]

This remark by the priest had made, Teresa later wrote in a letter to her spiritual adviser, Father Powell, (*vide infra*) "a great impression on me, though he did not think I had heard it, yet it sank deep down in my soul, for that night when we received our parents' blessing, when Papa put his hand on my head, he sighed and it went through me. Then, that same night, when Mama came to look at us last thing, she knelt down by my crib and cried, and when she kissed me the warm tears fell upon my face, and I was too much ashamed to open my eyes and felt unworthy of so good a mother. I mention this fact for it has never been forgotten, and I think our dear Lord had a great deal to do with it, though I did not then understand the meaning of it all, but I did beg of the dear little infant Jesus to help me to be more like Him, and never to let me do anything that would make my dear parents cry, for I loved them so tenderly. I don't know how old I would be then, but I must have been very young."

The sole records that survive of Teresa Higginson's early years are two accounts written by her in obedience to instructions from the priests who directed her spiritual life, Father Edward Powell and Father Alfred Snow. The tale she had to tell was of a very religiously perfect Catholic home. Albeit, the life that the children led there was somewhat over-sheltered, for they were not allowed to play with, or even get to know, other children, until they met them at the convent school of the Sisters of Mercy, in Nottingham, to which they were subsequently despatched. Their early education was entrusted to the hands of carefully-selected nursery governesses, in particular Miss Gosforth and Miss Featherstone, but in all matters relating to the respect for, and love of, God, they were taught and supervised

3. Convent of Our Lady of Mercy, Nottingham. Where
Teresa was at school, 1854-1865.

by their devout parents, who also familiarised them with the feasts and seasons of the Church, and made sure that they punctiliously observed them.

The young Higginsons were taught the virtue of charity by example: the first helping from the dinner dish was each day set aside to be given to the next beggar who knocked at the door seeking alms. If no beggar came, the dish was carried to the kitchen to be kept warm; and if by bedtime none had come, the parents would say, "We have had no visit from Our Lord today." Often, later in life, Teresa would recall, with wry smile, how in the course of one of these charitable dish-carrying excursions, from dining-room to kitchen and back-door, she had taken a tumble and scattered the food all over the floor.

4. The Chapel of the Convent of
Our Lady of Mercy, Nottingham.

Teresa remembered that one of the lessons that her mother had early instilled into them was what she called the practise of the presence of God. She would bid them to picture Our Lord as standing by their side, and, in her last illness, Teresa confided to a priest the comfort that this had brought to her throughout the whole course of her life. "I had only to put out my hand to find it ever in His." This statement surely gives us some idea of the strength and disciplined imaginative power which animated and sustained her throughout a life which would seem to most of us to have been a long Purgatory, punctuated by glimpses of Hell. It may also go towards some explanation of the visions which she is said to have seen so constantly.

Even as a small child, Teresa had been exceptionally strong-

*5. Interior of the Chapel of the Covent
of Our Lady of Mercy, Nottingham.*

willed. She exercised a great power over all those with whom she came into contact, and a dominance over her brothers and sisters, being always the leader, the one who decided which games they would play. She herself confessed: "I was very headstrong and almost always contrived to get my own way. I had such control over all in the house, and even strangers, that dear Papa and Mama say I led them whichever way I pleased, in spite of themselves, and this self-will grew as I grew. I used to weigh a thing well in my own mind, and, if I thought it should be, I would not rest until I had achieved my point. I used to propose it, and if I thought there was opposition, for a little I might argue it over, but dear Papa often said as long as I argued there was some chance, but when I became silent I had made up

6. Convent of Our Lady of Mercy, Nottingham.
Our Lady's Cloister.

my mind, cost me what it would, I would do it (through God) and invariably I got what I wanted."

This admitted quality of determination to have her way, to bend others to her will, is interesting, to say the least, in the context of her later conduct. The notion of her as a constitutionally shy, shrinking, little creature, too nervous to stand up for herself, is misleading. Her apparently deliberate fading away into the background, seems to have been the consequence of conscious and intentional self-obliteration, rather than of natural self-conscious reserve. Equally, it may have been the mortification of self by the suppression of the desire to dominate.

According to Teresa's own belief, the time when she arrived at the use of reason was on November 21st, 1848, the feast of the

7. Convent of Our Lady of Mercy, Nottingham.
Another view of Our Lady's Cloister.

Presentation of Our Lady in the Temple. "A strange feeling began to work within me … and I thought that I, too, must give myself to God as Mary did; and yet a strange feeling of dread was over me, and I dare not. A real struggle was going on in my soul. … I stole into the oratory, and, bowing myself down to the ground, I offered myself to God to be all His for ever. Then I realised God for the first time." She was just four years old.

Teresa goes on to tell of what to us may seem to have been, at that age, a mere whimsical act of childish disobedience, but what she regards as having been her first 'sin'. Father Snow, for so many years her spiritual director, used to say that, in his opinion, this was the only true matter she could ever have had for confession, and it would almost seem as though Almighty

God had allowed this fall in order that she should realise to the full the horror and malice of sin, and the anguish of repentance.

One day we had all been out for a walk as usual, and when we returned I stayed behind a little till the rest had gone upstairs and, instead of hanging up my hat, I was going upstairs dragging it after me ... and dear Mama saw me and called to me, and I pretended not to hear her, but went on humming to myself and trusting she would call me again. But she did not. And I did not go to see what she wanted, or tell her how naughty I was, and say that I was sorry; for I really was grieved the moment after it happened. The next minute I was called into the nursery, but I could not do anything; I was so ashamed of myself, and so sorry, that I could not learn my lesson, play, or take my tea, and they all thought I was sick, and everyone's kindness made me worse and worse. I really felt they would cry if they knew how wicked I was, and I longed to tell them and beg pardon, and yet I felt they would be so hurt with me, and when they nursed and kissed me I felt as though my heart would break, not so much because I had offended my dear Jesus, as it was for the wrong I had done so good a mother, and I felt I was so ungrateful to her ... I was put to bed and of course I could not rest; so, after a while, I crept out of my bed and came partly down the stairs. And there I sat crying to myself till someone saw me and told Mama, and I was carried into the room where they [Father H. Smith, of Sheffield, and her parents] were playing whist. I said I wanted to tell Father Smith something, and he took me on his knee, and when supper was ready he said he would stop a few minutes to see what I had to say, and there and then I made my First Confession. Though I did not get absolution from Father Smith, yet I felt so happy again, and he took me down with him and told my dear parents; and Father Smith, Papa, and Mama all cried. I cried, too, but now they were tears of joy for me, and I promised I would not be such a naughty girl again.

A storm in a stoup. It seems as though, even at that tender age, the little girl was becoming beset by scruples of the kind that torment the hypersensitive consciences of blameless nuns. In an atmosphere highly charged with Roman Catholic Christianity, wherein the most venial incidents can assume the aspect of gigantically disproportional acts of guilt, the self-accusing may, by a kind of Pavlovian conditioned reflex, shoulder a totally unjustified burden of guilt. Thus, for little Teresa, her minor infringement was, as witness this letter to her confessor and spiritual director, Father Powell, an exceedingly serious matter.

I felt that I had been the cause of all that our Blessed Lord suffered, and I tried each day to hurt myself in some way. I have cut my fingers and scalded and burnt myself as if by accident, trusting that, in union with His bitter torments, these little things would be acceptable in His sight. I often used to put my finger ends in between the door when it was about to be shut, and try to get my feet trodden on. I would entangle my hair purposely, so that when it was combed it would hurt my head.

This kind of self-mutilant mortification was in fact practised by many of those who became canonised saints of the Roman Church. There is, of course, a long tradition in religious thought of expiatory pain-causing behaviour – the scourge, the hair-shirt, and other inventive variations – arising clearly out of pious thinking, the desire to share in the Passion and agony of Christ, and offer the suffering to Almighty God.

There is no problem in differentiating the religious

mortification from the self-mutilation of the mentally ill. In the old days, and occasionally now when there has been no effective treatment, the most bizarre attacks on any region of the body were to be seen. The motivation for such attacks derives from disordered thinking, with delusions and hallucinations. Schizophrenia has usually proved to be the underlying illness, but manic depression can be the causal factor. Even severe neurotic depression is capable of triggering the hurting of significant parts of the body. In cases of personality disorder, often with hysterical attention-seeking features, "cutting-up" seems to give some relief to disturbed individuals.

It was also when she was four, that, Teresa asserted, God had revealed to her the mystery of the Blessed Trinity – "Not anything distinctly about it," she says, "but prostrating myself to the ground, I felt an overwhelming power and majesty, and when I was able to speak, I said over and over again: ' Blessed be the most holy and undivided Trinity, now and forever more. Amen.' She elaborated in a later letter to Father Snow: "I seemed to see and know the great Mystery of the Blessed Trinity and how Mary was the Tabernacle of the thrice Holy Trinity. I then really bowed in adoration and saw how the soul is made after their Image and Likeness. It seemed to me that God was in my soul in a mysterious manner, yet I knew Him and loved Him and gave myself to Him ... and though I did not understand all the offering I made, yet I daily renewed it."

Teresa was eight, although in her autobiographical fragment, written at the diktat of her spiritual director, she says that she was five years old when her young brother died. This must be a mistaken dating, for it would mean that the death took place in 1849. There was no recorded death in the Higginson family at that time. It was in 1852 when a terrible tragedy hit her family and her brother, John Edward, who had been born only the previous year, died, and, for all their sturdy belief in the afterlife and the child's happy transition to Heaven, those he left behind mourned his loss greatly, and this, her first brush with death, made a profound impression on Teresa. She later wrote: "I think someone must have said something about what a soul must feel when it has to be separated from Almighty God, when we feel so deeply the death of a person we love; but I don't remember who said it, only that ever after I used to beg our dear Lord never to let me be sent away from Him for one moment."

In 1854, Teresa was to experience personal loneliness of a more mundane kind. That was the year that the Bishop, Dr Roskell, made an episcopal visitation to Gainsborough to attend at a Confirmation service. Very likely he spent the night as a guest at the Higginsons'; he certainly heard the children's prayers and catechism there. Miss Featherstone had been obliged to leave in order to look after her aunt, who was sick, and Dr Roskell advised Robert and Mary to send Teresa and her sisters, Mary and Louisa, to the school conducted by the Sisters of Mercy at their convent in Derby Road, Nottingham, where Teresa was to remain, sporadically, for eleven years.

They arrived there on March 3rd, 1854, and, as it was a Friday in Lent, the Stations of the Cross was being celebrated in the chapel. Neither Teresa nor her sister had ever before been to this service, which represented, with appropriate meditation and prayers, each of the fourteen stations, or stages, of Christ's *via dolorosa* from Pilate's praetorium to Calvary, carrying His cross. The services of Benediction and early morning Mass were also new to them.

The convent, the work of Pugin, was an architecturally splendid building. It had an inspiringly beautiful chapel, and a wide cloister overlooked a quiet and sheltered garden, where, singing hymns, the children would walk in solemn procession.

At times during those first schooldays as a boarder, Teresa suffered from severe bouts of home-sickness, but after one of the

31

nuns told her that when she was three years old the Virgin Mary was taken to the Temple, and that she had never cried for her mother or pined to go home again, Teresa began to settle and to love the convent. But tragedy was again lurking in the wings.

Three months had passed. Now it was June, and everything at the convent was being made ready for the approaching feast of Corpus Christi. It was the custom to decorate the cloisters, and every place through which the procession bearing the Blessed Sacrament would pass, with archways wound about with fresh greenery, lilac, and laburnum. Teresa, always agile and inclined to tomboyishness, had climbed up a tree in order to bend the branches for Sister to break off suitable sprays of decorative greenery, when she suddenly fell crashing to the ground. Sister was much alarmed, but calmed down as Teresa, who thought that the good Lord had permitted the accident that she might have "some little thing to offer Him", persisted in her smiling assurances that she was unscathed. But ... "The pain went on increasing till at last I could not get out of bed, and the doctor was sent for, and he was very angry and said he should have been sent for before; that inflammation of a very serious kind had been doing its work for some days, and he was afraid he had no chance to do anything effectively; it was too late, and they must telegraph home at once."

Teresa was ill in bed at the convent for six or seven weeks. She felt, she said, quite disappointed when at last she got better. The doctor, however, pronounced her to be in decline, and she was sent home to convalesce. Her lungs were supposed to have been affected.

She had, as a matter of fact, had a previous fall – at home – the sequence of which she recounts in her own words:

A few weeks before I went to the convent I threw myself down into a sawpit, which hurt me severely, and through this fall, when I got to the convent, I had inflammation in my left side … (They were enlarging the house and a number of men were busy there and they had to saw up a quantity of wood, so they made this pit.) I did not say anything about it and my sisters dare not, until the doctor said I had been severely bruised. I was questioned and I said I did fall down in the pit, but I had done it purposely. I thought about the dreadful agony our Blessed Lord must have felt when His Cross was fixed on Mount Calvary and I longed for a chance to feel that dread shake and I thought I could then easily stumble as if by accident, and so I did.

Teresa did not remember exactly how long it was after her second fall – that from the tree – that she remained at home, but she believed that it was a full year. As she grew stronger, she begged and begged to be allowed to return to the convent, and when, eventually, she did, it was decided that she should not have regular lessons and should be out in the open air as much as possible. Reverend Mother, Sister Mary Aloysius Perry, who had had one of her legs amputated, also had to be out in the garden, so she and Teresa spent many hours in each other's company. Reverend Mother was very holy, and everyone looked upon her as a saint. She was a great comfort and companion to the eleven-year-old Teresa.

Seeing her suffer so patiently, I began to have a very great thirst for suffering and felt it so sweet, and I begged of our dear Lord never to leave me without it, and ever to give me more and more. I think the reason dear Rev. Mother liked me to be with her was because I hurt her most, for I used to jump into her chair and sit down at the side without the leg to thread daisies, and jump in and out. I never was still, and then I used to say I was our Blessed Lord, crowning her for

33

being so good and suffering so much, and she would caress me, I think now, because I caused her greater pain when I stood up, perhaps kicking or knocking against the stump, for she used to smile so sweetly and often kiss her crucifix and let me do the same. ... I think it was at or about this time that I made the resolution of rising in the night for the sorrowful mysteries of the rosary, and half an hour's meditation, and then go back to bed. This was very hard for me, and I was often tempted to give it up ... I did not undertake any regular corporal punishment until I was preparing for my first Holy Communion. Then I began to rise and lay under the bed (after Sister had put out the gas and gone down) till the bell rang at five in the morning for the nuns to rise – then I used to get into bed. Then I managed to get a piece of sacking and I pushed in bits of old knitting needles, little tacks, etc. I used to put it under me on the floor ... I was so often sick and the nuns took such great care of me that they seemed to notice every little scratch or mark, but I had an opportunity one day of getting some red hot cinders from the fire and I only just had time to pick them from the grate when Sister entered. I put them down my breast and they set my things on fire, but when I made the holy sign of the cross on the flames they went quite out, but Sister scolded me very much and told me never to do such a thing again.

Throughout her life, Teresa kept to herself such things as the nature of the physical penances which she privately practised." I thought our dear Lord liked to have secrets and I therefore tried to hide things." Any notion that she boasted of, or revealed her secret mortifications can be totally discounted. The sole reason that we are privy to such things as are revealed in the foregoing quotations is because, in 1888, she was asked by her spiritual director, Father Alfred Snow, to whom she was under a vow of obedience, to write to him a series of letters, in which she was required to provide a full account of her spiritual life and religious activities.

On Easter Sunday, April 12th, 1857, in the beautiful convent chapel, where she had made her first Confession, and where, during her schooldays, she would spend many hours before the Blessed Sacrament, Teresa made her first Communion. A rubric day in the life of any Roman Catholic child, it had, for some unexplained reason, been delayed until the extraordinarily late age of nearly thirteen.

Five weeks after, on May 17th, Reverend Mother, Sister Mary Aloysius, died. "This was a great trial to me," wrote Teresa, "for she had been such a great help and so excessively kind to me, and the dear Mother who succeeded her thought I had been too much made of and tried me in very many ways for my good." Under obedience to their new superior, the friendliness of the other nuns cooled. Teresa became confused and unhappy, and towards the close of the year of her first communion, she experienced a sudden overwhelming indifference, a sort of spiritual drought. Her love of God dried up. A far-ranging darkness fell upon her. She combated these alien feelings by forcing herself to spend longer and longer periods on her knees, determinedly praying.

But these were private anguishes. To all outward appearance, she was a happy, jolly schoolgirl. One of her friends was Fanny Cowlam, who was a couple of years younger. At fifteen, Fanny was a pupil teacher. At the time of the 1861 census, Teresa was staying as a guest with the Cowlam family at their home, The Mill, Toft Lane, West Rasen, in Lincolnshire.

Teresa could never remember which year it was, but clearly recalled that, "Father Faber came round and asked the children their birthdays and as mine was on St Philip's feast he said: 'You should be called Philippa. What is your name?' And when I told him Teresa he said: 'See that you are a Teresa.' And I wondered much what he meant, and I was greatly afraid and thought it a great pity that I had a name of such an extraordinary saint.' Later, she came to recognise its full significance.

It was in 1857, that the Higginson family's fortunes began to decline, along with those of the canals, whose life was being gradually but systematically drained away by the advent of the railways. Robert Higginson found himself obliged to move to Whaley Bridge, actually in Derbyshire, but close to the Cheshire border.

Earnestly seeking to lead a good and charitable life, the young Teresa embraced whatever small opportunities presented themselves to perform self-sacrificing acts of charity. There was, for instance, a child who sat near her in class who hated sewing, and did it very badly. Not only did the child suffer from hot hands, which made sewing difficult, but she was also at the time actually having trouble with one of her hands. The class were making things to give as a present to Reverend Mother on her looming feast day, and this child had done the decorative stitching on the top of a nightdress. The child was delighted, but when Sister saw it she said that it was so badly done that it must all be unpicked and stitched over again. The child dissolved in bitter tears and doggedly began unpicking.

"I thought I would take it and do it for her and give her mine," wrote Teresa, "but we were going to Robin Hood's Cave that afternoon, and I thought, 'No, I won't, it serves her right for not taking more pains,' and though I felt very sorry for her, you see I thought more of myself, though I now had a great chance to overcome myself. Without saying a word to anyone, this struggle went on within me for a while, then I took my name off my work and stitched it on hers, took her work and said I wanted to stop in, so she might let me have her work as an excuse, for Sister wanted it all finished that evening. She, poor girl, was overjoyed and said: 'How can you do it for me when I am always so unkind to you?' Then Mother Mary Walburga came in to see if we were all ready and right for going out, and when she saw me sitting sewing she came up to me and looked at the sewing and said she was ashamed of me, it was disgraceful for a child who had been so long at school to produce such work, and she said I must have tried how badly I could do it, and she scolded me very much and said I was not to go out the whole week for a walk (as penance) nor go to the playground, but stay in and learn to sew. They all went off and I was left by myself, and when they had all gone I began to cry, for I was much disappointed at being deprived of the walk and play, for I was a great romp and loved play. But I looked up at the statue of our dear Blessed Lady and the Holy Child, and I said: 'I unite every stitch with those you took when making the seamless garment, and the little disappointment as an act of atonement for sins against charity committed by children in this school, especially my own self-love.'"

Scruples attended her, even in the midst of her efforts to do good things.

I felt that everything that was not truth was the devil, and I hated everything that bore the appearance of a lie. And when I would take the blame for others, if not actually telling a lie I was acting one, and I was so blinded with self-love, etc., that I did not consider it a lie. ... For instance, I remember once Sister having to speak about something that was very disagreeable, and I felt what pain it must be to her to have to do it, and so sorry for the poor child who had done it. I felt all her confusion, and prayed that she might own it at once, and when she did not, Sister said she was very sorry to have to put the whole school in penance, that she felt obliged to do so. For an instant I struggled with myself, and then I stood up as if I had done it, but I was [so] filled with shame that I reeled over, and when I came to myself I found that the poor child had owned, and Sister said: "How could you stand up and own doing something that someone else had done?" But mind it was not sin that had been committed, I would not say I did not do it, I was trusting that she would think I did. ... when I hardly knew which would be more perfect of two actions I used to try and choose that which appeared to me to be the act of charity to my neighbour, and in this you may see selfishness again, for naturally I took a pleasure in these things, so I always was suspicious of these seeming kindnesses to others, for I doubt not but that in many cases it was greater kindness to myself.

As the time for her Confirmation approached, Teresa did not know which saint's name to take as her patron. Bishop Roskell suggested Agnes. Inevitably, it reminded her of *Agnus dei*, the sacrificial lamb. She had been toying with the names of her favourite saints, St Joseph and St John the Baptist, but she settled for Mary Agnes, and was duly confirmed by the Bishop in the convent chapel.

At the convent, as well as at home, Teresa stood out for her lively, gay, and energetic character. The nuns were amazed at her exuberance, because they expected to find only gentleness and tranquillity in a girl of such obvious piety. The fine, apparently healthy, happy Teresa would have been just coming up to her fifteenth birthday when, in April, 1859, she was suddenly taken seriously ill. She was in bed for nearly nine months and was given up by the doctors. The nuns, too, all thought that she was going to die, and told her their little secrets of what they wished her, when she died, to ask Our Lady to grant them. They slipped the blue ribbon and medal of the order of the Children of Mary on the sick girl's pillow, and pressed the little silver medal to her lips. Immediately, she lost consciousness, and was to remain in that state for several days. As she lay there, already like one dead, she was consecrated a Child of Mary, anointed, and received the last rites of the Church. On the morning of December 3rd, 1859, Bishop Roskell and Father Smith, who were in Rome with Father Powell, each said a Votive Mass to the Virgin Mary, begging her intercession on Teresa's behalf, and, on the octave of the feast of the Immaculate Conception, she came to herself again and began to get better day by day.

The Lord had, it seemed, still work for this Teresa Higginson to do.

NOTES

1 Richard Roskell (1817-1883). Born at Gateacre, Liverpool. Educated at Ushaw and the English College, Rome. After ordination served at St Patrick's, Manchester. In 1853, appointed the second Bishop of Nottingham. Resigned in 1874. Retired as titular Bishop of Abdera to Glascoed, North Wales, and later to the Vale of Whitewell. Died aged 65. Buried in the churchyard of St Hubert's, Dunsop Bridge.

2 The Honourable George Spencer (1799-1864). Born at Admiralty House, London, youngest of the eight children of the second earl Spencer. Educated at Eton and Trinity College, Cambridge. Ordained priest of the Church of England 1824, and became rector of St Mary's, Brington, on the family's Althorp estate in 1825. He was an ancestor of Princess Diana, the Princess of Wales. Received into the Roman Catholic Church in 1830, and went to Rome, to study at the English College for the priesthood. Ordained, 1832. When in Rome met Father Barberi. He returned to England and was appointed to Walsall, Staffordshire, in August, 1832. Following a serious illness in 1838, he began his life's work, his crusade for the conversion of England. In 1846-47, he entered the Passionist noviciate at Aston Hall, near Stone, in Staffordshire, taking the name of Father Ignatius. He became rector of St Anne's Passionist Retreat, at Sutton, St Helens. He died of a heart attack at Monteith House, Carstairs, Lanarkshire, on October 1st, 1864.

3 Frederick William Faber (1814-1863) Born in Calverley vicarage, near Leeds, in Yorkshire. The family moved to Bishop Auckland, where he attended the grammar school. In 1826, sent to Shrewsbury School, and the following year to Harrow School. Matriculated at Oxford and came into residence at Balliol in 1833. Elected scholar of University College, 1834. Ordained Church of England priest, 1839. After Newman was received into the Roman Catholic Church in October, 1845, Faber followed him in the November. In 1849, he became rector of the London Oratory, which, in 1854 moved to the Brompton Road, South Kensington, and died there, aged 49, of Bright's disease.

4 Lady Anne Cecil Kerr. Born: June 30th, 1883. Daughter of Major General Ralph Drury Kerr, son of the 7th Marquess of Lothian, and Lady Anne Fitzalan-Howard, daughter of the 14th Duke of Norfolk. Died: August 9th, 1941.

2

TEACHER

By the time, in 1865, that Teresa, at the age of twenty-one, finally left the convent in Nottingham, her family had moved from Newton-le-Willows, in Lancashire, to St Helens, where her father was now working as a commissioner or forwarding agent. Life seemed to be going smoothly. But the Higginson family prosperity was not destined to last long. Waiting at the garden gate of their Salisbury Street home one evening, as she usually did to welcome him back from the office, Robert's wife saw that her husband, deadly pale, was obviously deeply distressed. Without a word, he walked past her into the house, and began to pace, still silent, up and down the dining-room. Teresa, watching, and unable to think of any reason for such anguish other than sin, ran forward, threw her arms around her father's neck, kissed him, and said, "Oh, Papa, even if you have committed mortal sin, God will forgive you. Only do not lose your trust in Him." But Papa pushed Teresa away. "I am ruined. I have ruined you all," he said brokenly.

What had actually happened was that Mr Higginson had ventured into some speculative dealings in cotton, and, because of the American Civil War, his gamble had gone disastrously wrong, and he had lost everything. He had no alternative but to go bankrupt, and while the family moved into 8 Horne Street, Everton, in Liverpool, and dire poverty, he moved on his own into a boarding-house at 35 Hall Street, St Helens. Although she had always harboured a great dread of riches, and, indeed, actually prayed that her family might be poor, now, seeing her

8. Victorian Bootle. Litherland Road and Merton Road, Bootle Village.

father's misery, realising the familial implications of a dramatic descent into impoverishment, Teresa knew ambivalence. It was at this time that she, a highly skilled needlewoman, tramped from shop to shop around Liverpool asking for work. The Sisters of Charity at the convent in Beacon Lane, Everton, were, in this respect, extremely good to her.

The family's next move was over the water – that is to say, across the river Mersey to the Cheshire side – to Liscard, where they lived at 12 Poole Road, and it was while they were there that Teresa was to teach for a time in 1876, at St Alban's School. Her sister, Louisa, Louey as she was known, three years her junior, having completed her studies at the Pupil Teachers' Centre, at the Convent of the Sisters of Notre Dame, in

*9. St Alexander's Church, Bootle. The building to the
right is the presbytery. The large building
on the left is the school.*

Mount Pleasant, Liverpool, and obtained her teacher's
certificate, had duly embarked upon a her career as a mistress in
a Catholic school at Carmarthen. Frances (Fanny), who was
musical, gave lessons in music.

It was a terrible epidemic of cholera and smallpox in 1871
that first brought Teresa Higginson to Bootle. Father Edward
Powell, rector of St Alexander's Roman Catholic church, St
John's Road there, had come in a state of some distress to see
Sister Mary Philip (Lescher), who had charge of the teachers'
training college at Mount Pleasant. Many of the Bootle schools,
including that attached to St Alexander's, were, he told her,
closed for lack of teachers, and he was worried because his little
parishioners were running wild, becoming utterly impervious to

the good offices of discipline. Could Sister, he wondered, help him? Alas, she had, she said, no qualified, or even experienced, teacher available, but, after a minute's thought, added that there was Miss Teresa Higginson, the sister of one of her students. She happened to know that Miss Higginson, although she had never been a teacher, nevertheless had a wonderful way with children, and she had no hesitation in recommending her. Contact was established, and Teresa, totally unscared by the prospect of possible infection, hoping, in fact, that she might catch it and die, eagerly grasped at the opportunity to be of real service.

The temporary appointment was an enormous success. The children loved Teresa: Teresa loved the children. They succumbed rapidly and unprotestingly to the charm of her personality. A pupil teacher who worked beside her remembered for ever after a game of railways in the schoolroom, with Teresa puffing vigorously up and down playing the part of an engine. Moreover, she proved an absolutely first-rate teacher. Father Powell used to watch with high satisfaction as the benches of the Sunday afternoon catechism class filled with grown-ups alongside the children when she was giving her instruction. Neither was it only her teaching abilities that impressed him. A shrewd observer, he recognised the degree of sanctity to which she had already attained. He allowed her, and this was unusual, to take Holy Communion every day – this was a privilege of tremendous importance to her, for which she was profoundly grateful.

Edward Powell, who came from a well-known Catholic family of corn and provision merchants, was born on September 25th, 1837, in the village of Wavertree, on the rural outskirts of Liverpool. He was educated at St Edward's College, St Domingo Road, Everton, Liverpool. Clearly displaying a vocation for the priesthood, he was taken under Bishop Goss' wing. The Bishop, anxious at that time to have some priests proficient in foreign languages in his diocese, sent the young Powell and one or two others to a college in Bavaria. Here, he soon achieved fluency in German, and the following year, 1857, was sent to the English College in Rome, where he remained until 1861, spending four years studying theology and philosophy, and at the same time learning Italian and French, and winning a gold medal for his performance in a public examination in Hebrew. He was ordained priest at the Basilica of St John Lateran on April 19th, 1862, aged 29. On his return from Rome to Liverpool, in June, 1862, he was appointed secretary to Bishop Goss. Administering to the victims in the cholera-stricken neighbourhood of Eldon Street, hard by Scotland Road, he contracted a peculiarly virulent strain of the fever, and for sixteen days it burned within him. He was fortunate to survive. In 1866, difficulties at the new mission of St Alexander's, in Bootle, calling for the tactful ministrations of a prudent and zealous priest, he was despatched forthwith, and spent the succeeding nineteen years there. A thoroughly good and holy man, a dedicated parish priest, he was well qualified to act as Teresa's spiritual guide. Cecil Kerr recounts that the story is told of how, worried and distressed by the fact that although he had prayed and fasted for the welfare of his parishioners he discerned but small result, he had taken himself off to France to seek the advice of the saintly Curé d'Ars – Jean-Marie Vianney. The Curé listened to his tale of woe, then simply said: "Have you tried blood?" And when, many years later, Father Powell died, he was found to be wearing a hair shirt. However, there is an uneasy feeling as to the likelihood of this being so, for the Curé died in 1859, at which date Father Powell, would have been only twenty-two, and still unordained.

When the smallpox outbreak subsided, Teresa had been teaching at St Alexander's for about a year. The crisis past, Father Powell told her that he felt sure the Almighty was calling her to serve him as a teacher. Obedient as ever, Teresa trotted

10. Father Ignatius Spencer.

along to Mount Pleasant to see Sister Mary Philip, who informed her that she would need to do a year's study before sitting the required examination. However, Father Powell, upon learning that there happened to be such an examination taking place the following week, told Teresa to go and take it. She did so ... and passed successfully.

Her parents were not at all happy at the idea of her becoming a teacher. They were afraid that her rather fractious health would not stand up to the strain. Cecil Kerr relates in her biography (p.47) how, troubled, Teresa, went to St Anne's Retreat, at Sutton, St Helens, to consult Father Ignatius Spencer, the venerable Passionist, "who had been so fond of her in her childhood ... He encouraged her to continue her teaching and told her she had no vocation to be a nun, though she would, later on, live in a convent. He assured her that God had special designs on her, and that she must be very faithful and very open with her confessor, adding that if she were lost her damnation would be awful.

Unfortunately, Cecil Kerr seems to have been misinformed. But the source of her information is by no means clear. Whatever that source may have been is a puzzlement, for the interview between Teresa and Father Ignatius, which Kerr reports in all good faith, could not possibly have taken place, as she asserts, in the 1871-72 period. Father Ignatius Spencer was long dead by the time indicated by Lady Cecil Kerr: he had in fact died in October 1864. What we are looking at here must be a mere a slip of the tongue, mishearing, or *lapsus memoriæ*. Either the given time is wrong, or it may be that it was another priest that delivered the disappointing guidance that was to rule out the conventual life. Obedience, naturally, was her only option.

This is what her friend Susan Ryland has to say. "When Teresa would be, I think, about 25 [i.e. in 1870], Father Lennon was her confessor. She asked him about becoming a religious [a nun] which she wished to be. He sent her to Father Ignatius Spencer, who in better days had been a guest along with Father Dominic (Barberi) at her father's house. (Miss Carr [*sic*] says he did not seem to remember her and perhaps he did not). This is how *she* (Teresa) told me. As soon as she entered the confessional, and before she had time to speak, Father Ignatius had said aloud the *Gloria Patri*, and then said to her, 'Thank God you have come to me.' She told him what she wanted, and he said: 'No, you are not called to religion, you have much to do for your family.' He also said, 'Make no friends, God will send you a friend when it is necessary.'"

What is indisputable, is that any doubts as regards a teaching career which Teresa may have harboured were

11. St Mary's, Wigan.

somehow set at rest, and, in 1872, she arrived as mistress to the village school at Orrell, near Wigan. The requirements of government inspection as to her proficiency in the class-room having been there satisfied, she was duly granted her certificate, or parchment, as the young teachers used to call it, at Christmas, 1872, and, thus stamped with official approval, embarked upon the occupation which she was to follow faithfully until the end of her life.

At the start of term in 1873, she began work as one of the mistresses at the more important St Mary's Infants' School, in Wigan. A fellow-teacher, unnamed by Cecil Kerr, but most likely to have been Margaret Woodward, describes the new arrival.

She appeared about thirty years of age ... She was about five feet two inches in height, her body seemed much emaciated though her face was not too thin. She had what the people here call a wizen face, i.e. shrivelled and sallow. Her hair was dark, eyes also dark, small, very quick and bright, her general expression very pleasing; in conversation she was animated, witty, and humorous. Her movements were quick and sprightly and she seemed always on the alert and entered heart and soul into everything she took in hand. Her dress was often odd. She never cared whether her clothes were in taste or well-fitting, in fact never seemed to have a new costume and as she had literally no regard for money I came to the conclusion that her clothes were simply her sisters' cast off clothing, and that she squandered her salary in buying books and objects of piety for others and in charity, so that she never had the wherewithal to buy a decent outfit. Such was Miss Higginson as I remember her. ... From the first day I met her until we parted I could never find fault with her in any way. She was never cross-looking or out of humour and her pupils idolised her. She seemed to live in the presence of God and always introduced some religious topic into the conversation without boring one with an overdose of piety, or seeming to preach.

There could be no mistaking the new teacher's religious disposition. She fasted rigorously, seeming at times to live on nothing save the Blessed Sacrament, going without normal food for at least three days. She went to daily Mass. Often, she would be so weak that she had to be virtually carried to the altar rails to receive Holy Communion, but once she had taken the Host upon her tongue, her strength seemed immediately renewed, she would walk back to her place in the pew unaided, and would carry out her duties for the rest of the day just like any normal, healthy young woman.

The priest in charge, the rector of St Mary's, was Father Thomas Wells.[5] He was also at this time Teresa's confessor and spiritual director, regularly guiding her in the confessional. In the latter, not always easy, capacity, he would, with Teresa's consent, discuss her case with, and seek the postal advice of, the Reverend James Lennon, D.D., professor of moral theology at St Cuthbert's College, Ushaw, Durham, and would, in consequence of this tutelary correspondence, begin to impose trials and humiliations upon her.

"This," wrote Canon Snow, in his *Notes on the Life of Teresa Higginson*, "is a situation that has often arisen in the lives of the saints and other holy souls, arisen no doubt by the Providence of God for the greater purification of the soul, but one which in itself can hardly be considered consonant with the principles which should guide the confessor in his dealings with the penitent. It invariably happens in such cases that the priest consulted is never satisfied, especially where he has no personal knowledge of the penitent. He is ever in doubt and orders one test after another to be applied, one humiliation and trial after another, until the penitent and director are robbed of all peace. This is precisely what happened in the present case. Father Wells was one of those men, and there are many like him, who think that when they ask advice they ought conscientiously to take it. Hence he appears to have imposed upon Teresa all the trials and humiliations that Dr Lennon suggested. At one time he insulted her in public and drove her out of the church. This little affected her, for she and all who witnessed the event, knowing as they did the habitual kindness and gentleness of Father Wells, would know that he was only acting. The humiliation was too apparent. What proved to be a real trial and suffering was a much more simple thing. He put her under obedience to take off her scapulars and medals and carry no pious object on her person.

12. Father Thomas Wells, Teresa's spiritual director at St Mary's, Wigan.

This caused her very great suffering as she considered she must in some way have made herself unworthy to wear them, and, moreover, thought that they were means of grace which she had thought necessary for her salvation."

Before the school broke up for Christmas, 1873, a new mistress was appointed. Her name was Susan Ryland. She started work on Monday, January 5th, 1874, and at first shared a lodging in the town with Teresa, before they moved together to the little school-house attached to St Mary's, where, as was the custom at that time, they shared a single room, and even slept in the same bed. As Cecil Kerr rightly observes, "Hard-worked and poorly paid, there was much of sacrifice and no little heroism in the life of the Catholic teacher of those days."

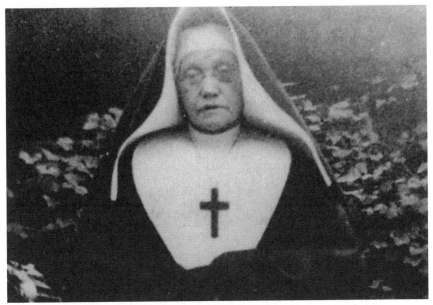

13. Susan Ryland – subsequently Sister Mary St Barbara.
Teresa's greatest friend.

Susan was to become, in Teresa's eyes, the friend in need whom God had promised her. For the next eighteen months they were seldom apart, and during the holidays Susan used to go home with Teresa, where Mrs Higginson greeted her, "I have longed to meet you. You are the only friend Teresa has ever had." And Mr Higginson and the rest of the family welcomed her with open arms.

Susan Ryland, the daughter of James and Elizabeth Ryland, of 31 Smithdown Lane, Edge Hill, Liverpool, was born on February 29th, 1852. She was with Teresa at Wigan from January, 1874, to July, 1875, a mere eighteen months, but during that time she witnessed some passing strange happenings.

She had been at the school only a couple of weeks when, at

about half-past ten one night, she and Teresa were upstairs undressing to go to bed. Suddenly looking round, she was horrified to see Teresa lying apparently unconscious on the floor. Unable to lift her on her own, Susan called for help, and managed to get her on to the bed. By 1 a.m. there was no change in Teresa's condition, so Susan went for the priest in charge, Father Thomas Wells. He came at once, but Susan was surprised by the calm and casualness of his demeanour. He simply sprinkled some Lourdes water on the unconscious young woman, whereupon she instantly came to. Father Wells sent Susan for the doctor. He was surprised by the patient's excessive weakness, but not able to account for it. The truth is that Teresa had not actually been ill; she had been in a condition known in terms of religious mysticism as 'ecstasy'. Susan was to see her friend constantly passing into this state. It manifested in two quite different ways. In one, Teresa's body remained supple and she displayed either inordinate grief or joy: in the other, her body became totally rigid and it was practically impossible to move her. Happily, the trance did not last long. Twice, when Susan was with her, it happened in the street – "Fortunately it was in a lonely part or it might have proved awkward. I could do nothing but stand at her side until she became conscious."

The word ecstasy is defined in the dictionary as "The state of being 'beside oneself', thrown into a frenzy or a stupor, with anxiety, astonishment, fear, or passion." It was applied by early writers to all morbid states characterised by unconsciousness, such as swoon, trance and catalepsy. Mystical writers use it as the technical name for the state of rapture in which the body was believed to become incapable of sensation, while the soul was engaged in the contemplation of divine things.

It is said to have been Teresa's constant concern to avoid arousing the attention of her fellow teachers, to disguise as best she could the peculiar things that were happening to her. But living in such intimacy with Susan, it was hardly possible to mask the strangeness of the events, and Susan was later to write of Teresa: "She received to my knowledge many favours from God; visitations from the evil One in person, also from our Lord, our Lady and the saints. In Lent, 1874, she was granted the following of our Lord in the details of [His] sacred Passion, the Crown of Thorns, like St Rose of Lima, the sacred Stigmata and many other favours."

Sometimes Susan would literally beg Father Wells to bring Holy Communion to a distraught Teresa, but he would not do so. With informed hindsight, the obvious reason for his refusal would be in order to try her.

Fill-dyke February had brought its waters of tears. Sad news. Teresa's sister, Clara Elizabeth, a 23-year-old school-mistress, had died, at 12 Poole Road, of pneumonia on February 3rd, 1874.

In the early part of 1874, there was much reference in the newspapers to a Belgian woman, Louise Lateau, being in ecstasy every Friday, and, wrote Susan Ryland, "we passed the remark (I mean Miss Woodward and I) 'That is nothing to this house. It is a daily occurrence here,' which it was at that time."

Louise Lateau was the youngest of the three daughters of poor working people living in the tiny village of Bois d'Haine, in the province of Hainault. She earned an exceedingly modest livelihood as a seamstress. In 1866, there was an outbreak of the cholera in her parish, and Louise, then sixteen, heroically devoted herself to the nursing of the victims of the disease, who had been abandoned by most of the villagers. At the beginning of the following year, her own health started to deteriorate. She suffered from crippling neuralgic pains in the head, spat blood, lost her appetite, and would take nothing but water and the medicine prescribed for her. Her exhaustion increased to such a degree that her death was believed imminent, and, on April 1st, 1867, she was given the last sacraments. From that moment she suddenly improved, so rapidly that, on April 2nd, she was able to walk to Mass at the parish church, three-quarters of a mile away.

After her miraculous cure, Louise became an object of curiosity, and crowds of people came to see her. Then something very strange happened. During the night of Friday, April 24th, 1868, blood oozed from the left side of her chest, from both feet, and, towards nine o'clock next morning, began to flow freely from the palms and backs of her hands, thus marking Louise with the sacred stigmata, which theologians believe to be mystic physical replications of the five wounds of the crucified Christ. In July, Louise began to experience weekly ecstasies. It was also said that she never slept, passing her nights kneeling at the foot of her bed, lost in contemplation and prayer; neither did she take any nourishment, other than the host at her weekly communion, and three or four glasses of water a week. On Friday, September 25th, 1868, blood issued from a circle of small punctures surrounding the forehead – such as would be made by a crown of thorns placed on the head. Revered to the last, she died, at the early age of thirty-three, in 1883.

Susan Ryland thought that "Teresa must have had some sort of communication with [Louise Lateau], for she said one day after coming to herself: 'Louise Lateau told me to read something in the life of St Teresa.' So I brought the book to her, but I don't know what she read. She had the same favours as that saint, one being the seraph's dart of love (St John of the Cross treating of the love of God, reminds us that the soul is attacked by a seraph who pierces the heart or soul with a fiery dart), but she said it did not seem to come from an angel, it was our Lord Himself. Once she saw something (I don't think it was the Passion) that caused her great grief, and a little while after something that brought on excessive joy, and I heard her say (for she spoke rather loudly): 'I can bear the grief, but I cannot bear this joy.' At another time she experienced some terrible fear, she was for a long time as pale as death and as if in an agony. She held her crucifix in her hand at a distance and passed it round in front as if to ward off someone. I got the holy water and used it freely. It brought about no change, so Miss Woodward went for Father Wells. He came down, watched her for a while, then called her by name when she immediately came to herself."

Miss Ryland bears interesting witness to a series of minor miracles.

At the bidding of Father Wells she cured a child of some chest disease. She used common lard (as an excuse I suppose). The child's mother asked her afterwards for some of the ointment. Teresa said to me: 'What shall I do? It is only common lard.' One night she came from church where she had been doing the altar, etc., bringing with her a duster or so to wash. There was no common soap in the house. I suppose we had forgotten it. She asked me had we nothing but the good soap and when I said no, she remarked it was against holy poverty to use that for dusters. I turned away but happened to turn back just in time to see a pound of common soap on the table and Teresa stretching out her hand to take it, as it was nearer to where I was standing than to her. I am not sure but I think she laid down the money necessary to pay for it. I am quite certain there was no soap on the table when I turned away. Another time I had forgotten, or did not notice, that there was no wood in the house. In the morning I wanted to light the fire. Teresa was in bed. I went in to her and said: 'We have no wood and I want to light the fire.' She said: 'There is plenty in the sacristy.' But I said: 'The church is not open yet.' 'Very well,' she said, 'ask St Joseph for some.' I said: 'You ask him, he won't do it for me.' Then she said: 'Have you been to such a cupboard?' I said: 'Yes, and there is none there.' 'Well, go and look again.' I went and found a quantity of nice pieces of wood not like the wood we bought. The key of the school was once lost. We kept it in the school-house, and when she wanted to enter it was not to be found. I searched the house for it, so did she. She then went up to the parlour and I think knelt by the table. Presently she came out with the key in her hand and looking very pale. I said to her: 'What on earth is the matter with you? You look frightened to death.' (It was unusual to see her like that.) 'Yes,' she said, 'I was frightened, because I saw nothing, but a white hand put the key down.' Another day after coming from Holy Communion she lighted the fire on the spur of the moment by making the sign of the cross over cold cinders. She said: 'This would warm the children's cans'. Then made the sign of the cross and I saw the flames come into the cold cinders. She did the same thing at home. Her sister, Fanny, said to me in Teresa's presence (they, like myself, used to tease her sometimes): 'Our Tess is very clever, she can light a fire without coal or wood.' I asked Teresa what she meant and she told me her Mama was ill that morning and Fanny wanted the fire quickly. Hence the result. Her brother said to me one day: 'Tess can do wonderful things. She can send up a tray before her.' He was teasing her. I asked her what he meant. She told me she was going to bring up the tray but it was too heavy for her, so her guardian angel took it from her and put it into her brother's hands. Then he saw her at the bottom of the stairs.

This personalisation of the guardian angel, this concept of the entity as an actual, knowable being, materialised, as it were, and performing concrete actions, is a distinctly worrying one so far as the normal mind and perception are concerned, and undoubtedly calls for a great stretch of credulity, or perhaps the word should be faith.

Another curious faculty which Susan noticed that Teresa seemed to possess was the ability to read her thoughts, and to be able sometimes to tell of things that had happened in her absence. For instance, Susan was on one occasion making pastry and dropped the rolling-pin on the floor. She picked it up, carefully washed it, wiped it somewhat perfunctorily with a moist cloth, and carried on rolling. When she had finished, she went upstairs, and Teresa, who had all along been up there in their bedroom, said with a smile, "My dear, never roll out pastry with a damp roller."

Amusing, in the mind-reading context, but very possibly apocryphal, is the story told of two old priests who, making their way together to pay Teresa a visit, suddenly mutually struck by a disquieting thought, decided that it would be the wiser and better part of valour to go to confession to each other before encountering her all-seeing psychic eye!

When, in the 1920s, Cecil Kerr was writing her biography of Teresa Higginson, she had scoured England – and Scotland, Ireland, and Wales – in vain for her fellow-teacher at St Mary's. But Miss Margaret Woodward had married, become Mrs Ashworth, and gone off with her husband to live in Australia. It was not until ten years later that her whereabouts became known. On December 19th, 1933, she wrote an explanation to Miss Isabella Arkwright, of Ormskirk, who had herself been a teacher at the Bishop Goss School, in Liverpool, and who had actually met Teresa Higginson.

Miss Arkwright remembered:

When I was thirteen years old I went as a pupil teacher boarder to Mount Pleasant Convent, in Liverpool. It was there I met another boarder, Agnes Donnelly, whose parents were friends of Teresa. Mr and Mrs Donnelly and Teresa all taught at the same school, St Alexander's, Bootle. Agnes also knew Teresa. I remember well Agnes speaking of a "very holy person" who lived on the Blessed Sacrament. This fact made a very great impression on my mind. ... One question all important to me was, "Is that 'holy person' living NOW?" to which Agnes replied, "Yes, NOW." I must tell you that Teresa was never mentioned by name. I knew her only as a "very holy person". Years went by, but I never forgot what was told to me concerning this "very holy person" by my friend. It was always more or less in my subconscious mind. I passed out of the Training College at Manchester and began my career in Liverpool. About this time my sister [Elizabeth] went as housekeeper to the Very Rev. Canon Snow (Teresa's spiritual director). When she first went there Teresa was supplying for the schoolmistress, Miss Garnett, who was ill. The schoolhouse was a distance away from the church so Teresa had a room at the presbytery. To my sister, on first meeting Teresa, she was just another teacher on supply but she very soon discovered that Teresa was much more than that. At that time Teresa was partaking of a little food, having become more normal from the time of her Mystical Union.[6] The only food my sister prepared was: Breakfast: Tea and two or three wafers of bread and butter. Evening Meal: Two dessert-spoons of mashed potatoes, tea and bread and butter. Before retiring: Tea and bread and butter. This was Teresa's daily food. She spent the night before the Blessed Sacrament (resting for about two hours in the early morning). My sister had to be told in case she heard any noise. The Canon told her much more concerning Teresa, and Teresa related many incidents in reference to herself. These she told so naturally that my sister was, as it were, put off her guard! When my sister paid her weekly visit home, she told us all she knew about Miss Higginson. We were keenly interested and sometimes awe-stricken. She told us how Teresa was persecuted by many people. Now, my sister did not know that I had heard of a "very holy person" living at Bootle, and I did not know the name of this same "holy person". I suddenly associated Miss Higginson with the lady of whom Agnes, my friend at the convent, had spoken. I asked my sister, "Did Miss Higginson ever live at Bootle?" "Yes," she replied, "all that I have told you happened to her whilst she was living there." I thought then that the "holy person" and Miss Higginson must be one and the same. And so they were. All that Agnes had told me eight years previously came back to my mind. I must tell you of my first meeting with Teresa. A cousin, Nellie Molyneux, and myself went to Aughton (Canon Snow's parish) to visit my sister, and, of course, to see Miss Higginson. This cousin in my presence asked Teresa to pray for her intention. Teresa with a twinkle in her eye asked humorously, "Are you going to be married?" To which my cousin replied, "Oh! no, no, Miss Higginson." Teresa then asked seriously, "Is it your vocation, dear?" No answer from my cousin. Teresa then said, "Yes, if it is God's Will." My cousin answered, "It must be God's Will." I said to myself, "You will be rebuked for that exclamation," but Teresa just smiled very sweetly and repeated, "If it is God's Will." My relative later joined the Order of the Holy Child of Jesus. Before I leave this account of my meeting with Teresa, I must relate what my cousin told me afterwards. Thinking that she wished to ask Teresa's advice, I left them together and talked to my sister. It seems Teresa went out of the room and came back toying with a pair of rosary beads. She showed them to my cousin, who is now Mother Philippa, and said, "These belonged to St Teresa." I believe they were brought out of Spain during the Carlist Rising by English relatives of a

Spanish family, and given into Teresa's charge as being the most worthy to care for them. That Teresa was in possession of St Teresa's beads is corroborated by a great living witness who also saw them. My relative and this witness are quite unknown to one another. Both gave me the same description of the beads. I have seen the beads so can vouch for the veracity of their statement.

It was in her capacity of Promoter of the Cause for the Beatification of Teresa Helena Higginson, that Miss Arkwright was the recipient of the letter from Mrs Ashworth, who was then living at 24 Stroud Street, Cheltenham, South Australia.

"A few years ago I had a rather serious illness, which resulted in my husband and self coming to live with my married daughter, where I expect to remain. My husband, of course, is past work, and I am two years older than Sister Barbara [Susan Ryland], I will be 83 in July, 1933. We have a small pension, 17/6d. [91 pence] per week, which gets our little necessaries, and we have a comfortable home. I have two children. My son is a Marist Brother."

Mrs Ashworth remembered: "We were three teachers, Teresa Higginson, Susan Ryland, and Margaret Woodward. We lived together in a small school-house. We noticed that Teresa, though she came to the table, did not eat, and when we remarked on it, she said eating made her ill.

One evening shortly after we came together, we were seated at the tea-table, the bell rang for the Angelus, we all stood up, and when finished Susan and I sat down, but Teresa remained standing, evidently unconscious of her surroundings. Several times we asked her to sit down, but to no avail; we then put her gently into a chair, where she remained till bedtime, when we carried her upstairs to bed.

That was the first intimation we had that she was a mystic.

After that, incidents multiplied, showing that she was one of the greatest saints, and we venerated her as such. During the evenings in Lent, she suffered the Passion, the Scourging, the Crowning with Thorns, and, though there was nothing to be seen outwardly, we knew by the prayers she kept repeating and by her movements, that she was suffering, and we took it in turns to sit by and take notes. At the Crowning with Thorns, she would cry out:

King and Monarch art Thou now
A Royal Diadem on Thy Brow.

And she often told Our Lord that she was quite willing to suffer for all eternity, if it would be for His Glory.

She taught the infants, and was a good teacher, and though so ill in a morning that one of us would help her to church, yet once she had received Holy Communion she was quite ready for her work. If she did not come in soon after the children were home, I used to go and look for her. On one occasion I found her cleaning the sacred vessels, she held the monstrance in her hand, and was in ecstasy, so I knew she would stay like that till Father Wells came and told her to finish up. She obeyed the priest at once.

I used to tell my children about Teresa as they grew up, but for many years after coming to Australia I did not hear of her. One day my son picked up a book – *The Life of Teresa Higginson.* He at once wrote to me and to Lady C. Kerr, who had searched England for me when she was writing the *Life.* She at once wrote to me, and at her request I sent to England my memoirs of Teresa, attested by a notary public and another lawyer. That was in January, 1932. Monsignor O'Brien was to take the papers to Rome. I left some of my notes with Susan, and when she went to the convent she gave them to Father Wells, that is how I came to be mentioned in the *Life.* ... I think [Sister Barbara] may not be able to write any more, as both her eyesight and hearing are very much affected."

A last letter to Miss Arkwright, dated November 13th, 1934, tells her: "I have had a long nervous breakdown, I received the last Sacrament, and thought I was going to die, but am still here."

The rest is silence.

NOTES

5 Thomas Wells. (1846-1889). Born at Heaton, Lancashire, the son of an agricultural labourer. Attended Ushaw College, Durham, where a fellow student was Alfred Snow.

6 vide post. Chapter 3, p.3

3

MAGNIFICAT

The year 1874 was Teresa Higginson's *annus mirabilis*. It was during the Lenten prelude to glorious Paschaltide that she had bestowed upon her the incomparable grace and favour of the sacred stigmata.

"On Good Friday," writes Margaret Woodward, "as Teresa was too ill to be got up, Susan and I went to church without her. On coming home, we ran upstairs and found her stretched out on the bed with wounds in her hands and blood in those wounds. We immediately got Father Wells, the parish priest, who was no way surprised, and I suppose he closed the hands, and he told us after that she did not know we had seen the wounds."

Teresa is said to have been determined to maintain a constant low profile, to hide, or disguise as best she could, all signs and symptoms of mystical favours. One of the things that she could not conceal were the extraordinary attacks of what her fellow teachers called 'debility', by which she was suddenly, especially matutinally, bereft of all her strength and energy. Susan, the silent witness of so many of her friend Teresa's spiritual adventures, was loyal, caring and, above all, uninquisitive; which is not to say that she did not draw her own covert conclusions. She testifies: "I have said little of Our Lord's visits. They were frequent but, as a rule, Miss Higginson did not speak to Him in such a way that I could hear. She told me once, however, that she was longing for the Day of Judgment that He might show men how much she had loved Him." Susan adds: "I recognised these words as having been said to St Teresa."

Does this carry a resonance of suspicion? She continues:

Our Lady appeared to her. ... I saw she was talking to someone. Of course, at these times she was unconscious of anything else. When Our Lady went away she said to me: "Isn't she beautiful?" I asked: "Who?" "Our Blessed Lady. Didn't you see her, dear?" When I said no, she was very quiet and only said: "She has told me I love Him more than I can tell." The second apparition was at a time when she was very ill and not able to help herself. I was kneeling by her side when she sat up and said: "Our Lady says I am cured, and I shall go to Holy Communion on Thursday morning." That was Tuesday night, and I thought why not the next morning since she was better, but in the morning I found she was weak as ever. I got her up before dinner and brought her downstairs. After dinner she became unconscious again. I had to leave her and go to school. Miss Woodward remained with her. A little before four o'clock, she (Teresa) came up to the school to me, although she had to mount a flight of stone steps. I said: "You have no right to come up here when you have been so ill." She said: "What God does He does well. I am all right," or words to that effect. She had also been to church and to see Father Wells. Miss Woodward told me that at three o' clock she came to herself and said: "Didn't Our Lady say three o'clock?" She then put on her hat and came out, going first to church. ... There were other visions which she only told me of, but I mention only those I was present for.

Susan Ryland's "being present for" a vision is veridically meaningless. She *saw* nothing. She merely reports what Teresa reported seeing while Miss Ryland was present.

Possibly explicable in other than supernatural terms, or the helpful activities of a guardian angel, is the following little incident, recounted by Susan Ryland.

"On Maunday Thursday, I was preparing the room for Holy Communion and had nearly finished, when the bell rang for Mass, and I had to leave to see to the children. There were clean sheets downstairs, which I was airing at the fire the day before, and a white counterpane we used only when she received. That was in my box. As I went downstairs I said to Our Lord: 'I cannot do any more. I must go now to my duty.' I locked the door of the house. When I came back the sheets and counterpane had been put on. It was done for her, but certainly not by her, as she was unable to leave her bed. Besides, the under-sheet was only halfway, as is sometimes done in case of sickness."

There are those who would argue that it is scarcely beyond the bounds of possibility that the invalid contrived to accomplish this 'little miracle' herself. Passing strange is the following sample of Susan Ryland's most seriously tendered testimony.

"Once, when Teresa was engaged in prayer for the Holy Souls, I saw four small birds, about half the size of our sparrows. I was not praying, I was standing facing the place where I saw them. Teresa was not, she was sitting, and had to turn her head in order to see them. I followed her gaze and looked up as they were nearing the ceiling. We were in the kitchen, one bird was in front, the next two were almost parallel, and there was another behind. Teresa was uttering cries of joy and longing. Each bird, before going through the ceiling (which they did without damaging themselves), bowed to Teresa, as if thanking her. After they passed through the ceiling, I saw no more of them. Ever since I have had a feeling that heaven and earth were connected, that although, like the cloud that hid Our Lord from their sight, we cannot see them, those in Heaven can see us, and it gives a more homely feeling."

Holy Week, 1874, was momentous. On the eve of Palm, or as

it is now called Passion, Sunday, Teresa was lying in bed. Susan was kneeling beside her. So far as Susan was concerned, Teresa was unconscious, although she was speaking, as though to someone present. She raised her right hand and held it up quite firmly for a minute or two, before letting it drop. Susan did not examine it. "I was strangely wanting, as I think now, in curiosity about these things, but next morning she kept that hand closed, placing her thumb in the middle. I think she washed herself that morning with the left hand, but I forget. However, when she handed me back the towel it was stained with blood. The morning after, both hands were closed. I washed her and she said to me: 'I can wash my own hands, dear.' So I gave her the same towel and she returned it to me again spotted with blood."

Passion Sunday (March 22nd), was the day on which Teresa received the Crown of Thorns. Susan Ryland was the only person present. She recalled:

> Teresa asked me to come upstairs in the afternoon. She was apparently suffering, and she went to lie down. She asked me to pray that she might be able to go to Sunday school, and at night she would bear all Our Lord wished. ... She was able to get up and went to Sunday school and also to Benediction. Towards night she got very weak, and after we were in bed became very ill. I wanted to go for Miss Woodward, who slept in the next room, but she would not let me, so I returned to bed. All at once she sprang up and I am sure she left the bed, for I sprang up too, to pull her down. For a while she spoke to her heavenly visitor. Then she put out her right hand towards Our Lord (for it was He) and said aloud: "No, not that, the thorny crown, give me the thorny crown." Then in a few moments she fell back again just as she had got up. I said to her: "Teresa, are you going to die? If you are, I must go for Father Wells." She did not seem to wish to get him up,

so I left it alone. Then she said to me: "Our Lord has given me His Crown of Thorns, and also the Wound in the shoulder." I saw no signs of it next day, except I thought there were pimples on the forehead, but I could not say whether they had anything to do with it or not.

On Good Friday morning, (April 3rd) Teresa's fellow-teachers went off to church, leaving her in bed and the door of the house locked. When they returned, they ran upstairs to find Teresa stretched out on the bed, her arms extended, in the form of a cross. And they could clearly see that there were wounds in the palms of her hands. Margaret Woodward threw up the clothes at the foot of the bed to see if Teresa's feet were also pierced. Susan ran off to bring Father Wells. When he arrived, he took one look at Teresa and told Susan to run for the doctor. When Susan came back with Dr Hart, Teresa was fully conscious and was talking to Father Wells. The doctor found her extremely weak, but was unable to make any kind of firm diagnosis: Father Wells did not hesitate to diagnose the unmistakable symptoms of the stigmata.

Teresa told her spiritual director that she had earnestly begged God to remove the outward signs of her holy wounds, but to give her, if possible, an increase in the pain. The wounds did not immediately disappear. They bled for a while, but before the end of her life they had finally vanished. Teresa told her confessor: "I have suffered much in the head, chest, and side since 1860, but the pains have been much greater since 1874, when our dear Blessed Lord conferred the great favour ... in the centre of the hands, feet, head and heart, they are at times very excessive, but I am relieved always when they bleed, which does not happen very, very often. I also have a severe pain in the shoulders. ... I did not at first think what was the cause of these favours, but some ten or twelve years back I noticed they were always worse on Fridays, feasts of Our Lord, and during Lent."

It was when she was at Wigan that Teresa vowed "never to go to any public amusement unless forced through obedience or charity... And although I always tried to mortify the senses, yet when I went to Wigan I made a vow never to indulge any of my senses in anything that was pleasing, only in obedience etc.; never to ask questions about ordinary things, I mean news; never to show if I was hurt; try always to be the same under every circumstance."

As Bernadette F.G. Hurndall well expresses it, [*By God's Command: The Amazing Supernatural Life of Teresa Helena Higginson*. Privately published, Great Oakley, Essex, 1987. p.29] "With Teresa, the secrecy she kept up throughout her life meant that her whole mystical life of suffering was a locked door which she shared with God alone."

There were other, physical, mortifications, disclosed only under vow of obedience and seal of confession.

> I could not adopt any method of mortification until after I had left the convent [in Nottingham] when I at first wore a cloth (in which I put twisted wire and tacks) but it was continually breaking, and I began to use a pair of goffering irons made red-hot to burn myself, and which I found very effectual, for when they would not really burn they would scar, and this I used in every part of the body that was not actually exposed to view. When I had a very sore burn I used to put on some cobbler's wax on a piece of leather which I had for the purpose, and once I had two large holes into which I used to pour turpentine. Two or three times when I had crushed toes and felt them sore, I pulled off the nails by wedging in small splinters, and so dragged them out. Then another time I saw some of that steel wire cloth ... and I got a small piece and wore it round my arms, then I procured enough for the waist, but I think the heat and discharge from

the sores rotted it, for it broke into small pieces and I was
some time before I was able to get enough to make another.

A pair of wire stays which she wore broke into little pieces that
ate into her flesh so deeply that she could not get all the
fragments out for months. One reason why she thought these
"little nothings" she took upon herself were "pleasing to Our
Blessed Lord was this, that on several occasions (when I have
been taken suddenly ill and others have undressed me) He
concealed them so perfectly that neither chain nor sores have
been noticed."

Such self-mutilations seem exceedingly gross, but many of
the canonised saints and Fathers of the Church indubitably
practised them. Lay psychiatrists would identify all such
mutilative acts as symptomatic of mental disorder. Self-
flagellation was – and still is – a common penitential practice.

The second immensely significant event of that year took
place on the feast of the Sacred Heart – the Friday following
Corpus Christi. It was the Mystical Espousal – clearly akin in
some respects to the phenomenon of stigmatisation, opines
Herbert Thurston S.J. in his *The Physical Phenomena of Mysticism*.
(Burns Oates, London, 1952.) It is the spontaneous appearance of
a miraculous ring upon third, or marriage, finger of the left hand
of certain virgins of holy life. In practically every case, the
outward physical manifestation is preceded by an ecstasy
wherein the favoured soul believes herself to have undergone a
ceremony of mystic espousal, which is to say a betrothal,
engagement, or promise of marriage, with Christ. As Dr
Dauvergne, who had seen such a ring appear on the finger of
Célestine Fenouil, born at Manosque, Basses Alpes, in 1849,
observed in his report of her case in the *Annales de Dermatologie*,
"Imagination and science become lost in inextricable confusion
when we study manifestations of this sort." Célestine's ring

consisted of a vivid red line, with tiny crosses occurring at intervals, encircling the finger. The bezel represented a heart pierced by three swords. The ring was not composed of small blood clots adhering to the skin, but was simply a red mark, most likely involving epidermal thickening.

Teresa told Father Powell: "On the feast of the Sacred Heart [1874], when I was making a visit to the most Blessed Sacrament, Our Lord placed a small crown of thorns, joined by a cross of unspeakable beauty, as a ring on the finger next to the little finger on my left hand, giving me to understand that thorns and crosses are the portion of those He chooses for His own, that He had accepted the offering I had so often made of myself, and that I must consider myself for the future to be entirely His, even as He had given Himself entirely to me, and, as proof that this was no delusion, He told me that I should feel the thorns and cross which this little ring symbolised. And so I have, for since then He has sent me desolation and dryness and crosses of every description which before I knew not."

In a later letter she embellishes: "Our dear Blessed Lord placed on [my] finger a small circle of thorns with a small cross of magnificent stones in the centre, and He gave me to understand I should suffer much for Him from that time to the end and that I must now regard myself as the 'Spouse of the Crucified'."

Canon Snow writes in his *Notes on the Life of Teresa Higginson*: "During this period she underwent many trials and much suffering. Our Blessed Lord allowed her more fully than before to participate in the sufferings of His Passion. ... She was also much subjected to many trials and tests on the part of her [spiritual] director." At this time Father Wells was fulfilling that rôle. One night Teresa came into the house looking to Susan Ryland, who thought it best not to speak to her, "much disturbed." Teresa broke the silence with, "I was nearly overcome that time!" What had happened was that she had gone, as she usually did, to ask Father Wells' blessing before retiring for the night, and he had brusquely ordered her out of his room. "I think he would have thrown me over if I hadn't got off my knees quickly." Father Wells was, of course, behaving in this way so as to try her.

Later, Father Powell, although he firmly believed in her, also put many a deliberate humiliation upon her. He had given it out that under no conditions were collections to be made in the parish without his permission. He just happened to mention one day within Teresa's hearing that he most urgently desired something and only wished that he had the money to buy it. She promptly set to work, and in no time had gathered the required sum. When she brought the money to Father Powell he expressed considerable displeasure at her having contravened his specific instruction, and told her to take every penny back to the donors. This she most humbly did, asking pardon for the scandal she had given by her disobedience.

In July, 1875, Susan left Wigan. Before they parted, Teresa confided to her how, prior to her arrival, the Devil had warned her that she was coming, and that he had tormented her, saying that she, Teresa, would no longer be able to keep her secrets, as the new teacher would soon find them out. The two young women walked together to the railway station. Susan was in tears. On the way they met one of the curates from St Mary's. He asked what was the matter. Teresa told him that Susan was leaving and she was seeing her off, adding with a dry-eyed smile: "I think it rather I who should cry, for I am losing my friend and being left all alone."

Thereafter, they corresponded and met occasionally in the holidays. They saw each other for the last time on the platform of Liverpool's Exchange railway station. Teresa's final words to her were: "We may never meet again in this world, but we shall on the Day of Judgment. Let us say together, three times, 'Glory be to the Father', and, three times, 'Thy Will be done', for all that will happen to us till we meet again." She and Teresa never met again. Susan Ryland, known now as Sister Barbara, lived on, afflicted latterly in her sight and hearing, to the age of eighty-eight. She died in 1941.

When, in the late 1870s, Susan Ryland had first decided to 'take the veil', she contrived a disastrous entry into an order of nuns for which she had found herself totally unsuited. Her second attempt proved no more successful. This time, she managed, to join an entirely wrong order; a contemplative and not, as she had thought, an active one. This order was newly founded. It had received the Bishop's approval, together with his instructions to its Reverend Mother that she was to base her rule on that of the Carmelites. When Susan, along with the Reverend Mother of the new order and an attendant group of postulants, arrived at a Carmelite convent in Paris, she was bewildered at finding herself walled in, as it were, in the stronghold of an enclosed order. Alone in her cell, and in great distress, she prayed most earnestly for guidance. It was then that she distinctly heard a voice – a human, exterior voice – say to her, "Ask to write to Father Wells." She did so, explaining her dilemma. He wrote back, saying that he had made arrangements for her to go to the Convent of the Sisters of Charity of St Paul of the Cross, at Selly Park, Birmingham. She entered there on August 7th, 1879, made her first vows in 1881, and was finally professed in 1884. Henceforth she was to be known as Sister Mary St Barbara. The Sisters of Charity was a teaching order, and over the course of the next half century Sister Barbara taught at Batley (1881-1892), Llanarth (1892-1899), Newcastle upon Tyne (1899-1901), Hounslow (1901-1902), and Stourbridge (1902-1940). She was admitted to the Infirmary at Selly Park, where she died, on January 20th, 1941, just weeks before her ninetieth birthday. She is buried at Selly Park.

Subsequent to having written to Father Wells, Susan received a letter from Teresa, in which she wrote: "Do not worry. Have confidence and He in Whom you trust will cause the sun to shine, and the storm to cease, and lull you to repose in the sure haven of His Sacred Heart."

Long afterwards, a friend[7] asked Sister Barbara whose voice did she think that it had been. She smiled and said, "It may have been my guardian angel's." "But," said the friend, "you do not really think so." "No," she answered, "I think it was Teresa's."

Teresa did not linger on long at St Mary's after Susan's departure: less than six months. A younger girl, a pupil teacher, came to replace Miss Ryland. She stayed in the school-house with Teresa, but did not, it is believed, share her room. Teresa, unattended, is said to have had to use a rope tied to the bedpost to pull herself up in the mornings. She had wanted since the onset of autumn, 1875, to leave St Mary's, but Father Wells was loath to the point of refusal to lose her. In the end, she had to resort to circuitous strategy. When she went home for the Christmas holidays she took the keys of the school with her, returning them to Father Wells by post, along with her letter of resignation. Regretfully, he had to accept her decision, and posted back to her a suitably appreciative testimonial:

> Miss Teresa Higginson has, during three years, sustained a most exemplary character as a teacher in St Mary's R.C. schools, Wigan. (signed) Thomas Wells, Manager. February 22nd, 1876.

It was not in Teresa's nature to remain idle at home for any length of time. For a while, she taught at Father Lynch's school, Our Lady and St Joseph's, at Seacombe. Things did not go satisfactorily for her there. When the school inspector paid her a visit, he "became vexed and threw over the ink on the desk."

Teresa said that when he did this she knew she had "got her parchment!" She then moved on to St Alban's, Liscard, also in the Wallasey area of Cheshire. A hard coming she had at St Alban's, but an easy going, for the priest did not take to her; they got on badly. This circumstance may not have been unconnected with some sort of poltergeistic trouble that manifested itself – pictures were lifted off classroom walls by invisible hands and thrown at Teresa. A slate, snatched from a little boy, was also hurled at her. Such commotion did not at all meet with sacerdotal approval, and blame was doubtless levelled at the new teacher, whose speedy banishment may be thus accounted for.

And still she refused to take her slippered ease amid home comforts. Tidings came of the opening of a new school by the Jesuits at Sabden, near Clitheroe, in the Lancashire hinterland. Sabden and Clitheroe are about five miles apart, with the witches' hill of Pendle between, which made it an arduous journey to hear Mass at Clitheroe. So primitive were the conditions of the small village of Sabden, that great difficulty was being experienced in finding a schoolmistress willing to work in what was generally regarded as a rough and Godless place.

St Mary's Mixed School opened there on June 18th, 1877, with Teresa as its headmistress. There were 19 children who came on the first morning, plus 3 more pupils who came in the afternoon only, making a day's total of 22. Of these, Teresa classed eleven as infants. The remaining eleven she split up into three standards. The children were very backward. They were also decidedly unruly. The school equipment consisted of six new desks, a handful of old books borrowed from Clitheroe, and seven slates. There was no blackboard. To be fair, it had been ordered – from Heywoods, of Manchester – but so remote was Sabden at that time, that it was not until almost a month later, on July 13th, that the blackboard and other goods were delivered. Teresa tried to ease the situation by borrowing certain necessary

14. St Mary's Church, Sabden.

items, but her requests were rudely refused. The trouble was that in the Sabden of those days the non-Catholics had no love for the Catholics, and she was badly received. Someone said to her in the street, with plain aggression, "How is the Holy Ghost? How is the Virgin Mary?" A further off-putting factor was the lack of a proper teacher's house. The only available lodgings were of very poor quality, and kept by a non-Catholic. The salary, too, was abysmally low, £30 a year.

None of this, of course, mattered to Teresa. Her parents were less happy about it. They had, in fact, been strongly opposed to her going. They thought her too delicate. But, as usual, she had her way, though her father could not be persuaded to give his blessing to the enterprise. She went,

15. St Mary's School, Sabden.

kissing him goodbye. She was destined never to see him again. On October 13th, 1877, he collapsed in the street in St Helens, and died almost immediately of what was described as a seizure, probably a heart attack – a myocardial infarction or something of that kind – but not before he was able to receive the Last Sacraments. In a letter to Susan, Teresa told her how she had had a vision of her father lying in the street in St Helens, dying, and when Father W. Lea, S.J., the priest in charge of the mission at Sabden, had brought the telegram to her, she had said: "You need not tell me what it is, Father, I know Papa is dead." Her calm must have been only superficial, for she wrote letters to all the priests she knew asking them to say Masses for him, and to the end of her days she always commemorated his anniversary by arranging Masses in his memory,

There had been a family death in August. Teresa wrote to Susan Ryland on August 20th, 1877: "Our dear little Freddie died on the tenth of this month at 25 min. past eleven in the morning. He was dying all Thursday [August 9th] but he went very quietly just as though he was falling asleep. Papa, Mama, Fanny, Louey and Willie were present. His mama came over on Friday [August 10th] evening. She seemed nearly distracted, He was buried on Monday (August 13th). They telegraphed for me and wrote on Wednesday, and I did not get the telegram till Friday morning, and I did not get word of his death from them till Monday, though I ought to have got the letter on Saturday morning. They are quite annoyed with me for not going home. They say they did not think I could be so indifferent, but it certainly was not God's Holy Will for me to be there, for I did not go to Clitheroe, but missed Mass and Holy Communion waiting for that letter, and after all I did not get it. I am sure you will say a fervent prayer for Freddie and get all your little ones to do the same. ... The Saturday I returned, Pat Dolan, one of our Sunday scholars was killed in the mill. It was his fifteenth birthday. The poor boy had not made his first confession. Pray for him and all our poor people."

"Our dear little Freddie" is something of a mystery. His full name was Frederick William Hallifax. He was born in 1869, in Manchester. In the 1871 census, when he was two, he was living with the Higginson family in Horne Street, Everton, Liverpool. He was eight when, on August 10th, 1877, he died of what was certified as *Tabes Mesenterica*, an old term for a form of tuberculosis, at the School-house, Little Neston, where he was continuing to live with the Higginson family. His death was registered by Louisa Higginson, his "aunt." His father, Frederick Fothergill Hallifax, is shown on little Freddie's death certificate as a seaman in the Merchant Navy.

16. Lamb's Lane, Sabden. Teresa lodged in the second house to the left.

Teresa's elder sister, Mary Ann, seems likely to have been Freddie's mother. Certification of her marriage to Frederick Fothergill Hallifax has proved impossible to trace, but, her actual marriage to a man called William Henry Jones *is* certified. She describes herself on their marriage certificate as a spinster, aged 26, and Jones, a bachelor, aged 25, a printer, is the son of John Jones, eating-house proprietor. William and Mary, both of Temple Street, Birmingham, were married at St Philip's Church, Birmingham, on March 31st, 1872. They had four children: Minnie Matilda, born December 27th, 1872; Clara, born *c.* 1875; Blanche, born *c.* 1878; and John Percy, born 1880, died 1949, aged 67.

There is a clue on Minnie Matilda's birth certificate, where Anne [*sic*] Jones, her mother, describes herself as "late Halifix [sic] formerly Higginson", though whether indeed any such previous marriage ever took place seems extremely dubious. W.H. Jones, the father, is a compositor, of 9 Geelong Place, Bridge Lane, Birmingham.

However, a Fothergill Hallifax, aged 35, whose occupation is given as that of a salesman, which could well be a misreading of "seaman", of 36 Birchall Street, Deritend, Birmingham, is recorded as having died of congestion of the lungs on July 18th, 1871. A Fothergill Hallifax married Clara Butler, in London, in 1869. In April, 1871, a Fothergill Hallifax was living with a woman of the name of Annie [*sic*], possibly *in loco uxoris*, at the house of his younger brother, Joseph, and his wife and daughter, at 228 Moseley Street, Birmingham.

On March 5th, 1878, Father Lea, who had received a letter from one of Teresa's sisters telling him that their mother's health had been much affected by the shock of her husband's sudden death, that Mrs Higginson was longing to have Teresa with her, and begging him to allow her to return home, replied:

> I hardly know what to say about Teresa. If your mother is ill and really requires her at home, there is nothing for her to do but to go home and help her mother. It would be a very terrible loss to Sabden in every way, but duty to her mother must hold the first place. If she does go home now I am sure she will apply for another school as soon as her mother can spare her. Now, under these circumstances, could you not as a great favour to me make arrangements for her to remain where she is if her mother can spare her. As to her lodgings, I will do what I can to better them the very next time I go over to Sabden. With your well-known kindness, I am sure you will do all you can to oblige me.

Teresa stayed on at Sabden. It was at the house of a Mr and Mrs Noble and their daughter, Mrs Bramley, that she was a lodger, when a most unfortunate incident occurred. At a time when he and Teresa were the only persons present in the house, Mr Noble had brought out a bag of sovereigns, his savings, which he had carefully counted in front of her. Shortly afterwards, on November 13th, 1878, the bag of gold, containing coins to the value of over a hundred pounds, was discovered to be missing, and Teresa was accused of stealing the money. The Nobles called in a policeman, who searched Teresa's room and her boxes. Mrs Bramley then insisted that Teresa should be searched. The police officer refused to do it himself, but stood by while Mrs Bramley did so, Teresa submitting quietly to the indignity. It was only then that Teresa demanded to see the officer's warrant, and, on his admission that he did not have one, she reprimanded him very severely, and told him that he must never take such a liberty again. It is said to have later transpired that Mr Noble had himself hidden the money away in a safe place, and forgotten both that he had done so and where he had put it.

Apropos the above, Miss Cottam, of Southport, told Miss Arkwright that when Teresa first went to Sabden the Cottams lived there also. Teresa and Miss Cottam became friends. The family eventually left Sabden, but it came to their ears that Teresa had been accused of stealing £100. So Miss Cottam went to Sabden to condole with her, and see what she was going to do about the accusation. Miss Cottam had been indignant, knowing well that the accusation was false. She remembered how Teresa smiled and said, "It is in the Father's hands and everything will be all right", and added, "I thought He had forgotten me," meaning this to be so if she were without a trial or suffering. Miss Cottam thought that by "the Father" Teresa meant the priest in charge, and was satisfied, but later realised that Teresa had meant her heavenly Lord and Master, because she would not allow any action to be taken. Her only concern was for the sins that the accusation had caused to be committed.

17. Teresa used to walk over Pendle Hill, from Sabden to Clitheroe, to hear Mass. She told Miss Elizabeth Arkwright that once she was so severely buffeted by the wind that she felt she could go no further – when she suddenly found herself in the porch of Clitheroe church.

Mrs Quick, of Bognor Regis, a relative of Miss Cottam's, said that she has been unable to glean any further details from Miss Cottam, other than those "about the boxes and baskets Teresa got and used to put the babies in, while the elder children were at their lessons." She also knew that it was rumoured that Teresa was known to have been giving away expensive presents following the disappearance of the £100. It was said, too, that a relative of Teresa's landlord (Mr Noble), a Protestant, who had become a Catholic, had found the lost money, and that it had helped him to carry out his desire of being ordained a Roman Catholic priest. A nice story, but, sadly, it is contradicted by Miss Arkwright's cousin, Father William Arkwright, who was headmaster of a school at Belgaum, in India, and attached to the

Jesuit College there. He informed Miss Arkwright that Father Bramley (Mr Noble's grandson), who was at the Belgaum Jesuit College, had declared that to his knowledge the missing money had never been found. [Note: There are other sources which claim that the bag of gold was subsequently found.] He had also stated that his grandfather, Mr Noble, had converted to Catholicism.

Teresa's friend, Susan Ryland, who went to spend a week with her at Sabden, recounted how, when they happened to pass the house where she had lodged with the Nobles, and where the accusation of theft had been made against her, she stood stock-still and silent beside it before telling Susan that St Peter had appeared to her and was bringing the Faith to that house. And, sure enough, as Father Bramley had said, his grandfather *did* become a Catholic.

"On Sunday we had a long way to go to Clitheroe to go to Mass," said Susan, "and we breakfasted in a house opposite the church. We returned to Sabden, but did not go the same way back to Teresa's lodgings. She went a long way round, to different places, collecting for the priest, Father Lea. I was very tired, and I told her so. There was a grass plot, and she said, 'I have to visit. You sit down on the grass till I return.' She was a long time. On the way back home she told me, 'People say they saw me at the altar rails going to Holy Communion. I was not there. I was in bed. Can an angel Communicate you?' I said 'Yes', because I had read somewhere that St Barbara sent Holy Communion by an angel to St Stanislaus. Teresa told me that she had had to miss Holy Communion, and even to miss Mass on holidays of obligation, and that she had spoken to Father Lea about this. She said she thought she ought to leave and let someone who was obliged to teach take her place. Teresa was, I remember, coming home for the holidays, so we travelled together. We passed a field where a man was working. Teresa said to him, 'I hope you will have nice weather for the crops.'

And he replied, 'Oh, we are sure to have that now.' 'Oh,' said Teresa, 'have you been to the weather office then?' 'No,' was the man's answer, 'but the Lord will not let a good 'un like you have bad weather for your holiday.'"

A woman who lived in Clitheroe and knew Teresa in her Sabden days remembers:

As there was Mass but once a month, she came to Clitheroe each weekend. She had a standing invitation to come to our home, and a room was kept for her whenever she chose to come to us. My recollections of her are most vivid. She was sweet and gentle and quite homely, so much so that the younger members of the family usually found their way to her and they would crowd round her while she told them stories or sang hymns, sometimes amusing the babies by making her Child of Mary medal whistle. Her attitude at prayer especially struck me: she knelt motionless, her eyes fixed on the tabernacle. If ever I chanced to go to Mass alone, I invariably knelt where I could see her instead of going to our own bench in church. On one occasion she got permission to take myself and my eldest cousin to the Mass at Sabden. She entertained us the whole day, showing us her school, etc. I well remember the caretaker of the school chapel, a woman, saying she spent the whole of every Thursday night before the Blessed Sacrament, which at this time was reserved, and that she had seen drops of blood upon her forehead on the Friday. The children too, she said, saw it, and had become quite used to the sight. I remember hearing much of the instructions or expositions of the Catholic doctrine to non-Catholics which she used to give on some evenings in the week. Numbers came to listen to her, but of the results I remember nothing.

There was an old man, John Nixon, who always used to meet

Teresa at Whalley station and carry her bag to Sabden for her. He eventually became ill with tuberculosis. One evening, all his family wanted to go out, but did not like to have to leave him alone. He said: "I'll be quite all right. She'll be coming in a while." They wondered what he meant. He told them that Teresa often came to keep him company. Many sick people claimed that Teresa came to them if for any reason they had to be left alone. These would all be cases of bilocation. The curious matter of bilocation will be discussed later.

One of the rather more charming reminiscences of Teresa's time at Sabden comes from the pages of a little diary kept by Father Snow. "While at Sabden she used to call the sheep and they came in great numbers to hear the Holy Name."

Among the many staunch and lifelong friends that Teresa made at Clitheroe was Elizabeth Dawson, who had first met Teresa when she, along with a number of other mill-girls from Clitheroe, began attending the catechism evenings at the Sabden school, which she used to give in the evenings. And Lizzie was one of several whom Teresa persuaded to take daily Communion; no mean feat, for they started work at the mill at 6 a.m., so that it meant sacrificing the half-hour allowed them for breakfast at eight in order to hear Mass, and left them precious little time to snatch a bite before going back to work.

Actually, it was her deprivation of daily Communion that had been one of Teresa's own greatest problems at Sabden.

Susan Ryland wrote of the signs of intense suffering which Teresa exhibited when she was unable to get Holy Communion. "I could only liken [her sufferings] to a person dying of hunger with food before them which she could not touch. When I came from Holy Communion you would think she would devour me, and to listen to her craving was most painful. I went to Father Wells about it and all he said was: 'She has no business to go on that way. Tell her from me she is not to do it.' I had to tell her, of course, and after that she became perfectly silent." Eventually, responding to her ardent prayers and pleadings, Our Lord Himself would come, bearing to her the "Bread of Life", visiting her sometimes three or four times in a day, bestowing upon her the supreme favour of Miraculous Communion.

Here, in her own words, is Teresa's description of one such Miraculous Communion. The occasion was early in the morning, before her departure on a visit to Burnley.

"I know not the hour, but I think between two and three, my Lord and my God, Jesus Christ, appeared to me verily, and indeed, His Sacred Person shone with that brightness which is indescribable, and I think He wore a stole (but of this I could not be positively certain), He said to me: 'What wilt thou, my loved one?' and I, sinking in the depths of my utter misery, could have faded into nothingness before Him. Oh, my God, who can describe this annihilation of the spirit. Then He said, holding the Sacred Host in His hand (I know it was a real Host): 'Ecce Agnus Dei ...' etc. And gave me the Blessed Sacrament of His love."

But it is not only upon her word that we must rely. These Miraculous Communions took place frequently down the years, and were witnessed by many people. Teresa's fellow-teacher, Minnie Catterall, for instance. She testifies:

"On one special evening my assistant [actually her companion was Helen Nicholson. See Chapter 5] and I had been arranging something in the bedroom. We came downstairs together singing the hymn to the Blessed Sacrament, and found Teresa to all appearances quite unconscious, looking quite dead to the world. I stood to look at her, and in a moment I distinctly beheld the Sacred Host quite stationary in the air just above her head. I could see the print of the crucifix on it, and after what seemed to be a few seconds, she opened her mouth and it slowly descended and alighted on her tongue. She swallowed it and remained in a most peaceful attitude for some considerable time.

We had both dropped on our knees without knowing it, so awed were we at beholding such a tremendous miracle. I know I felt a thrill of delight. Our Blessed Lord was feeding her Himself."

Miss Catterall writes to Father Snow: "I scarcely know what to make of her ... On Monday evening [May 16th, 1887] she seemed very weak (a little before six) and said she did so much wish to receive Holy Communion. In a few minutes she popped off; about five minutes after, I saw her open her mouth and I distinctly saw the Sacred Host alight on her tongue. She seemed all anxious to get it, and at once closed her mouth. Then she seemed as though she was dead, except that she seemed to have a most beautiful smile on her face."

A week later, she reports to Father Snow: "Since I wrote to you I have three times seen her receive the Sacred Host. On last Friday evening [May 20th, 1887], Father Mussely's[8] housekeeper [Margaret Murphy] came to see Teresa. While she was here, Teresa got ill, as it were, and both Margaret and myself saw distinctly the Sacred Host alight on her tongue. But neither of us could see where it came from."

Teresa herself, writing under vow of obedience to Father Powell, at this time her spiritual director, told him: "Of course I did not get in to 1st Mass, for when the Angelus bell rang I was lying on the floor unable to rise, but I managed to get in for the 8 o'clock Mass. I was very weak, and I begged our dear Lord to give me strength to get in for the Holy Sacrifice about six, and Jesus, my beloved Jesus, gave me Holy Communion Himself."

In another letter she elaborates: "Then He really came and gave me Holy Communion Himself, and drew me entirely into Himself, even as a raindrop into the ocean, and there He represented to me the great desire He had to have the Seat of Divine Wisdom [the Sacred Head] honoured, and He instructed me in this manner; that the Uncreated Wisdom of God is God the Father, Son and Holy Ghost, and that God the Son becoming

Man and being the Image of the Uncreated Wisdom of God, built for Himself a house; which is the Sacred Head (for Wisdom has built Herself a house), and as Jesus has promised to remain with us for ever, so He, and Spirit of Truth, etc., will guide and govern and enlighten His Church to the end of time. And I saw Him as the Sun, drawing up vapour from the earth; so will souls warmed by the heat of this Sun of Divine Justice, and guided by its Light, ascend to the great white Throne to adore the ever-blessed Trinity in Persons, and Unity in essence."

In 1879, her health, undoubtedly undermined by all the years of savage mortifications, finally broke down, and she had, for the time being at least, to give up teaching. Father Lea was sad at her going, but there could be no doubt about it, this time she had to leave Sabden and go home to her family. They were now living in the school-house, St Winefride's Cottage, at Little Neston, Cheshire, where her sister, Louisa, had charge of the Catholic village school. From now on this would be the home of the Higginson family.

Teresa spent the summer months at Neston. Then, coming once more in contact with Father Powell, confessed to him that the question of having a religious vocation had returned to her very strongly, and she had been making enquiries as to the rules of various orders. "Of my own choice," she told him, "I should certainly enter a convent in which prayer, austerities and mortifications formed a great part of the rule, but I leave the matter entirely in your hands."

His response was to offer her a position as a teacher. She promptly accepted it, and, on October 1st, 1879, found herself back where she started – at St Alexander's School, in Bootle.

NOTES

7 Miss Isabella Arkwright.

8 Father John Constant Mussely. 1842-1910. Born: Henly Flanders, Belgium, December 23rd, 1842. Died: November 13th, 1910.

4

DIABOLUS

Teresa Higginson's Liverpool was the Liverpool of Silas Hocking's *Her Benny*, the last peterings-out of which I glimpsed in the skin-and-bone little children in tattered ganseys [Liverpudlian Scouse dialect for jerseys] running barefoot over the cobbles. Although Bootle in 1879 was markedly better than the disease-raked Bootle of 1871, it was still neither the most desirable nor the most salutary of places, but to Teresa, who knew and respected Father Powell, and loved St Alexander's Church, it offered the warm feeling of a homecoming.

For the first few weeks, she found temporary accommodation with a Mrs Carter, before settling in, cosily enough by her Spartan standards, in a room above a small grocery shop kept by Mrs Mary Nicholson, a recent convert, whom Father Powell had just received into the Church and had persuaded to have Teresa as a lodger. Mrs Nicholson was a widow, her husband, Edwin, a foreman joiner by trade, had died, untimely young, at the age of thirty-nine, in 1872.

The Nicholsons' shop – No.109, subsequently No.169, St John's Road – stood almost adjoining St Alexander's Church, and the tiny first-floor-back which Teresa occupied looked out straight on to the church wall. One can well imagine it. The narrow iron bedstead with pristine white counterpane. The small wardrobe. The wash-stand with its flowered jug and bowl. The little table and chair by the window, discreetly lace-curtained, whereat she would sit, hour after hour, writing those quite extraordinary letters to Father Powell which have been described as the autobiography of her soul. And against the wall, on her right, an altar, in the centre of which stood a bright-painted, full-length statue of the suffering Christ, His hands tight-bound, His head thorn-crowned. How gladly at work day's end would she make her solitary way up the narrow stairs to the room like a monastic cell, wherein, a visionary, she met and talked with her God, and in its Purgatory rejoiced to share physically in His sufferings.

Mrs Nicholson had a 10-year-old son, Robert, and a daughter, Ellen, a girl of twelve. Teresa persuaded her mother to let Ellen study for a career as a teacher, and she entered Everton Valley Convent, for training. Teresa was a great help in every way, especially in assisting Mrs Nicholson in getting Ellen's outfit for the convent ready. Ellen (or Helen, as she subsequently renamed herself) later recalled: "When we had the First Friday devotions at the Convent. Miss Higginson used to attend, and I can remember how the girls and teachers were excited about her coming, and how they wanted to see and know more about her. They had heard such a lot about her. Some believed in her and others did not, but we were not allowed to talk about her in any way. I was always up in arms if anyone spoke against her. In fact, I felt and knew that she was so different from anyone else, and I loved her much."

The Nicholsons became very attached to Teresa; Mrs Nicholson in particular, who was anxious to do all she could for her. Helen Nicholson wrote of Teresa: "She was exceedingly kind and gentle with everyone, and her goodness was a great attraction to each of us. Miss Higginson at this time was not very strong and seemed especially weak in the mornings. Each morning she went to Mass and Holy Communion, although sometimes she could hardly manage to walk. I have seen my mother helping her downstairs by walking before her, Miss Higginson resting her hand on her shoulder for a little support, and many times Mother or I have taken her to church."

There, she would settle into her favourite seat, which was the right-hand corner seat on the epistle side of the altar, and Helen notes what so many others who knew Teresa over the years have remarked; how strange it was that "after receiving Holy Communion she would be much better. She was able to come home without help, and would afterwards teach all day in school. She also had a great influence over the children, who were very fond of her and regarded her as a friend. They often came to her with little troubles and pains, and she was always ready to help them. She had a lovely crucifix which she always carried in her belt and with this she would make the sign of the cross over them, and their pains, such as toothache or earache, would cease."

Helen says that Teresa was ever cheerful and happy and full of fun, and entered into all the sports and games of the children, telling them tales and singing songs and rhymes to them. "She had the same influence with adults as with children and was often able to get them to come to Mass and their duties. She was on such an errand when I once accompanied her to a very poor and rough part of Bootle – dock labourers lived there mostly. We went down some steps into a cellar where the men were quarrelling and fighting. She approached them and, raising her crucifix, she struck one man on the arm. He turned as if to strike her back, but, seeing her, his arm dropped immediately and he became very quiet. They listened to her very calmly and looked quite ashamed."

People often came to visit her, asking for her advice and prayers. Miss Elizabeth Dawson, from Clitheroe, and Mrs Bamber, from Preston, two very old friends of hers, frequently visited her, and, knowing her devotion to the Blessed Sacrament, had the greatest respect and confidence in her ability to help them."

In the last week of June, 1883, Helen's mother was very ill

*18. Ellen Nicholson on her wedding day,
1892, aged 25.*

and Teresa obtained permission for her daughter to come home from the convent. "I arrived home on the Thursday [June 28th], and on the following Saturday [June 30th] Miss Higginson had an appointment to meet her sister in Liverpool which she had to keep. After she had gone, Mother became much worse and we knew that she was not going to get better. Father Powell administered the last Sacraments. Meanwhile, Miss Higginson had returned. While out with her sister she had turned to her saying, 'I must return. Mrs Nicholson is dying.' How she knew we could not understand, for we did not know where she was. It was a great comfort to my brother and me to have her with us, but especially so to my dear mother during her last hours. My mother held Miss Higginson's crucifix and a blessed candle, and

19. Mrs Helen Lonsdale (née Ellen Nicholson),
who died in 1940, aged 73.

when she turned to Miss Higginson for help she told her not to be afraid. My mother died in the early hours of the morning of the feast of the Precious Blood, July 1st. What a privilege to die in the presence of, and helped by, such a great saint as I feel sure Miss Higginson was."

Helen never forgot how, after her mother died, Teresa, who had been her godmother at her Confirmation, "took charge of my brother and me, in fact of everything, as we had been left in her care and Father Powell's. She stayed with us until all was settled, then took us to her home in Neston for about ten days, where I met her dear mother and her sisters. Before I returned to the convent our home was broken up, and we made our home with Mrs Blackburn, a very dear friend."

20. St Alexander's, the interior.

Living at that time with his uncle and aunt, Edward and Margaret Blackburn, in their house at 7 Keble Road, Bootle, was 19-year-old William Lonsdale, whom Helen was to marry in 1892. Mrs Blackburn was sacristan at St Alexander's. Teresa was a great friend of the family and was very often a visitor to their home. Many years later, William Lonsdale would recollect: "Horses were then used as a means of transport. On this particular occasion Teresa wished to visit her spiritual director, Canon Snow, then at St Mary's, Aughton, near Ormskirk. She asked Mr Blackburn to drive her there in his trap, as he had often done before. However, Mr Blackburn not being free to go, I was given the privilege of driving Teresa accompanied by her friend, Miss Catterall. On arrival at Aughton, we found Canon Snow was out on a sick call, so Miss Higginson and Miss Catterall were invited into the presbytery to await his return. I stayed in the stable, where I put the horse and trap. When the Canon returned, his coachman came into the stable to put up his horse, and told me how very frosty it had become on the roads. They were like glass, he said, and it would be impossible to travel without screws in the horse's shoes. On hearing this I was perturbed, knowing my horse was not so shod. I went round to the kitchen to speak to Miss Catterall and told her the position. She asked Miss Higginson what should be done, and she replied, 'Tell Willie not to worry, everything will be all right.' In passing, I would just like to say this: whenever Teresa was asked to make a decision or answer a question for you, one always took her word as final and had no further doubts. On this occasion, when, a little later, we set out for home, although the roads were still very glassy, the horse simply flew along without a slip, Miss Higginson sitting next to me in the front of the trap."

Helen was one of those who was aware of, and a witness to, the fact that Teresa was a stigmatic. "She suffered a great deal during the holy season of Lent and was often very ill, especially in Holy Week.

One good Friday, it so happened that Miss Higginson was very ill in bed. Mother went to the Stations of the Cross at three o'clock, leaving me to stay with her. It was whilst doing so that I noticed how she was suffering. Her tongue was terribly swollen and black, and her face quite distorted with pain. She could not speak and as I looked at her I saw that her forehead was pierced with holes from which blood was oozing and trickling down her face. I knelt beside her and taking her hands in mine I noticed that they too were stained with blood. I was dreadfully upset and tried to comfort her by telling her that Our Lord would soon come to her in Holy Communion and that she would then be all right again. During Holy Saturday morning

*21. Edward Blackburn's trap in which Teresa was driven to
Aughton by William Lonsdale.*

she prayed and begged Our Lord to come to her and after
receiving Holy Communion she became well again and full of
joy and happiness."

Helen was much attracted to Teresa and loved to spend time
with her. An intelligent, sharp-eyed child, of whom Teresa
herself had observed that after she had lent her a life of the Curé
d'Ars, who suffered so many attacks of the Devil, Helen, newly
aware, noticed many strange occurrences, curious sounds and
smells, and came to her own conclusions.

"She [Teresa] was frequently tormented by the Devil. One
evening Miss Higginson, Mother and I were in the kitchen when
suddenly I heard a terrible noise. It sounded like the little coal
wagons they used at the pits running round and round the room.

95

22. St Alexander's in its heyday.

I looked up startled, but apparently Mother had not heard. The noise continued, but I could see nothing. Then I became conscious of the most horrible smell like sulphur and brimstone, which almost suffocated me. I was terrified and did not know what to think. I asked Miss Higginson, 'Does the Devil come to you?' but she did not reply. The next day I was called in by Father Powell, who questioned me closely about what had happened. He then told me that it was the Devil and that sometimes Almighty God permitted him to tempt and annoy very holy people, but that I need not be afraid because he could not harm me, or do more than he was allowed." He also told Helen to ask no questions.

The Devil was, if Teresa is to be believed, no new personal

23. All that remained of St Alexander's after the May, 1941, Blitz.

acquaintance. He had manifested his pomp and circumstance to her when she was a schoolgirl at the Nottingham convent. She wrote to Father Powell: "I feel certain ... that different things that then happened in the convent were done by the Devil, for sometimes the whole building seemed to have fallen in by the noise that was made, and the place shaken to its foundations, and on more than one occasion all the nuns, as well as all the children, were so afraid that they got up and dressed. The nun who is Rev. Mother there now, was a boarder at the time. She, I am sure will remember it well (she is my Godmother in Confirmation). Her name was Eliza Cowlam, in religion Sister M. Xavier.[9] It was always worse when I made an especial offering of myself in reparation or for the conversion of sinners,

*24. Father Edward Powell. Teresa's
spiritual director.*

and I noticed how enraged the Devil was in after years when I really saw and felt him, and so I connect the two facts, though I really don't know."

She had had unwelcome truck with Beelzebub in her Wigan days also. She told Father Powell:

I think the first visible temptation which I had at Wigan was as soon as I went. I think you know that without any permission I used to rise as soon after twelve as I conveniently could (I had not a bed to myself) to make my meditation etc. and each time I commenced the Devil used to beat and ill-use the body, and spit horrible filth upon me in the face and eyes, in fact, completely cover me which made me very sick, and the stench was almost poisoning. And this I told to rev. T. Wells who told me he thought I had a very fertile imagination, and as far as I can judge he did not believe me, but he told me to tell him each time I fancied it, and when he saw that it still continued he asked me could he write to some priest of great experience about it. But in the meantime he said, you must not rise to make your meditation. Night is the time to sleep and rest so that you may be able to do your work as duty requires. And so I did not rise intentionally, but several times I found myself rising, and when I at once returned the devils would shriek and yell and laugh in a most dreadful manner and mock me and say: "Most obedient maid how firm are your words of promise to the King of heaven!"... Then [Father Wells] said I must sleep a certain time, I forget now but I think he said four hours, and under obedience I did so, and when I slept the Devil would rouse me. Sometimes he cried as though some poor child were out upon the doorstep; sometimes he used to throw me completely out of bed, throw things at me that were within the room, and make awful noises, and I used to be afraid at first that ... the people of the house would hear. And several times when I awoke I perceived a smell of something burning, and the house being filled with smoke and brimstone, I thought surely the house was on fire. And other times I saw the whole bed and room full of flames and heard the crackling and I am afraid in this case I proved a coward, for I was frightened more than I can tell at first for there was no holy water: the Devil threw something against the bottle and broke it.

For all her fears and misgivings, it was not until she got to the St Mary's school-house that Teresa's diabolical visitations became quasi-public knowledge.

The Devil knew I did not like anyone to know these things and so he often told me he would let the other mistresses see and know all ... At length Miss Ryland and Miss Woodward soon saw and heard everything almost; at least I don't know what they knew, but as they were frightened Fr. Wells told them the Devil could not hurt them etc. I think I had temptations against every virtue while there ... I think the reason why the Devil used to spit and throw that abominable filth of such awful stench at me was because at that time I was resolved to mortify the senses more rigorously ... Certainly at times I was almost suffocated ... the Devil used to be infuriated and beat, drag and almost choke me. ... The Devil used to make me strike myself as I have seen children playing with each other. He used to appear in hideous forms sometimes and also as man very often (I think he used the bodies of damned souls) and I remember particularly on two occasions him opening the bedroom window and talking as if he had a companion. Miss Ryland heard him too, but she did not see him and she became much alarmed. It was in the night and she said she could not help listening ... the Devil was so exasperated that he commenced to throw the things about the room at me and make a terrible noise. Then it seemed as though a great explosion was taking place and he seemed to set the room on fire – she [Susan Ryland] could smell the burning and she said: "Oh dear, he is burning the bed, what shall we do?" I told her to take no notice, to sprinkle a little holy water and let us get on with our prayers, or else try to go to sleep, he could not hurt her and the bed was not mine, he had no power over Fr. Wells' things. So he threw something against the holy water font and broke it. Sometimes [the Devil] would follow me about as a fox, and sometimes part a fish, part a fox, and part a pig. I mean a thing with a serpent's head, a pig's head and a fox's head and tail and a bird's wings and head with hooked bill, in church and out, but I never took much notice, I mean I appeared not to notice. I used to be much afraid at first, but Fr. Wells told me it was not sinful, it was the natural consequence of the supernatural coming in contact with the natural.

Called in to supply confirmatory evidence, by Father Powell in June, 1880, by which time she was a professed nun, Susan Ryland, now Sister Barbara, wrote from St Paul's Convent, Selly Park, Birmingham, stating that while living with Teresa at Wigan she had heard at times extraordinary noises and seen Teresa ill-used, although she never saw by whom. She had found the holy water stoup and bottle broken in a strange manner, but she had not seen it being done. She had never seen Teresa actually being thrown out of bed, but she had "found her almost out and unable to replace herself." She had seen smoke, but not flames. And "the bed was not set on fire as far as I know for certain. I believe there were marks as if an attempt had been made to do so." She saw a strange light on the wall, sometimes on the bed, and covering Teresa's face. She saw, though indistinctly because of the dark, things hurled at Teresa. She saw Teresa's own hands thrown violently against her face, and saw no one there to do it. She found water which she (Susan) had left by Teresa for her to wash with, thrown over her, but did not see it done. She heard noises as if everything *in the room above* was being dashed against the ground, and on going up the noise then seemed to be *in the room below, where Teresa was.* She heard at times a rushing noise as if animals were in the room, sometimes footsteps, knocking, voices of people (once only) speaking in an undertone. She heard a noise made by Teresa as though someone had hold of her by the throat. She had been wakened by, as she thought, hearing shrieks, but when fully awake she did not hear

*25. Father Alfred Snow. He succeeded Father
Powell as Teresa's spiritual director.*

them. Once or twice during the day she heard a noise as if Teresa
had been struck by a hand.

"As to the effects on myself," she told the priest, "it did
cause me fear which increased until I spoke of it in the
confessional and received advice about it. Afterwards it was
much lessened. I never asked Miss Higginson's advice. I told her
in the beginning I was afraid of that strange light, that I did not
know what it was, but I don't remember ever asking her what I
should do. I never asked anyone. I used holy water. "

Sister Barbara relates further instances of ceaseless and
petty attacks during this period which she ascribes to the Devil.
Often, she says, there would be a knock at the door, and when
Teresa went to open it she would receive a violent blow in the

face from an unseen hand. When Miss Ryland went herself, no one would be there. On one occasion, Teresa had staggered back into the room with a great swelling down one side of her face, which gradually turned black and blue. One evening as she and Teresa sat together in their house opposite St Mary's school, they heard a child sobbing bitterly. Thinking that it must have been accidentally locked in, Teresa ran in some distress for the school key. The two young women searched the building from top to bottom. There was no sign of any child. Suddenly, the sobbing changed into mocking laughter. Satan was up to his tricks again, they decided. On another night, when Susan and Teresa were in bed, they heard what sounded like two men whispering at the foot of the bed. It seemed as if they were hatching a plot of some sort. "Yes," said Teresa, " it is the Devil, and he is planning to send a man in at the window to attack us." She got up and fastened the window securely with a rope. A little later there came a terrifying rattling and knocking on the pane. But the window remained tight shut.

Father Thomas Wells, writing to Father Powell on June 28th, 1880, confirms: "I certainly saw the signs of the stigmata upon one of her [Teresa's] hands upon the Good Friday afternoon of 1874, and I was quite aware of the many and extraordinary temptations to which she was subjected, and saw the effects, afterwards, as broken articles in the room she occupied, and notably the holy water stoop. Upon one occasion she had been absent from school through sickness for nearly a week, and the doctor had been in attendance upon her at my request and seemed unable to afford her any relief, and was of opinion that her case was very obstinate and very dangerous. She was all but unconscious when I visited her at twelve o'clock, noon, and bedfast. I said, as I thought the school was taking harm through her absence, that she must get up and take her place in school by three o'clock that afternoon. Though then unable to stand, I saw her at a quarter to three walking up alone to the school to make a visit, and by three she was teaching in the school, apparently as well as ever. These things recurred repeatedly and I was in constant communication with Mgr. Lennon of Ushaw, who helped me by his advice very much. I wrote at once to the Bishop about her. I got Miss Ryland to write down the occurrences during Holy Week which she and I witnessed."

Writing to Sister Barbara from Neston, where she was home for the holidays, on July 12th, 1880, Teresa told her: "Fr. Powell has gone on the Continent and he expects to see the Passion Play[10] before he returns. We are having our holidays. Louey [Louisa] goes to Liverpool for the students' retreat … All last week dear Mama, Fanny and myself were at Holywell. I bathed each day. I think the out [sic] has done us all good. We saw all there was to be seen for miles round. Twice we went to Pantasaph. We kissed the relics of the true Cross, St Francis of Assisi, and Blessed Lawrence at the Franciscan Monastery, and those of St Winefride at Holywell. We made the Stations [of the Cross] at Pantasaph. I did not forget you when I was in the holy well."

Importantly, the letter goes on to make references to the Sacred Head.

"We have a new devotion here which is I am sure most pleasing to our dear blessed Lord, it is to honour the Sacred Head as the seat of 'Divine Wisdom', the reason that overruled all the motions and affections of the Sacred Heart, and the shrine of the three powers of the holy and immortal soul of Jesus Christ. We say morning, noon, and night, 'Oh Wisdom of the Sacred Head guide us in all our ways, Oh love of the Sacred Head consume us with thy fire', and three times 'Glory be to the Father', in honour of the three powers of the soul. We have had several sermons preached on the same subject and I am anxious that you should have a share in promoting this heavenly devotion and be among the first to fulfil the ardent desire of our dear blessed Lord in

26. Winter Scene. Bootle in the 1890s. Linacre Lane and Litherland Road.

honouring it. Do all you can towards this end."

That July, Teresa writes to Father Powell: "While I was at home [at Neston], most of the time I had no control over myself at all, and I think they are a little alarmed about me. At first, they thought I went to sleep, and then thought I was fainting, and dear Mama asked me this morning if the doctor told me that I had fits, for, she said, 'There is something very strange the matter with you.' She says I go quite stiff, but I have asked our dear b. Lord not to let them be uneasy about me, and I feel sure He will do as I ask Him, at least He always has done so before. Mama seems afraid that it should get out that I have fits, but I have given myself entirely into His hands – I care not what anyone thinks, in fact I am very pleased they do think so, but

27. No.15 Ariel Street, Bootle.
Where the Devil came calling.

even Ellen Nicholson notices things very quickly, and asks questions which are rather difficult to answer. When I bathed in the holy well, I noticed that both my feet and hands bled, and I was tempted not to go in any more after the first time, but I put on, or rather went in the second and third time in, stockings, and yet a person who was present said, 'You have cut your foot, see how it is bleeding!' And then I feared that I had done wrong, and I humbly beg pardon if I have."

Generally speaking, Teresa paid little or no attention to her own physical comfort or appearance. Her mother, tall, slim, neat, fastidious, used to say that she could not understand how any daughter of hers could be so careless of her personal appearance. The fact is, of course, that the vow of poverty, which she had taken very early in life, meant that Teresa regarded absolutely nothing as her own. She claimed no possessions. The very clothes she stood up in she thought of as being on loan, and she was ever ready to give them to anyone whose need she believed to be greater than her own.

Once, during her time in Bootle, she took off her flannel petticoat to give it to a ragged woman. The woman went round in triumph to St Alexander's Presbytery to display her new-found finery to the priests' housekeeper. She, outraged, promptly bore it in to Father Powell, who, sharing her dismay, told her to give the woman something in its place, and, sending for Teresa, ordered her to go home and put her petticoat back on at once.

Her mother would complain, "I don't know what Teresa does with her clothes. Each time she comes home I get her things, and when she returns to me she has nothing to wear." When she went home on visits to Neston, her sisters would do all they could to renovate her wardrobe. Minnie Catterall remembered Teresa's return from one such family shopping expedition, bearing the gift of a new bonnet, trimmed with a rather splendid ostrich feather. She remembered, too, how, by some strange mischance, that large feather soon got burnt in the gas, and how thereafter Teresa seemed much more partial to the bonnet! When going through Teresa's meagre possessions after her death, Louisa remarked that she could not help wondering what, if she had recovered, Teresa would have had to wear. The clothes cupboard was virtually bare.

To return to Bootle. After the death of Mrs Nicholson, Teresa had perforce to find new lodgings, and she joined three of her fellow-teachers at St Alexander's – Kate Catterall, her sister Mary "Minnie" Catterall, and Elizabeth Roberts – in their lodgings at No.15 Ariel Street., where their landlady was a Miss Joanna Flynn. Here, as at Mrs Nicholson's, Teresa occupied a

*28. Teresa at the time she was fighting
the Devil in Bootle, 1884. Aged 40.*

back room looking out on to the sanctuary of the church, St Alexander's, and her fellow-lodgers soon well knew that once its door was closed its occupant would brook no disturbance. Great dramas would be here played out. Assaults of the Devil. Divine favours of the Almighty. There would be swooning ecstasies, so frequent, that they would provoke no comment from her sympathetic companions other than "She's off again!" Her face, at these times, in the happy words of Miss Catterall, "Suddenly looked as of the finest alabaster; then her heavenly look and serene smile, directed as I thought to something far distant, amazed me."

And it was here, on that manifestly inappropriate stage, that the Devil – if indeed it *was* the Devil in Bootle – made his grand

29. Minnie Catterall. Teresa's friend and fellow-teacher. Taken with a group of teachers at Holy Cross School, Liverpool.

entrance, gave his most spectacular pantomimic performance. All those in that modest little house trembled before his scarifying antics.

Father Powell, who had been called in by one of the Catterall sisters on the night of September 20th, 1883, when Old Nick was presumably up to his tricks in Ariel Road, wrote from his first-hand experience: "They said they heard a noise as if a person was sawing in their bedroom and soon afterwards in the parlour underneath. They all rose and ran downstairs; as they were descending they heard as if from the top of the stairs a long mocking laugh like descending the musical scale. They ran out, Miss Roberts without her slippers, and sent for me. After I had been in the kitchen some time with them all, I heard as if in the room above where Miss Higginson was as if a body had been dashed to the ground, worse than if a person had fallen. It shook the ceiling, the windows and the kitchen. After some minutes, I heard as if a person was dragged across the room and her head bumped two or three times against the floor. I stayed some time after but all was quiet."

Kate Catterall, teaching at St Alexander's School, writes of the afternoon of Thursday, August 23rd, 1883, how "the blackboards in the room over the one I was teaching in seemed as if being continually dragged about. I went upstairs wondering why there was so much noise and asked about the blackboards, but was assured by both teachers that they had not been moved at all. I felt certain that they had, as the effect of the moving about shook the partition, against which I was sitting, twice over. The noise was heard continually during the afternoon, even when the children from the room overhead (Standard 4 room) were out in the playground. Sometimes it sounded like the low growl of some wild animal or a rumbling of thunder. I asked one of the boys in the room if he heard any noise and what it was like. He said, 'Yes, they are rolling something on the floor upstairs.' In the evening there was a fearful smell in the kitchen as of sulphur and something else, I cannot describe what, but it was quite sickening."

Her extra-curricular duties, so to speak, desirable activities beyond the bounds of the schoolroom; Teresa saw them with clarity. "Which," she asked Father Powell "is the worst street in the parish?" adding, "I have promised Our Blessed Lady to say the fifteen mysteries of the rosary for fifteen days (I mean an extra fifteen) and do all that you would allow me for their benefit."

A few days later she was able to report: "I have been through all the houses in Mordan Street, and 27 of the people have promised to come to confession, and many of those have been here today, and nearly all are entering or re-entering the

Holy Family Confraternity. ... Our dear little ones are coming a little more regularly to school and are trying to be good pious children. Ask their guardian angels to let me know quickly each child's character and see his little faults, that with his help I may correct them, and pray that I may do my duty to them in every respect, and may never scandalise them in word, look or action."

Minnie Catterall could never forget the delight she felt when Father Powell introduced Teresa to her as her new assistant, "to think that now I really saw the person of whom I had so frequently heard from an aunt of mine in Wigan, who keenly interested me by the things she told me in connection with this very wonderful and holy creature who was then Head Mistress of St Mary's Infant School, Wigan.

On her arrival in Bootle, we soon became great friends. I was very attached to her and seemed to feel I had known her for a very long time. I spent a good deal of time with her in going about, always on some mission of mercy or kindness. Her conversation keenly interested me. It would sometimes relate to ordinary topics or current events, and I was often puzzled as to how conversant she was with the general doings of the country and her sound judgment on them, for I never remember seeing her reading a newspaper.

When I came to work with her in school, her general conduct and instruction to the children confirmed in my mind that she was in some way miraculous, for I had never heard even the priests give quite the same points of instruction that she was able to put forth, and on many occasions I felt she could almost see the state of each child's soul. She could tell if a child was telling a lie, although she had no knowledge of the facts concerning the case in point. The little ones coming to school with aches and pains, were often cured by her almost immediately.

Outside school, from my experience, her influence among the people of the parish was most marked. She spent her time visiting the sick, helping and comforting people in their various troubles, oftentimes taking upon herself their physical ailments to free them from suffering. All that she did was done in a most humble and hidden manner, she being always calm and collected. She never appeared to be put out or alarmed at whatever happened, and never by any chance got out of patience.

She had not lived long with us when I was very much alarmed and frightened. My sister and I occupied the double bedroom next to that occupied by Miss Higginson. On a certain night we had just retired to bed and extinguished the light, when I was terrified by a terrific noise on the landing and walls which I could never describe. My sister and friend, who also shared the room, were more than astonished at me as I was trembling with fear and could not help exclaiming, for neither of them, though wide awake, had even heard the slightest noise.

On another occasion, I heard [the Devil] walking with a tremendous foot on the landing and wriggling the handle of the door most dreadfully: and again, as if someone, suspended over the door of Teresa's room, was laughing and screeching with the most hideous and fiendish laugh, so that I cold not refrain from quite loudly exclaiming – 'That is Hell!'

I was so terrified by the things I constantly heard that I was always very careful to have my crucifix in my hand when I retired. I had just settled myself one particular night, when suddenly I felt the warm breath of a huge crawling beast coming stealthily towards my hand with its rough tongue and large teeth. I was struck with fear and instantly snatched my hand away. It appears that the Devil had told Teresa – which, of course, he never had – that he would teach me for taking a crucifix to bed and that he would do other things to me.

I well remember on another night I could hear repeated noises and upset in Teresa's room, which at one time sounded as if her head was being banged on the floor. This filled me with dismay, so that I persuaded my sister to come with me and try to get into her room. After repeated knocking, we succeeded. What a sight! There she appeared, hair dishevelled, herself and bed in a most ruffled condition, as if she had been tossed or pulled about. There were pieces of burnt candle lying about, and the walls were disfigured by marks of burnt candle and grease, which had been thrown and then dropped on to the floor. We looked around in such dismay that she told us it was the Devil, who, when she was trying to light up her little altar, had snatched up the burning candles and paper from her and thrown them all about.

Many times, when I have heard anyone speaking disparagingly of her, I have been very much annoyed, but she has at once declared she was most grateful to them for their revilings, looked upon them as her best friends, prayed hard for them, and invariably did them a good turn. She certainly had many enemies and was looked upon by some, even including some of the priests, as the greatest impostor imaginable."

NOTES

9 Eliza Cowlam, born in 1838, was the daughter of Thomas and Elizabeth Cowlam. He was a miller and the Cowlams lived at West Rasen – "The sleepiest town in England", as Dickens designated Market Rasen – in Lincolshire, where Teresa used to visit them. Six years older than Teresa, Eliza was a pupil teacher at the Nottingham convent. She became a Sister of Mercy.

10 At Oberammergau, the Bavarian village where the Passion Play has been acted since the middle of the seventeenth century. Most of the villagers are wood-carvers, and one of them, Anton Lang, played the Christus for many years.

5

CHIMAERA

Unsurprisingly, tidings of such weird 'goings-on' could not in that circumscribed ambience be suppressed; the news was bound to get out, the gossip to escalate, strident camps of believers and doubters to arise in increasingly belligerent confrontation. The epicentre of this emotional hurricane was the small, shabby little schoolteacher, staggering by under the weight of two wooden pails of pea-soup for the hungry, or scurrying about the mean streets dispensing to their disadvantaged denizens charity, tinctured with gentle pressure towards the observance of their religious duties. She passed with eyes averted, praying for those who hurled after her such abusive epithets as "Old hypocrite", or loudly proclaimed her a drunkard, swearing to have smelt drink upon her breath, as she swayed off down some dark alleyway

For all her outward show of indifference, Teresa felt insults very deeply. Indeed, she confessed to her friend, Alfred Garnett, that in Bootle, where insults were heaped, Pelion upon Ossa, on her, her mental anguish was so great that, for a passing second, the temptation came to her to give up her mode of life and, instead of responding to God's grace, live an ordinary life like anybody else. But she heard a most triumphant laugh – the Devil – which only served to help her to persevere.

As Father Snow sorrowfully acknowledged, in a letter to Father A.M. O'Sullivan, O.S.B., author of the pioneering memoir, *Teresa Higginson: The Servant of God*, (Sands, London, 1924): "The number of those who regarded her as a holy woman were few, and the number who regarded her as a 'lying hypocrite' were many."

Rumours of the clamour in Bootle inevitably came eventually to the ears of Dr O'Reilly, the Bishop of Liverpool, who did not at all like what he heard and expressed the firm desire that the case should be submitted to the consideration of several competent priests and learned theologians. This was accordingly done, and in the following lengthy epistle Father Powell makes his position in the matter clear. He is writing on August 17th, 1882, to Father John Fisher, President of St Edward's College, St Domingo Road, Everton, who was one of the Bishop's elected scrutineers.

The Bishop desires me to ask you kindly to enquire into the following case, and to give your opinion whether it comes from God or not. I may mention in the first place that Miss Teresa Higginson is one of my teachers in the boys' school, that I have known her for about seven years or more, that she has given me full permission to make use of any information derived in the confessional, and that she does not know about her letters having been copied. When first she came under my direction, perhaps nine or ten years since, though perhaps only seven, I found she had the prayer of union, and after some time I gave her permission to communicate daily. This was the reason why she so loved St Alexander's. Once I found out that she had obtained the church key from my housekeeper, and spent from four a.m. to Mass at 8 in the church. At the *Quarant ore*, she stayed there from ten o'clock Mass until 8 p.m. without ever leaving. She had received Communion at the 8 Mass.

I did not at first know about her extraordinary life, as she kept all to herself, thinking as she said, Our b. Lord wished all to be kept secret of His extraordinary favours. I found it most difficult for her to explain anything by word of mouth,

115

so it struck me to put her under obedience to write something I could *not* understand. I then made her explain other matters in the same way, and, though it was a terrible struggle and trial to her, to write about all her mortifications etc. Her life has been a most innocent one, very few even venial sins, she mentions most of them in her letters – from when she was four years old Our blessed Lord seems to have called her in an especial manner, and I never read in the lives of the saints of anything equal to her austerities. A wire belt of some instrument used at Neston to clean something or other, which, when ordered to stop any mortification as she was ill, it took her three months to extract from her flesh, boring holes with a hot iron and putting in vinegar and salt. I tried the truth of this once granting at her request leave to touch the arm just above the wrist with a hot iron, asking next day to see it, and finding a ghastly wound. She did not know I would ask to see it.

Eating putrid dripping, rotten eggs, and the water in which herrings had been cleaned, etc. For three weeks I tried to make her eat, and found everything was vomited: at last I asked her, as she was very ill and the doctor could make nothing of her, if she knew what was the matter. She replied when asked, but never a word before: " I think our blessed Lord does not want me to take anything." I gave her leave to take nothing and next day she was quite well again.

I got one to watch her for a week. She – Miss Higginson – pretended to eat but Ellen Nicholson, who lives in the house, watched her closely and noticed she never swallowed anything. She saw she was watched, and when urged to eat used to pretend to eat by chewing india-rubber, etc. In answer to my enquiries she told me she never eats now, except when at home at Neston, and then very seldom. She never sleeps either, I really believe, but for that I have to take her word.

It is now over three years that I began to know of her extraordinary life. I have known her to find out a boy who stole a sovereign in another part of the school and tell him exactly how he took it. Once she was wrong about a person whom I asked her to pray that he might live: she said he would recover, but he died. She has often been totally insensible, always unconscious to all else after Holy Communion. I once sent a pin into her arm, but she evinced no feeling. But whenever in that state she always obeys her confessor.

I have known her to be most outrageously abused by a priest here, and others who overheard the abuse, told me she never said a word. When I had a chance (in her desire to protect another teacher, believing too readily what others said and speaking unfairly of another – that she gave the dullest boys to her fellow-teacher, etc.) of finding fault with her before the other teachers, she took it most humbly, and, I found, apologised at once.

Once, when accused of theft in another place, her parents, when they heard of it a year afterwards, wished to prosecute the calumniators, she was miserable until she got them to give it up. She got me to say Mass for this enemy of hers, though I did not know then the accusation. For a long time I was in doubt, but her inspirations are not, or very seldom, external appearances. She speaks of them as "Seeing with the eyes of the soul: knowledge impressed upon the soul: infused into the soul." I believe there is no instance of deception with such revelations; that such is beyond the power of the Devil. I was told how St Gertrude had been under delusion for thirty years, that the deception was at length discovered by her confessor forbidding her to have any extraordinary communications with Our blessed Lord, yet they continued. I forbade Miss H. to have any communication until I gave her leave. I did not then advert that she was going to Neston that week, where they have not always Mass. On other occasions similar, Our blessed Lord brought her Holy Communion; on this occasion two angels brought it. Thinking this was also forbidden, she refused it, and there was no communication until I withdrew the prohibition.

I am sorry to give you so much trouble, yet I think you will find it a pleasure as well. Father Snow, of Aughton, and Father Bertram Wilberforce said they never read anything so beautiful as many of her letters. The narration of the Passion will, I think, well repay perusal. It taught me a very great deal indeed.

If this is all the work of God, Our blessed Lord wishes His sacred Head to receive special adoration, and that, as with the devotion to the sacred Heart, He chooses one most insignificant and plain in appearance to make His Holy Will known. In these days of pride, self-will, rebellion against His Church, and intellectual pride, He wishes that sacred Head, treated with such mockery and crowned with thorns, to be publicly and specially adored as the special Seat of Eternal Wisdom, the Shrine of the Will – so tortured (as man sins especially with the will) by His taking upon Himself all the sins of the world, so awful for the will of an all-pure God to do; of the memory clearly cognisant of every sin of every individual; of the understanding grasping iniquity by the full knowledge of God's Justice and Holiness. These powers of the Soul of Our blessed Lord being specially dwelt upon complete the devotion to the sacred Heart, thus revealing the springs, so to say, of His love.

Lately, He has let her participate in the sufferings of His divine Soul. Unspeakable as were the sufferings of His Body, yet they are but like a drop in the ocean compared with what His Soul endured. As man's soul is the seat of guilt, Our blessed Lord through all His Passion, but particularly in the Agony in the garden, took upon Himself the punishment due to every sin that would ever be forgiven – in fact, equal to an eternity of Hell for each mortal sin. Her letters, I certainly think, give a most wonderful completion to the whole of the Incarnation.

I send you some prayers composed by her, and my first request is that if you find nothing objectionable in them, I may get the Bishop's leave to have them printed. Finally, if there is anything further you wish to have explained I shall be most happy to do so. It may give you great trouble, but if it is from God, the promises are that all that aid in promoting this devotion shall receive the choicest blessings in return from our divine Lord.

Two matters referred to in the foregoing letter require explanation. Firstly, her letters. Teresa was a voluminous letter-writer, and a long series of those addressed to, and at the behest of, her spiritual directors, Father Powell and Father (later Canon) Snow, carefully gathered together by Canon Snow, were bequeathed by him to Father A.M. O'Sullivan, O.S.B. a monk of St Augustine's Abbey, at Ramsgate, in Kent, where they are still preserved.

The subjects of the letters are many and various. Typically, she is asked to write of her accompaniment of Our Lord through his Passion; to describe the Dolours of Our Lady, the Incarnation, the Trinity, Purgatory, and the state of the soul after death. She is required also to write what amounts to the history of her own soul, and the ways in which the Almighty revealed himself to her, instructed her, and interacted with her.

The letters are even more remarkable in their way than the seemingly supernatural eruptions of violent phenomena which punctuated her life, for they frequently deal with abstruse areas of theology, propounding definitions and providing illuminations in connection with matters which might normally have been expected to be completely alien to Teresa's knowledge and explicative capacity. Yet, most critically examined by experts, their content was found to be faultless, her propositions unchallengeable. It is these letters, rather than the fireworks on the psychic landscape, which are perhaps the greatest enigma. It has been observed that throughout her life Teresa Higginson was scarcely ever seen with a book in her hands. She was not a reader, not well equipt with what used to be called 'book learning'; indeed, her fellow-teachers would often, half-humorously, complain that she seemed to be able to deliver her lessons with such bookless ease, whereas they had to spend hours poring over their text-books in preparation.

Secondly, the Devotion to the Sacred Head.

Although it had been generally believed that the first revelation in this matter had taken place on the feast of the Sacred Heart, 1879, at St Winefride's Cottage, the school-house at Neston, where the Higginson family were then living, shortly after Teresa's return from Sabden, Margaret Woodward was able to contradict that assumption. She had been with Teresa at Wigan from 1872 to 1876, and says: "I think I was the first she told about the devotion to the Sacred Head, as I met her coming out of church and she seemed as though she had just received the commission. She said, 'Our Blessed Lord wishes His Sacred Head to be honoured.' I replied, ' 'tis the very devotion wanted in the world today, when men seem to be worshipping their own brains.'"

From this time forward, the establishment of a devotion to the Sacred Head of Christ as the Seat of Divine Wisdom, as the Sacred Heart was venerated by Catholics as the source of Divine Love, became the all-absorbing interest of Teresa's life.

"When I went into the church a little after five on Easter Sunday morning," wrote Teresa on April 9th, 1880, "I had hardly knelt to adore Him ... when the powers of the soul again began to act. He represented Himself to me (I think) as we see Him in pictures of the Sacred Heart and His Sacred Head radiant as a sea of light and a glorious sun shining to its very depths and acting on the affections, motives, and entire workings of the Sacred Heart and raising them even as the sun draws up the vapours from the ocean. In this light, I saw distinctly formed the figure of a silvery dove which I understood was the Holy Ghost, and rolls of glory (I was going to say clouds, but that is hardly correct) or pillars, as a rainbow appeared above which I felt represented the Eternal Father. The whole formed an Eye, which I knew was the Eye of God in unity. And from it I understood that our dear Blessed Lord wished His Sacred Head to be specially worshipped as the 'Seat of Divine Wisdom' and the powers of His Human Soul adored therein, as it is the seat of the intellectual powers of man."

And in a letter dated April 27th, 1880, she continues: "Our dear Blessed Lord has shown me, too, how the head is also the centre of all the senses of the body, and that this devotion is the completion, not only of the devotion of the Sacred Heart, but the crowning and perfection of all devotions. ... Our dear Blessed Lord did not positively state the precise time that this should be made a public devotion, but He gave me to understand that whoever should venerate His Sacred Head in this manner should draw down on themselves the choicest gifts of Heaven; and those who shall try by words or means to hinder or reject it, shall be as glass that is cast down, or as an egg that is thrown to the wall, that is that they shall be shattered and become as naught, and shall be dried up and wither as grass on the housetop. Our Beloved Spouse also let me know that it was in this church [St Alexander's] that He would manifest to the world the manner, etc. etc. that He wished to be honoured, and the time, and all concerning this most wonderful Devotion."

Then comes this tantalisingly perplexing passage:

And I think it is *that soul* that is drooping as the vine under
the weight of heavenly gifts and saturated through and

through with the Precious Blood, that in His infinite Wisdom He has ordained to make known His holy Will to the world. For He continuously shows me this precious soul so dear to Him, and frequently before He makes known to me anything concerning this heavenly devotion (to His Sacred Head) He comforts me also with it. For when I feel my poor heart breaking with sorrow at the coldness with which He is treated, and the way He is betrayed even by His priests, He shows me this soul as His consoler and refuge, this lily in which He delights, and the will of this holy one blending so completely with His that they seem as one, this understanding in which the light of God shines as the midday sun in the clear waters of a spring, and that memory that is always recollected in God, that heart that pants and languishes for Him and wastes itself away in longing desire to be dissolved and be one with Him for all eternity.

Oh my God, how much You have taught me in this soul which You drew from the same abyss of nothingness as myself, and yet, through her ready compliance with Thy adorable Will in all things, Thou hast raised her to a pinnacle of perfection which but very few saints have ever reached.

Oh my God, how wonderful are Thy works and how incomprehensible Thy judgements and unsearchable Thy ways. For this jewel of Thy house is a wonder to the angels and Thou Thyself hast shown me that (she) *this soul* is one of the centre pieces of Thy Sacred Heart. I know not whether *this soul* is a priest, or even a male or female saint, but I know you will join with me in thanking God for all He has done for it, and allowing us, unworthy as we are, to live and worship before this same tabernacle where in His Love He deigns to listen to us as well as to this great servant of His Sacred Heart. I think our dear Blessed Lord shows me this soul to humble me, for I always feel I am sinking away in the abyss of my own nothingness whenever He allows me to see it, and yet my whole soul seems to overflow with gratitude to Him for raising this soul to such perfection, and love and admiration at His work and delight beyond utterance at His reserving her (I mean the soul) to comfort and console, to love and adore Him as she does.

And this last week, after our beloved Lord has shown me the greatness of His gifts to this saint, He has made me feel what black ingratitude it would be if she refused to fulfil His designs. I understand that of course it will be a great humiliation for her to undertake the great work which I think He intends, and I pray for and compassionate her exceedingly, yet I burn with desire to see His holy Will accomplished and say with her, and for her, 'Thy holy Will be done, for Thou art my light and strength, Thou art my Protector and Helper, what shall I fear.'

Although I have no curiosity to know who this chosen one is, yet I feel an ardent desire to be near her and to render her some service, to go and meet her as St Elizabeth went to meet our Blessed Lady, our dear Mother Mary, at the time of the Visitation.

Cecil Kerr comments[11] that this is "the first allusion in Teresa's letters to this wonderful soul, though she seems to have known about it as far back as Wigan, [Note: 1874-1875 was the duration of Susan Ryland's stay there.] for Miss Ryland recalls her asking quite simply one day: 'Do you know that Father Wells directs a saint? I wonder who it is. If I knew I might do something for her, perhaps wash for her. Have you any idea who it is?' "

Teresa often writes to Father Powell regarding this "chosen one", earnestly entreating his prayers and expressing urgent desire to be allowed to do something for this innominate saint. In fact, both Father Powell and Father Snow felt certain that the 'unknown soul' was that of Teresa herself. With sagacious, imaginative insight, Father Snow concluded: "And so it came about in the mysterious designs of Providence that Teresa learnt humility from the vision of her own sanctity, and that her mighty prayers, so pleasing in the sight of God, were offered, all unconsciously, to herself, for the perfecting of her own soul."

Something of a riddle arose. Teresa had mentioned to Father Powell that St John somewhere speaks of the Sacred Head as the Seat of Divine Wisdom, and he asked her for the when and where of the reference. She told him: "After Holy Communion this morning [May 23rd, 1880] I asked our blessed Lord ... and He did not tell me what text or words. He gave me to understand that it was spoken of in the last two chapters of the Revelations and with this mark were sealed the numbers of His elect."

Very early on Ascension Day morning, 1880, she saw another vision.

Around His Sacred Head shone a light of indescribable brilliance and beauty: as it were a sun in which sparkled twelve magnificent crystal stones reflecting all the colours of the rainbow. And in the Head I saw as it were an ocean of fathomless depth, smooth and clear, and the brightness of the sun's rays penetrated to its very depths, and in it were reflected all the beauties of the sun and twelve stones like diamonds in which were reflected the green, yellowish green, purple, red, etc., and all the colours that sparkled in the sunny rainbow, and nearly in the centre was an eye ...

She revealed, too, that Our Lord had told her that it was His desire that the first Friday, after the feast of the Sacred Heart, should be dedicated as a festival day in honour of the Sacred Head, which He wished to be publicly worshipped.

The devotion to the Sacred Head is in some ways akin to

that to the Sacred Heart, for both are devotions to the humanity of Jesus. It was a very ordinary young woman, Margaret Mary Alcoque, of the ilk of Teresa Higginson, who was elected as its champion. Born in Janots, in the Burgundy region of eastern France, in 1647, she, like Teresa, suffered from poor health. A rheumatic illness kept her bedridden in her Poor Clare convent school for six years. Unlike Teresa, she contemplated marriage, then discovered a vocation, taking the veil after a vision of Our Lord, joining the Visitandine nuns in their convent at Paray-le-Monial, at the age of twenty. Shortly after her profession, she heard Our Lord, of whom she was aware as a sensible presence, telling her that she was His chosen instrument for the dissemination of a devotion to His Sacred Heart. She was, moreover, told that there should be established an especial feast of the Sacred Heart, to be observed annually on the Friday following Corpus Christi. Margaret Mary was generally dismissed as delusional. Further shades of Teresa. But she found a powerful supporter in a newly appointed confessor to the convent, Father Claude de la Colombière (canonised in 1992). Margaret Mary died, aged 43, in 1690. The devotion to the Sacred Heart spread throughout the Catholic world, but conservative official suspicion lingered, and it was not until 230 years after her death that, in 1920, she was canonised.

Among those who were asked to examine and pronounce upon Teresa's writings was William Ullathorne, O.S.B., (1827-1905), Bishop of Birmingham. He refused, excusing himself on the basis that he was much engaged, and, anyway, felt that without a personal knowledge of the writer, a perusal of the letters would not be of much avail. He appended to his diplomatic refusal a word of warning. "Extreme caution with respect to females who are liable to mistake imagination for revelation!"

Edmund Knight, (1806-1889), Bishop of Shrewsbury, was cautious, too. After reading Teresa's letters, he opined: "The impression they convey to me is first of all that they are the outcome of a mind deeply impressed with religious feeling and sincere in believing what she writes. So much of it is purely subjective that the evidence is intrinsic only, or else dependent on the character of the writer, and while this is known to *you* others would be without it in forming a judgment. The devotion she is especially drawn to is of course unexceptionable as being one aspect among many of the cultus of our Lord's Humanity."

Father Bertram Wilberforce, O.P., on the other hand, was deeply impressed by the devotion to the Sacred Head, adopted it himself, and did all in his power to spread it. He forwarded a long memorandum to Father Powell, which will be discussed later, together with a letter telling him: "I think much of what she writes is, especially for a person of her education and little reading, very wonderful and that it shows great illumination of mind. Her humility, obedience and mortification are wonderful, and, on reading the letters, my mind seems to *feel* they are true."

Also consulted by Bishop O'Reilly was Monsignor Alfred Weld, S.J. Professor Superior of Stonyhurst Seminary (1823-1890). He reported:

If all the information I have received is correct (a matter which would have to be tested with very great rigour if circumstances which do not at present present themselves rendered a juridical examination on the part of your Lordship necessary) she presents a case of extraordinary love of God and zeal for the salvation of souls, profound humility, unhesitating obedience, love of mortification and suffering only to be paralleled by that of some of the greatest saints. This seems to date from her infancy. If all this is true we should not be surprised if our Lord bestowed upon her some of the favours which He usually bestows upon such souls. He seems to have been prodigal to her in this way and what she relates with great reluctance by order of her director to whom she is bound by vows of obedience, is beyond the power of invention of one who has not made a deep study of the writings of the more mystic saints, and at the same time is so varied that only a profound knowledge of theology could enable one who was not exceptionally enlightened by our Lord Himself to vary what she has copied to such an extent as to oblige the reader to admit that all that can be said is that the favours are analogous to those of the saints, but not identical with them. She fulfils faithfully the duties of her state as a teacher, she influences all the other teachers, etc. with whom she is brought in contact, unostentatiously for great good and piety, she strips herself of everything and gives all her earnings away. As far as I have read of her extraordinary favours, I have seen nothing to which I could take exception.

One may interpret a remark dropped by Monsignor Weld in a letter which he wrote to Father Powell as expressing his surprise at the absence of any confirmatory miracles. He wrote: "I am struck by the absence of the more tangible signs by which our Lord generally conforms the truth of a great work when He entrusts it to the charge of a soul."

A point picked up by Father Snow. "As to miracles, I have to say that both Father Powell and I quite expected that important miracles would take place and that these would be of great help in furthering the Devotion to the Sacred Head, and at the same time be useful if, hereafter, there was question of her canonisation. But I never mentioned this subject to Teresa, nor did Father Powell to the best of my belief."

Father Thomas Smith, of St Francis de Sales, Walton, Liverpool, consulted in the matter of the validity of Teresa's phenomena, was for a time sympathetic, but later withdrew.

30. Father Thomas Smith. He blew hot and cold.

Also at first favourable to Teresa was an account which was to be rendered to Bishop O'Reilly by Father John Placid Hall, O.S.B., of Grassendale, Liverpool. He informed Father Powell, in November, 1882: "You will be glad to hear that after having read all Miss T.H.'s letters and thought over her case, I shall have to report to our good Bishop that T.H. has been, and is, supernaturally favoured and illuminated. As regards the Devotion to the Sacred Head, the arguments pro and contra are similar to those advanced and answered in connection with the Devotion to the Sacred Heart."

A mere week later, however, Father Hall underwent a change of opinion: "From her letters I had concluded that T.H. was exceedingly clever (seeing that she teaches in your school)

31. Higginson Family Group. Neston. 1884. Sitting: Louisa, Mother, Fanny, Teresa. Front: Minnie Matilda Jones and John Percy Jones.

had had a good education in a convent, possessed a lively imagination, etc. Our mishap the other evening enabled Father Snow to undeceive me somewhat." Father Hall had missed his train, and was on that account able to have a long talk with Father Snow, following which he wrote: "We cannot question T.H.'s truthfulness, but it seems clear to me that her vivid and strong imagination accounts, and is accountable for several statements in her letters." It seems that what stuck in the good Father's throat at the time was his reading of Teresa's alleged adventures in bilocation.

The report which, the following August, Father Hall submitted to the Bishop, surprised and disappointed Father Powell, who, clearly rather hurt, wrote to Father Hall: "On

Monday last week the Bishop told me he was satisfied I was duped by Miss T.H., that in your report you ascribed something to hysteria, some to delusion; and that 'assuming certain things narrated to be true,' that there was something supernatural or preternatural. His Lordship further added that in a conversation he had with you, you were stronger against this being the work of God even than in your report. I thought this was very different from what you led me to understand. I have not seen your report. I think you often said all rested on her individual testimony. Before I saw the Bishop, three other of my teachers, and Miss Flynn with whom they lodge, as well as Miss H. heard such yells, blows, unearthly noises, that they could not sleep at all for three nights; that they sent one of their number to me ... to give orders to Miss H. to tell the Devil – to whom they ascribe these disturbances – that he was not to frighten them any more, or to let them hear anything. The four were really very ill with terror. I send you what they wrote, describing what they each heard. Please return the book to me. I have to thank you for all your trouble in the matter, though, of course, I grieve for your decision."

The practical upshot of all this commotion was that Bishop O'Reilly pronounced Teresa a pest, and advised the clergy of St Alexander's to lock the church door against her. The curates needed no second bidding. They had always regarded her with unreasonable harshness. One had, indeed, refused her admission to the church on a previous occasion, saying that she was mentally defective. Becoming aware of what was going on, Father Powell had then let her in through the presbytery door. Another time, when Teresa called at the presbytery to sell some raffle tickets, one of the curates told her never to come again, and said that if he saw her loitering there at any time in the future he would send for the police.

The Bishop also wrote to Father Powell, telling him that he

was satisfied that he had been duped by Teresa, although, backing his bet both ways you might think, he added, "If it is the work of God it will prosper in spite of opposition." He wished Miss Higginson to change her confessor, and said that she must write no more of those letters of hers.

Originally trained for the legal profession, before abandoning it to become a priest, Alfred Snow who had served as a curate under Father Powell at St Alexander's since 1874, and had moved away to take charge of the mission of St Mary's, at Aughton, near Ormskirk, in Lancashire, persuaded by Father Powell, agreed, with some diffidence and after making a retreat, to take over as her spiritual director and confessor, which he was to remain, supremely satisfactorily, to the day of her death.

NOTE
11 p.108.

6

EXODUS

The clamour against Teresa had been growing in intensity. Insults were being hurled at her in the streets. Garbled reports circulating about the ructions going on in Ariel Street were met with superstitious head noddings and mutterings about the Devil having come to claim his own. On a more earthly, and earthy, plane, she was said to have been seen gorging herself greedily and lurching drunkenly down dim-lit courts. They said that under a masking cloak of bogus sanctity there lurked a thoroughly vile and evil woman.

Father Powell wrote to a friend: "I rather like the idea of so many turning against her. I never read of them doing this with a hypocrite; in such cases the Devil sees that she is honoured to the end, until suddenly, the hypocrite or the Good God flashes the truth out. But the conduct towards Miss Higginson is exactly the way St Teresa, Blessed Margaret Mary, St Francis, St Philip Neri, and almost all the saints were treated. So I look upon it as the best sign that the whole is from God."

A decidedly eerie happening experienced by Father Powell in Teresa's company is recounted by Cecil Kerr: "It was the custom at Bootle to toll the church bell when anyone died so that all might join in the *de profundis* for the departed soul. On one such occasion there was no one about, and Teresa went into the church wondering whether she could ring the bell herself. As she stood there a little boy came in, and running up the belfry steps, began to ring the bell. Just then Father Powell arrived and asked who it was who was ringing. Teresa answered, 'That little

32. Canon Snow and Jumbo, his Great Dane, outside the church and presbytery of St Mary's, Aughton.

boy: it is the little boy who helps me to carry the big candlesticks when I am not able. I often see him in front of the altar praying.' The bell stopped, but no little boy came down. Father Powell said: 'No little boy could carry those candlesticks. It must be an angel or the Child Jesus.'"

Returning to Ariel Street one afternoon quite exhausted and thoroughly ruffled by the things she had heard being said about Teresa, whose reputation she had been stoutly defending, Minnie Catterall found her friend sitting quietly knitting some sort of garment.

"Who's that for?" she asked her.

"Mrs M.," replied Teresa.

"What," Minnie's voice was a positive shriek, "Mrs M.?

*33. St Winefride's Cottage, the
School-house, Neston.*

Why she's always crying out against you."

"Hush, she has five children."

"I don't care, why should you do this work of charity for one of your bitterest enemies?"

"They are my greatest friends," came the strange answer.

Comments a writer in the *Catholic Times*,"Anyone who added a drop of gall to her bitter chalice was her friend. She absolutely refused to defend herself, saving to the confessor who was responsible for her soul."

Young Helen Nicholson made no bones about it: "She suffered so much in every way. Many people began to notice and remark about her and some were not favourably inclined. In fact, she was most cruelly spoken of and unkindly treated, although she herself was so kind to everyone and always ready to help in every way."

And Helen remembered how, even at Everton Valley Convent, where she was studying to become a teacher, and where Teresa used to attend the First Friday devotions, some of the girls and teachers believed in her and others did not, "but we were not allowed to talk about her in any way. I was always up in arms if anyone spoke against her. I felt, and knew, that she was so different from anyone else, and I loved her much."

Another witness to those Bootle days is Miss Agnes Donnelly. She was only a schoolgirl at the time, but her parents were on the staff of St Alexander's School and knew Teresa well as a colleague. "My parents always spoke of Miss Higginson as a saint ... my mother knew her for many years and spent many hours in her company. On her death-bed she suddenly said, 'I wonder when the Church will recognise Teresa's sanctity.' " Agnes Donnelly's father was once heard to declare: "If Teresa had been in an order of nuns she would have been canonised long before this." St Margaret Mary Alcoque might not altogether agree!

A good example of how, in those troubled days of Teresa's life, misinterpretations might arise: it is told of how, having met a beggar boy in the street and learnt that he was a lapsed Catholic, Teresa succeeded in persuading him to go to the Sacraments. The lad was weakly, half-starved, and she thought it would be a good thing to have a bit of food ready for him after he had been, fasting, to Communion. So, off she went and bought some bread, a little meat, and a few biscuits for him. But when she went in search of the boy she could not find him. Not wishing to waste the provender purchased out of her slight means, she stowed it away temporarily in her tin trunk under her bed. During Teresa's absence, a suspicious, inimical female of the species – most likely her resentful landlady, Miss Flynn –

34. Louisa Higginson. Headmistress at Neston.

stole into her bedroom, rooted around and triumphantly came up with the 'hidden' comestibles which *proved* what nonsense it was to say that this fraud never ate.

Miss Flynn, according to Bernadette Hurndall, regarded Teresa "as an object of curiosity, and seeing Teresa sitting in ecstasy, oblivious of her surroundings, she would trundle the chair around the room to show her friends the queer state that enveloped her lodger." [Note: *By God's Command*, p.57]

Another one who had no time for Teresa was her fellow-teacher, Miss Shuttleworth. When blood trickled down from her forehead on to her scarf, as at certain seasons it did, she made no bones about saying that she thought Teresa had been doing something to herself, as it was a Friday.

One last Teresian mystery of the time – a high scandal which took eleven years in the solving.

The tale is told by Father Snow: "A Mrs Banks, a lady in the parish [of St Alexander's], presented Fr. Powell with a surplice. It so happened that Miss Higginson made one for him of exactly the same pattern. Not wishing Fr. Powell to know from whom it came, she took it into Cook and Townsend's of Liverpool and asked a young woman at a counter to add some little detail to it and to have it got up at the laundry and send it to Fr. Powell without any word as to whence it came. Some time after, the housekeeper, Mary Kelly, was getting up the surplice Mrs Banks sent, and called Miss Higginson's attention to some alteration or repair that was needed, and Miss Higginson, having no other thought than that she had made that very surplice, referred to some difficulty she had had in making it, in short she said she had made it and had it sent to Fr. Powell. Mary Kelly, knowing that Mrs Banks had presented it, considered that Miss Higginson was lying and taking credit to herself for the gift. Miss Higginson could not explain the mystery, nor did she try to solve it, but left the matter in the hands of God.

Eleven years later, in 1897, the following letter was sent under cover to the Bishop 'to be forwarded to the Rev. Mr Powell, late of Bootle.'

Rev. Sir.

About eleven years ago I was forewoman in a Liverpool drapery establishment and while there I undertook to send off by our delivery van a box to you given in by a lady customer, but yielding to a strong temptation I kept it and sold contents which was a linen surplice with deep crocheted lace in Marie monogram for 30/-. I was then a Protestant but have since become a Roman Catholic and wish to make restitution and beg your Reverence to pray for me and to

137

forgive me. I am heartily sorry and beg God to forgive me and I wish to atone for this and my many other sins and ask you holy Sir to pray for me. I enclose p.o. for 30/-.

In all probability, Mrs Banks was the person to whom the surplice was sold for thirty shillings.

Father Powell commented, in a letter to Minnie Catterall: "So this clears up that mystery. I think this is one of the tales Fr. Tom Smith [of St Francis de Sales, Walton] got hold of. Please let him know the truth."

This, incidentally, was also one of the things cited against Teresa in the turn-coat priest's report to the Bishop in June, 1886 [see below]. Immediately after receipt of the 'surplice confession' letter, Father Snow wrote to the erstwhile complainant cleric: "I send you a copy of a letter received last week by Fr. Powell. ... The matter concerns you more than me. I had at the time such overwhelming proof of her sanctity and high gifts that I paid little regard to the many wicked things said about her. All the saints have had to suffer such things and Benedict 14th says that they are 'essential to a saint that has to be canonised.' I will only add that all that has happened since that time (1886) has confirmed me in the conviction I then had that she is not only a great saint but one of the greatest saints Almighty God has ever raised up in His Church. On the last page I have copied your remarks on the surplice contained in your letter to me in June, 1886. You see you as it were give the Almighty five years in which to clear this matter up. He has taken eleven. *Mirabilis in sanctis Suis.*"

Teresa was at home in Neston during the summer holidays of 1884, and was with her mother when, on September 28th, she died, very peacefully and fully fortified with the Rites of Holy Church. The natural great grief of her loss was assuaged for Teresa, for, as she afterwards said, she could not really feel unhappy about it, knowing what a welcome Our Lord had given to her mother.

At the end of the summer term of 1885, Father Powell was moved from St Alexander's to the Church of Our Lady, at Lydiate, in south west Lancashire, where he took charge on October 9th, 1885, and where he was to remain until his death, at the age of sixty-four, on December 26th, 1901.

In October, 1885, Teresa became a Franciscan Tertiary. The Franciscans are members of the Order of Friars Minor, founded by St Francis of Assisi in 1209. The rule was to apply to three component orders: one for men (Friars Minor Conventuals and Friars Minor Capuchins); the second order for women (the Poor Clares); the Third Order for lay persons of both sexes. This last is an association recognised by the Code of Canon Law, and is dedicated to the promotion of Catholic life and action.

Teresa wrote to Father Snow in May, 1886, telling him: "I went to Liverpool yesterday and saw," she names a particular priest, "and he told me he felt very dissatisfied about all he had heard. I need not tell you how hurt I was, although I am truly grateful for it. I did not think I could care so much, but when our dear Lord sends a cross of course He knows how to make us feel. ... He[12] is going on his retreat tomorrow, so please say a little prayer for him, and when he returns he says he is going to devote some time in thoroughly investigating things." The reverend father, who had formerly been her staunchest admirer and done all that he could to promote the devotion to the Sacred Head, had now been metamorphosed into one of her most rabid opponents. He wrote to Father Snow: "I have just sent in to the Bishop at his command a full report of the investigations I lately made into the case of Miss Higginson. He told me to write down all I knew about her and all that I have lately found out about her. This I have done at considerable length and I think that the case I have handed in to him is most damaging to her unless you and Fr. Powell can prove that the statements in it are all

139

untrustworthy. For this purpose, namely to give her every opportunity of clearing herself from the accusations made, I have petitioned his Lordship to place what I have written in your hands that you may show it up or confirm its statements. I am sure that from what you know about her you will easily be able to bring the truth to light and I have no fear in abiding by your decision, after you have examined into the facts that I have had to state to his Lordship. Above all, I trust that you won't be angry with me for not previously stating to you what I was preparing to send to the Bishop for I was afraid that you would perhaps wish me to make omissions which my conscience would scarcely permit me to make. At any rate I have every belief that her case will now appear in its true light, for you can easily prove the matter."

The matter was not, in fact, going to be at all easy to prove. One of the most tiresome stumbling-blocks was that Teresa was not prepared to make the slightest effort to clear herself, except, under the seal of Confession, to her confessor.

She told Father Snow: "I have thought that perhaps it may please our dear b. Lord to allow people to really consider me guilty of the different sins I have offered myself to expiate and let me feel the shame and confusion that the persons would feel at these things being known, and if I could save one from shame on the last dreadful day, how willingly will I submit to more, for I did not think these things could affect me so keenly. I do not intend to contradict one of the accusations, only to you as you are answerable to God for my poor soul."

On April 17th, 1886, Father Snow was constrained to write to her:

My Dear Child,
Another little cross for you. Almighty God has been pleased to allow someone to enquire into certain things concerning you

140

with a view to trying your truthfulness, more especially with regard to your not eating or drinking. You must therefore give me an explanation of the three following things.

1. It has been said that there has been found a piece of something that appeared to be masticated meat in the vessel that contained the gargle you used recently for your throat.

2. Some bread and meat was seen in your box. Tell me how it came there and what became of it.

3. Miss Flynn has said that in the mornings to gargle your throat there was provided for you a quantity of tea equal to two cups full and that after you had finished there remained a quantity equal to one cup full. Write me an explanation of these things and send this letter back along with your own.

To this Teresa replied:

Dear Rev. Father,

I duly received yours of yesterday and in obedience and in the Holy Name of Jesus and Mary I answer as far as I can.

1. With regard to something looking like meat. I remember Miss Flynn passing the remark about it appearing like a piece of flesh, but I think it was a piece of clotted blood. I have often got up something like it before. I know positively it was not meat.

2. The bread and meat you mention was in my box, but I did not know that anyone saw it. I got a barm cake buttered and a quarter of meat from Miss Smith's shop one Saturday night for a poor lad who promised me to go to Confession. He was begging and I found out that he was a Catholic and had not been to the Sacrament for a long time. I got him to go and thought to give him the bread and meat afterwards. I saw him go into Fr. Rigby, and then went to Miss Smith's and bought

the above, telling her about him, either her or Mrs O'Hara, and asking them to say a little prayer for him. Then I went to wait for him coming out, but I missed him, and I put the cake etc. inside my jacket, and left it there. On Sunday morning, I put it inside my little tin box intending to give it to some child, but I forgot it and left it till Tuesday morning. I then took it to school and gave it to one of the boys to give to someone who had hens. I think it was T. Macmanus who took it.

3. As for the missing cup of tea, I really do not know what became of that without it was the day I upset the basin, or that one of the Miss Catteralls emptied it away before I gargled my throat a second time, for Miss Flynn would bring me some tea in a jug and leave it so that she need not come up more than about twice a day, or Miss Catterall was very kind sometimes bringing warm fresh tea and throwing out the cold, and always helping me by raising me and holding the cup for me.

I am not surprised about the questions you have asked me, and I have answered them as far as I can. I expected more, a great deal to have been said, and I know the Devil will do his best, and Almighty God will permit a great many things to be sifted, and I am only waiting His divine pleasure. You need not mind my feelings – do what you think is best, but I feel convinced that our dear Lord will not gratify vain curiosity.

It is recorded, written on the back of an old photograph of Canon Snow and his dog, Jumbo, outside St Mary's Church, Aughton, how, staying there as the Canon's guest, Teresa was in church one night making the Stations of the Cross, when "she was joined by two souls, who followed her round the church. She recognised them by their voices. One was a Miss McDonald, whom she knew, the other a priest of her acquaintance. Next morning Teresa asked the Canon to remember them in his Mass, as, she told him, they had died the previous night. Both the deceased were known to Canon Snow. Later, he received news of their deaths."

The charges against Teresa continued to accumulate. Father Powell's successor at Bootle, Father Michael Beggan,[13] was by no means partial to Teresa. Frankly, he disliked and distrusted her. He refused to bring Holy Communion to her. His behaviour in respect, or rather disrespect, of her was savage, thoughtless, and uncaring. Not to put too fine a point on it, with scant concession to charity he threw her out, with sacerdotally unbecoming indifference as to what was to become of her. His carefully cultivated self-excuse: henceforth he would be employing masters in the place of mistresses in the Boys' school. Teresa, uncomplaining, unprotesting as ever, packed up her small parcel of personal belongings and softly and silently vanished away.

Father Thomas Smith, of St Francis de Sales, Walton, facilitated Teresa's escape. He arranged temporary shelter for her with one of his parishioners, with whom she stayed until Easter Sunday. She then went home to her sisters at Neston, where, just to add insult to injury, to ensure that she really felt that she was being ignominiously booted out of Bootle, the postman delivered this nice little *billet amer* from her former landlady, Miss Flynn:

> Dear Miss Higginson,
> You are not to come to 15 Ariel Street any more except to take your things. I think home is the best place for you. If you like I will send your things to Birkenhead. Rev. Fr. says you need not come back and whether or no I could not do with you any longer.
> J. Flynn.

When the whole ghastly business had burnt itself out, Teresa wrote in a letter: "I do not think any Liverpool priest would have me in their school, for I know many reports are circulated among them, so in charity to their children they could not permit me to go in among them, much less to teach them."

It was during her visit home to Neston in November, 1876, that Teresa encountered what seems to have been a strange revenant. During this particular stay of hers, the parish priest, Canon Daly, had gone away, leaving the keys of the church in her charge. There was a shortage of wicks for the sanctuary lamp, and although Teresa had written off for more, they had not arrived, and she was worried in case the lamp should go out. That was when there came, early one morning, a sudden knock at the door and standing there was an old priest whom she did not know. Without a word, he handed her a box of wicks, then walked past her into the sacristy. Although he did not at any point actually speak, he somehow managed to intimate that he wished to say Mass. He seemed to know where to find everything. Teresa prepared the altar for him and lit the candles, noting with some surprise that he appeared to be strangely familiar with the place. She served his Mass and received Holy Communion from his hands. When the Mass was finished, she asked him if he would prefer tea or coffee for breakfast. He did not reply, so she went off to get his breakfast. She asked the milk boy, who had just arrived, if he would kindly go to the sacristy and tell the priest there that his breakfast was waiting. The boy came back and said there was no one in the sacristy, and he had not seen a priest anywhere around. Teresa went herself to the sacristy. She found the vestments there all neatly folded, but of the celebrant there was not a sign. Thoroughly puzzled, she made inquiries in the village, and drew a complete blank. Nobody seemed to have seen him. When Canon Daly returned, she retailed the matter to him, and he in turn told the Bishop about it. His Lordship remarked that the description of the

35. *St Winefride's Church and presbytery, Neston.*

stranger tallied exactly with that of a priest who used to serve St Winefride's many years before, and who, indeed, had lain buried many a long day in the church's graveyard.

This story is told by Montague Summers in the Introduction to his *Supernatural Omnibus* (Gollancz, London, 1949), where he says: "It is, if I mistake not, on this event that Miss Grace Christmas founded her story 'Faithful unto Death' in *What Father Cuthbert Knew*." The tale also features in *Haunted England*, by Christina Hole (Batsford, London, 1941).

Over the course of the nine months succeeding her unceremonious sacking from Bootle, Teresa took two teaching jobs – at Eccleshall, a market town in Staffordshire, and, back in Lancashire, at Osbaldeston, near Blackburn.

36. The interior of St Winefride's Church, Neston.

She was at first delighted at the prospect of Eccleshall – "It is close to Stone, so I can go to the convent there, I am so pleased about that, though I feel it more than I can very well say leaving all that has been so dear to me, but I am glad of a chance of a little self-denial. We do not know how much attachment we have for persons and places until we are obliged to leave them." But Eccleshall, where she started work in August, proved a sad disappointment. The mission there was not as yet fully established and there was no daily Mass. She made the best of it though, whenever possible setting off for Stone – "but it is a long way for me, three miles to Norton Bridge Station and then four and a half in the train." – where she could rely upon a cordial welcome from Father Wilberforce. And to be fair, Father

E. Tunstall, the parish priest at Eccleshall, left the church open for her, so that she could pay morning, dinner-time, and night visits to the reserved Sacrament.

At the end of September, 1886, the Eccleshall school having temporarily closed, Teresa returned to Neston. A month later, she found a place at Osbaldeston. Here, she again encountered difficulties about hearing daily Mass, but on a considerably lesser scale than at Eccleshall, and the good, pious people with whom she boarded pleased her immensely by saying prayers to the Sacred Head each night. As Lent approached, a fearful agony of dread and fear overcame her. But merciful relief was at hand. In March, 1887, she received a very welcome letter. It was from her old friend and fellow teacher at St Alexander's, Minnie Catterall. Minnie, who had left St Alexander's some time before Teresa's engineered dismissal, was now the mistress in charge of St Peter's School, at Newchurch, then a rather quaint village on an eminence overlooking the Rossendale Valley, some two and a half miles from Rawtenstall, in Lancashire. She had taken there with her as her assistant, Helen Nicholson, who, after completing her pupil-teachership at St Alexander's, had gone on to Bishop Goss Memorial School, but, owing to a bout of ill-health, had had to leave, and had for some time been unemployed.

Helen recalled:

As it was a branch school, away from the main church at Rawtenstall, we had a little school-house to ourselves near our little school. We had to walk about two to two and a half miles to Mass on Sundays. Miss Catterall and I were very happy there together, and we often talked about Bootle and our friends, especially dear Miss Higginson, whom we both loved so well. She was then at her house at Neston, and we often wished we could have her with us for a visit. Eventually Miss Catterall wrote and asked Father Snow, who was then Miss Higginson's director, if he would allow her to come and visit us at Newchurch. We promised to take great care of her and look after her well. At first, he would not consent, but after several more urgent appeals he promised, on condition that she was to be kept quiet and not annoyed by visitors nor inquisitive persons. Readily we agreed, and we were delighted to be so privileged. We were soon busy preparing for her arrival. She came, and her visit to us proved of great importance. She was very happy with us and we spent many pleasant hours together. She never went out, but was always anxious to do all she could for us while we were at school. ... She was so interested in the school and the children, anxiously enquiring about their religious habits and those of their parents. What she felt most of all was being unable to go to Mass and Communion daily. Although Father Mussely, the rector, was most kind and brought her Holy Communion once or twice each week, the distance was so great he could not come more often. We always arranged for Sunday Mass, though it was sometimes difficult to get a conveyance. We often stayed the whole of Sunday at the presbytery, and in this way we became acquainted with Father Mussely's housekeeper, Margaret Murphy, who became greatly attached to Teresa. Teresa too was very fond of Margaret. She was such a good, holy soul and so humble, and Teresa soon realised her goodness.

Margaret got permission from Father Mussely to visit Teresa at the school-house to keep her company while we were at school. They became great friends. Teresa, knowing that Margaret was very prudent, talked to her most confidingly. We were forbidden to discuss her in any way or to speak of what we knew or had seen. Miss Catterall suggested to Father Mussely that if he wrote to Father Snow he would be able to tell him about her, since he was her director and knew her well. This he did, and they became the greatest of friends and stood by Teresa to the end of her days. Both these good and holy priests realised Teresa's great sanctity and what a privileged soul she was and how dear to Our Lord.

During Teresa's stay with us she suffered intensely, and we were often grieved to see her in great pain, but she herself never murmured a word of complaint.

There had been no hesitation in Teresa's reply to the letter that invited her to come and stay with Minnie and Helen and look after them at the Newchurch school-house. She arrived there, tin trunk and all, on March 24th, 1887.

This was a happy time. Minnie Catterall remembered: "We had a very nice school-house and Father Mussely was very kind and often visited us. … When I first introduced Teresa to him, he appeared keenly interested in her and asked me if there was not something in her of an extraordinary nature, for he considered her a very holy and wonderful person, though he had not seen or heard of her before."

Described [Cecil Kerr, p.199] as "a practical minded Belgian and a very holy priest", he was from the first "much impressed by Teresa, struck chiefly by her wonderful eyes which seemed to see so far." His housekeeper, Margaret Murphy, " a simple soul who possessed the golden gift of silence", and who had been a factory girl, was likewise entranced by Teresa.

Margaret would tell how one day she had knocked loudly and persistently on the school-house door, and, although she knew that Teresa must be in, could get no answer. Challenged the following day as to why she had not opened the door, Teresa's somewhat odd reply was, "Oh, my guardian angel never told me you were there! He must have been busy getting the tea!"

Teresa, who was an excellent cook, took great pleasure in preparing tasty surprises for Minnie and Helen's high tea, which she had ready for them when they came in from school. She remained at Newchurch for four months, and, as we have already seen, it was there that Minnie Catterall and Helen Nicholson both witnessed her reception of the Miraculous Communion.

Another mystic experience reported by Teresa to Minnie Catterall was a visit which she said that she had had from a lady with a most beautiful child, and the whole evening she could speak of nothing but this mysterious visitation. A few days later, Teresa said that the lady had paid her another call, and that this time she had been allowed to hold the beautiful child in her arms. Margaret Murphy subsequently confided to Minnie that Teresa had told her that Our Lady had been the visitor, and she had shown her the chair upon which she had sat. That chair has been preserved to this day.

Father Mussely and Margaret Murphy both came rapidly to regard Teresa as a saint.

Teresa's stay was not by any means all pleasure, for her Lenten sufferings were exceptionally severe that year. Minnie Catterall informed Father Snow: "She has been in bed all day today and can scarcely articulate a word. Her throat seems to be in a fearful condition and I cannot persuade her to gargle it. She has not done it once since she came. She has been bad more or less every day. I think she is worse this year than she has ever been before." Teresa afterwards echoed that opinion, referring to Lent, 1887, as "the very hardest I have yet known."

Sometimes Minnie Catterall's feelings approached panic. "It is fearful to see her and to feel the presence of God," she tells Father Snow. "I never used to have such feelings as I have now [when] she gets bad. I am not afraid of her in any way, for I stay by her side all the time waiting to see if I can do anything for her. Do you think there is any fear of her dying? I have heard her exclaim several times: 'Let it break!' and it seems to me that her heart is really going to break … I do get so frightened sometimes."

For all these interludes of high drama, there was nothing gloomy about Teresa. She is universally limned by her friends as bright and cheerful, full of fun, very merry, spreading an air of happiness, even singing and dancing on occasion. She was never seen to open a book or read a newspaper, yet she seemed able to more than hold her own in conversations upon any topic of the day. She was a good listener and ever ready to enter with intelligent interest into all the details of her friends' daily lives.

Another eighteen years of living stretched before her, and the greatest event of her entire life lay hidden just around the corner.

NOTES

12 This is almost certainly Father John Placid Hall, O.S.B.

13 Born c.1842, he was Ireland's gift to the Roman Catholic Church in Lancashire. In 1871, he is to be found at Our Lady's Church in Great Mersey Street, Liverpool. In 1881, he was the priest in charge at St Sylvester's, Silvester Street, Liverpool. He died, aged about 65, in 1906, by which time he had been rewarded with a canonship.

7

BRIDAL

Towards the end of July, 1887, Teresa moved from Newchurch – gratefully, for she had found the distances there for church attendance proving difficult – to Clitheroe, where it had been arranged that she should go to stay with her old friend the mill girl, Elizabeth Dawson, now retired, and living in a modest stone dwelling at 53 Lowergate, with her adopted sister. This visit was the realisation of Lizzie's one great ambition; that Teresa should stay with her for a while.

In the tiny house, literally a stone's throw from the Church of St Michael and St John the Evangelist, Teresa was given a first-floor-back, from the window of which the church's sanctuary lamp could be seen, its living flame burning steadily away the long watches of her nights.

"Since I came to Clitheroe," she told Father Snow, "I feel as if I had all I could desire on this earth. Two Masses every morning and a visit to our dear blessed Lord whenever I like to go in church, and I go in school every day, and I can see the tabernacle from my bedroom window. I shall feel as if I were going into Purgatory out of Heaven when I have to return."

But it cannot have been all idyll, for Lizzie's 18-year-old cousin – a Miss Bolton – was later to testify: "We used to hear terrific noises in the small room occupied by Teresa which we now know was the Devil."

The things which marked Teresa apart very soon became evident. Lizzie saw her guest receive Miraculous Communion. She testified that the Sacred Host "seemed to come through the

37. The Church of St Michael and St John the Evangelist, Clitheroe.

roof." She saw, too, Teresa's forehead speckled with small blood-spangled woundings, as from the penetrative spicules of thorns. And Sarah Ann Orrell, who lived in the house with Lizzie and her sister, discovered that Teresa, who suffered so much herself, could banish pain from others. The two were out walking together one day when Miss Orrell was struck on the head by a cricket ball. The pain, she said, was intense, but when Teresa put her hand on the spot it stopped immediately.

For Teresa herself, though, pain was to diminish her otherwise unalloyed pleasure in her visit to Lizzie's. That September of 1897, was to prove a month of the most awful anguish. "I have never before experienced such terrible sufferings as I underwent last night. … I feel I really could not

38. No. 53 Lowergate, Clitheroe, where
Teresa stayed with Lizzie Dawson.

go through the same again. … One five minutes of such agony I am sure outweighs all united pains and sufferings of my life."

It was to be the final purifying fire, the conflagrant prelude to the raising of the curtain of suffering upon the greatest spiritual event of her life. The scene of this grand and glorious happening was humble, humble as the stable at Bethlehem: a tiny back bedroom barely bigger than a box-room. On the night of Sunday, October 3rd – Monday, October 4th, 1887, there was celebrated on this unlikely stage what the Latin Church hails as the closest union with Jesus Christ possible to a human soul upon earth – the Mystical Marriage.

Teresa, the Bride of Christ, described the ceremony as best she could to Father Powell:

"In the Name of the most august and blessed Trinity and in holy obedience I write of the unspeakable favours which Jesus Christ, true God and true Man, my divine Spouse and only Treasure, through the excess of His infinite Love has bestowed on me, the very least of His little ones. Oh my Father, how can I find words to express this wonderful mystery, this excess of His mercy and love, which is more astounding to me than the great mystery of the Incarnation. Oh my Love, my Love, my beautiful One, my Jesus, my Own, my All, my God my ... (the writing trails off into illegibility).

Oh my Father, it seems to me almost impossible to continue, or rather I should say I am unable to begin and describe what I would. This is the third paper I have spoiled; I am carried away at the recollection of His wonderful condescension. I have twice before written the four pages, and when I read them over I found it full of little prayers, and now again I find myself like one only half awake, for my whole being seems lost in His infinite immensity, His wonderful attributes, the unspeakable dignity to which He has raised this little nothing. And so, prostrating myself before the thrice holy Trinity, and before Jesus, my own Jesus, my spouse, and my Treasure, I beg of Him to guide my hand and my understanding, that I may write without these little wanderings, and make clear to you all that you would wish to know, to the praise and glory of His holy Name. Oh my soul, bless the Lord and magnify, for He has regarded the nothingness of His handmaid and has had compassion on my weakness and misery. He has drawn up this little drop of water from the earth into the ocean of His infinity, into the Essence of the Unity and Trinity of the Almighty God of Wisdom and Love, the all-pure and uncreated One, and made me one with Himself in the most holy and solemn bond of marriage. He has really and truly united Himself to me in the presence of the whole court of heaven, presenting me as His beloved Spouse to the Eternal Father and the

39. The Room of the Mystical Marriage,
at 53, Lowergate, Clitheroe.

Holy Spirit, and His blessed Mother, St Joseph, the Cherubim, and Seraphim, etc., etc., and making me feel and understand how this sacred alliance was as real and as true as the union of His divine and human Nature in the one Person of Himself, Jesus Christ the Coeternal Son and the Son of Mary since the moment of the Incarnation. And in His Name and with His help, I will tell the way as far as I can that all has been accomplished.

Remember, oh my Love and my Lord, that I am all Thine, and Thou art the God of Truth, the Word that is God, and that now I am one with Thee, as the body and soul of man are one person, so my words must be a reflection of Thine, must be, as Thou hast said to me they shall be, Wisdom and Truth, as the honey that drips from the hive, pure and sweet, and all men may confess that these things are the works of Thy Wisdom and Love.

Since the feast of our holy Father St Francis, when my divine Spouse gave me the general absolution {as I complained to Him that I had not been able to receive it from the hands of a priest and we had no Franciscans here), He caressed my soul, as it were, and told me that He would give me the absolution, not to take away sins from which He had preserved me, but to saturate me with His most Precious Blood and make me more like Himself. And He let me feel that my soul (through His presence and the holy Sacraments) gave great glory to the adorable Trinity and was a reflection of Themselves, in the powers in which He had, and they had taken up their abode, and which was glistening and saturated with His adorable precious Blood. He told me frequently that as I had given myself wholly to Him to be His entirely, so He would be all mine, and that He would glorify me in the sight of the angels and saints, because I had emptied myself and become as naught to myself and had gladly clothed myself with the sins of others for the price they had cost Him and for the love of His image and likeness. And because I desired Him with a longing nigh unto death, He would unite Himself to me in the closest union possible and clothe me with the brightness of His glory, and because I had rejoiced and united myself to Him when I was reviled by men and had clothed myself in the fool's garment (as it were) as He was during His bitter Passion, so He was about to clothe me with the wedding garment of Purity Charity and Truth. He also shot those fiery darts of love from His sacred Heart into the very centre of my poor soul so frequently that I felt as though my breast was a liquid fire: a boiling seemed to be going on in and through my entire being, and the pain it caused was so excessive that I continually cried aloud to Him for pity, and told Him again and again that He knew how I loved and desired Him, and begged of Him to burn away all that was not Himself, and so unite me and make me all His own, though never for one moment dreaming of the unutterable favour which His love has accomplished. In this fire which burns very clearly, for there is no smoke or wet fuel – in this consuming flame, all is brightness, and the light thereof is very pure so that the soul sees very clearly what God is and what He has done for her and that she has nothing of her own, all being the gift of her great and wise Creator and Redeemer, and she knows and understands how the Holy Spirit has sanctified her, and seeing what she is, and what God is, she is, as it were, annihilated in His sacred presence. Oh how He has taught me what I am and what I owe Him and His excessive love!

Well, on Sunday the 23rd, the feast of our Holy Redeemer, I thought of the holy Sacrifice being offered for me, I tried to make the same act of oblation to God of myself as my divine Spouse made to His Eternal Father during His most bitter Passion, and I felt that He graciously accepted the offering I made. Then, in the evening, I begged of the angel Raphael to guide me to my divine Spouse, as he did of old the young Tobias, and I sent the angel of the Incarnation to present my soul to Him with all its affections, my body with all its senses, to be all His forever, and I begged Him to present me through the hands of Mary, His Queen and my Mother, as a clean oblation in His sight. Then I repeated several times: 'Oh Wisdom of the sacred Head guide me in all my ways, oh love of the sacred Heart consume me with Thy fire,' when I found my soul fluttering on my lips almost, and my spirit softly stealing through the gates of death, and I was fainting away with desire, and yet such a calm, sweet peace was in my soul that it seemed to check the throbbing of my poor heart, that tried to break, because it was overwhelmed with His goodness and love, and yearned to be united with Him whom it loves with all its affections. Oh how I hunger and thirst after Him, for He alone can satisfy! And as I was thus literally dying, I think, of desire of Him, He appeared holding the b. Sacrament before me, and I thought He had come, as He so frequently does, to feed me with His adorable Body and refresh me with His most precious Blood, but refrained for some time, (it seemed an age to me) and stood gazing into the very centre of my poor trembling soul, which would have left this poor prison of the flesh if it could to fly to and rest in Him her only Good.

Then He gave me Himself in Holy Communion, and the Sacred Host liquefied, and I seemed to drink of the precious Blood, till I was saturated through and through. And it changed all into Itself, and my divine Spouse spoke to my soul and said He would now fulfil the promise He had made to me so often and present me to the adorable Trinity, and unite Himself to me in the presence of the whole court of heaven. I felt annihilated at these words, for I felt my nothingness and unworthiness, and I think I would really have died if He had not supported me by a new miracle of power and love.

Then He said, 'Arise my Beloved that I may glorify the triune God in Unity and espouse thee in Their adorable presence.' And turning then to His blessed Mother, He gave me to her as her daughter, and Mary taking hold of my hand gave it to Jesus, and He withdrew the ring that He had before placed upon it, and then replaced it on the same finger, saying: 'I espouse thee in the Name and in the presence of the uncreated Trinity and in the presence of My Immaculate Mother, and I give you to her as a daughter and My Spouse for ever.' "

All this, the dialogue and the ritual, must have emanated from Teresa's brain, presented to her in the form of a vision. That is not to deny its validity, nor to dismiss the possibility of both being of supernatural implant, but merely to account for its apparent substantiality.

For most of us, these phenomena of the Mystic Espousal and Mystic Marriage are concepts so far removed from our daily life and experience that they prove difficult to apprehend. The fact of the matter is that they are both widely recorded historically, having featured in the lives of many of the saints, and are described by the Reverend Herbert Thurston, S.J. in his classic study *The Physical Phenomena of Mysticism* (Burns Oates, London, 1951.) as "closely akin in some respects to the phenomenon of stigmatization, but in other features very different".

Let us take a closer look at the essentially mysterious phenomenon of the stigmata.

First of all, make no mistake, stigmata are genuine, if still definitively inexplicable, woundings of the living flesh. What they are not, by definition, are miraculous religious occurrences, hall-marks of sanctity, tokens of divine favour. A saint may be a stigmatic, but a stigmatic is not necessarily a saint. A relatively small number of stigmatics have been beatified or canonised. The brutal truth is that many stigmatics have been more distinguished for their hysteria and other neuroses than their sanctity. What is also true is that you do not need to be religious – or even a Christian – to manifest flesh changes of a stigmatic kind.

Some stigmatics suffer the entire Passion of Christ – the agony in the Garden of Gethsemane, which involves tears of blood or sweating of blood; the scourging; the crowning with the mocking crown of thorns; the infliction of blows and beatings; the carrying of the cross, with bruised and abraded shoulder; the crucifixion and its five associated corporeal wounds.

The first recorded stigmatic is generally held to be the thirteenth-century saint, Francis of Assisi (1182-1226). But it is possible that another thirteenth-century religious may antedate him. Blessed Dodo, a Premonstratensian monk, of Hascha, in Frisia, who died in 1231, was reported to have open wounds on his hands, feet and in his right side.

After the thirteenth century, stigmatics proliferated. Their temporal distribution spans more than seven centuries. Their geography is world-wide. As a rule, the stigmatic is a woman, and a member of a religious community, but Blessed Dodo, St Francis, and the twentieth-century Capuchin friar, Padre Pio, are exceptions. No stigmatic had made an appearance in Britain before Mary Ann Girling (1864), a Methodist,[14] and Teresa Higginson (1874).

A factor common in the lives of many, if not most, of those who bear the stigmata is that they have meditated for protracted periods on the Passion and sufferings of Christ. The suggestion here is that the explanation lies not in theology, but psychology; of mind over matter; that by some, as yet not understood, psychological mechanism physical changes are brought about. Experiments in hypnosis, for instance, have unequivocally demonstrated that flesh can undergo changes to an extraordinary degree in response to mental activity. Crucifixion-type imaging in an hypnotic state caused Dr Alfred Lechler's subject, Elizabeth K., to develop crucifixion wounds and to bleed, in an experiment carried out in Germany, in 1933.

Sensory upsets include blindness, loss of hearing, paralysis, specific body part anaesthesis, states of dissociated consciousness, such as trances, hysterical catalepsies, seeing visions, hearing voices, and miscellaneous hallucinatory episodes.

The manifestations of the gift of second sight, the ability to sense the oncoming of death, to practise bilocation, to go without, or with only very little, sleep, the power of healing, and the curious production of a sweet perfume betokening the stigmatic's presence, are further established characters.

But *do* the stigmata replicate Christ's wounds? Was He nailed to the cross through His wrists rather than through the palms of His hands? Through His ankles rather than through the centre of His feet? Those would certainly appear to have been the Roman crucifixion techniques. Was the soldier's lance plunged into His left or His right side? The wide variety of locations presented by various stigmatics' wounds is not consistent with the replication

40. Louise Lateau, the nineteenth-century Belgian stigmatic.

of any firm original pattern. It complies more closely with religious art, and cannot on that account be regarded as unquestionably authentic. And, indeed, not all stigmatics exhibit the full complement of crucifixion wounds – the crown of thorns, the nail-marks to hands and feet, the hole in the side where the lance entered, the bruised shoulder from the carrying of the weighty cross, the lash-marks and weals of the scourging. Moreover, spontaneous haemorrhages – psychogenic purpura – have been recorded, and the sweating of blood – haematidrosis – can occur at times of gross stress.

There are certain other abnormalities, too, which appear to be characteristic adjuncts of the stigmatised. One of the most challenging to belief is the claim of nutritional survival without the taking of food or drink, and with the sole daily ingestion of the Host in Holy Communion. Louise Lateau is reported to have neither eaten nor drunk, the Blessed Sacrament apart, from 1871 until her death in 1883. Dr A. Imbert-Goubeyre, the eminent French medical professor and author of the great nineteenth-century, two-volume, standard work, *La Stigmatisation, l'ecstase divine, les miracles de Lourdes, réponse aux libres penseurs*, testified that she produced nothing from her bowels, and a urine output of no more than two spoonfuls a week, though her menses remained normal. Conversely, Dr M. Warlomont, stated that a cupboard full of fruit and bread was found in her room.

Introducing an unexpected vein of humour is the fraudulent Alfonsina Cottini, of Caravaggio, Lago Maggiore. Claiming inedia, and that all her bowel and bladder activities had consequently ceased, she was nonetheless rumoured to be getting up in the dead of night, raiding the larder, and performing normal bodily functions. A special commission set up by Church authorities confirmed her errant conduct, as well as her production of eliminations of a remarkable potency!

Somewhat suspicious, too, one uncharitably feels, is the circumstance that, while Teresa Neumann (1898-1962), the Konnersreuth stigmatic, initially rendered her hearing of her Saviour's words in her native Upper Palatinate German, after her acquaintance with the linguistic scholar and priest, Dr Wutz, she began to supply hallucinatory phrases in Aramaic.

Latest accusations of fakery have been levelled at Padre Pio (1887-1968), canonised by Pope John Paul II, in 2002, by the Italian historian Sergio Luzzatto.[15] Padre Pio had reputedly all the stigmatical gifts. He could heal the sick, prophesy the future, be in two places at once, and exuded a powerful perfume compounded of violets and roses. During the last years of his life he ate hardly anything. The stigmata themselves appeared on his hands and the left side of his rib cage on the morning of September 20th, 1918.

But in 1919, a young pharmacist, Maria De Vito, said that, demanding of her the utmost secrecy, the priest had bought from her four grams of pure carbolic acid. This damning testimony was presented to the Vatican. The ecclesiastical authorities banned him from saying Mass, but the pilgrims continued to flock to him. It was some 26 years before he was again permitted to celebrate Mass. He survived another 23 years, and even predicted the very moment of his death, at the age of eighty-one.

From the earliest centuries, Christianity has regarded virginity as a special offering made by the soul to its spouse, Jesus Christ, and such virginal saints as St Catherine of Siena, St Teresa of Avila, St Colette, and St Catherine of Ricci, are said to have been accorded the supreme distinction and grace of the Mystical Marriage. The invariable prelude to the Marriage is an ecstasy, in which the woman believes herself to have undergone a form of Mystic Espousal with Christ. In the year 1367, St Catherine of Siena had a vision. She saw Jesus with His Mother, Mary, St John the Evangelist, St Paul, and St Dominic, and Our Lord spoke to Catherine, telling her of His intention of "espousing her soul to Him in faith." Whereupon, Our Lady took Catherine's right hand and held it out to Jesus, who placed a ring on her ring-finger. Her espousal ring, of gold, set with four pearls and a diamond, was invisible to all eyes but her own. The spontaneous appearance of a miraculous ring "upon the finger of certain virgins of holy life" is not infrequently mentioned in hagiographical records. The ring which appeared on St Veronica Giuliani's [1660-1727] finger was adorned with a raised red stone the size of a pea. Its presence was testified to by Sister Mary Spanaciani and Sister Florida Ceoli, both candidates for canonisation and beatification, respectively.

It is the accepted portion of wives to share in the lives of, and provide support for, their husbands, and the Bride of Christ must perforce enter into intimate participation in the sufferings which he endured for the redemption of mankind, and, in three cases out of every four, stigmatics have been granted the favour of the Mystical Marriage.

Father Snow, who had made a close study of the phenomena of mysticism, harboured no doubts in his mind as to the reality of Teresa's experience, and penned a charming congratulatory epistle to her:

My Dear Child,

I praise and thank our dear Lord exceedingly for His great goodness in bestowing this unspeakable favour upon you and I rejoice with you and congratulate you with all my heart upon your marriage with the Lamb, for that is the name of the degree of union to which in His goodness He has now raised you, and it is the highest union to which any soul can attain upon earth. You are now, more than ever His. You must now have but one thought – how can you please so good a Spouse. You must think only of His interests and He will take good care of yours. By all our dear Lord's dealings with you I knew He was preparing you for this union and I referred to it sometimes in speaking to you, and told you of the change it would make in your soul – how you would have more courage and think less of yourself (when people praised you, etc.) and only of Him and His honour. I was away Wednesday and Thursday, and only read what you wrote last night, but I have had great joy and consolation ever since. But I feel like Lazarus in the presence of Dives and I beg of you and your divine Spouse that I may have some of the crumbs that fall from the rich man's table. With every good wish to you and your friends I remain my dear child yours affecly.

In Christ

Alfred Snow.

For all her wonderful spiritual advances, the material prospect for Teresa was far from satisfactory. Father Mussely did his best to help, offering her a teaching post in his school. Fathers Snow and Powell both, well meaningly, advised acceptance. But Teresa did not relish the prospect of a return to Newchurch. It was the trouble that she had had there in getting to church and the Sacraments that had turned her against the place. However, as a matter of duty and obedience to the Will of God, she accepted the position. In the event, she was not needed, and made her relief clear in a letter: "I am not going to Newchurch, for which I am most grateful ... for it would have been like penal servitude for me, and though I made the sacrifice I still hoped it would be Abraham's sacrifice, and so it has proved, *Deo gratias*."

Teresa was delighted to be able to stay on a while longer at Clitheroe, but, worryingly, no further teaching opportunities seemed to be coming up on the horizon, and, in what looked like developing into an *impasse*, it was Father Snow who came to the rescue. Fortune so decreed that his sister happened to be the Reverend Mother of St Catherine's Convent of the Sisters of Mercy, in Lauriston Gardens, Edinburgh. He wrote to her asking if she would be prepared to give shelter to this very needy soul. Reverend Mother did not for a single second hesitate.

NOTES

14 *The Other Christ: Padre Pio and 19th Century Italy.*

15 vide: *England's Lost Eden: Adventures in a Victorian Utopia.* Philip Hoare. Fourth Estate, London, 2005.

8

CONVENTUAL

Teresa was forty-three years of age on the November morning in 1887 when she set off for Edinburgh. On the 26th of the previous month she had written, from 53 Lowergate, Clitheroe, to Father Snow: "I am really grateful to you for all your kindness. I should be most pleased to go to Edinburgh, but I think it is too much to expect, though I have a feeling which is more than a fancy that I have to go to Scotland and do something there about the furthering of the Devotion [to the Sacred Head] or the good of souls." And she does not forget to send "a pat for Donna," Father Snow's dog.

St Catherine's at 4 Lauriston Gardens, was a large and busily flourishing convent. Teresa was received with the utmost cordiality by Reverend Mother and all the nuns, although Father Snow's expressed desire that she should be left as far as possible unnoticed was, in the beginning, loyally observed. She was to remain there for nearly eleven years. She found it a very happy home. She was overjoyed when she discovered that the accommodation allotted to her was a little room partitioned off from the organ gallery, not only overlooking, but actually *in*, the chapel. This, she quickly realised, meant that she could pass the night "in secret commune with Our Lord in the tabernacle".

The conventual life suited her. There can be absolutely no doubt about that. Perhaps she *should* have been a nun, but Father Spencer had told her all those years ago that she had no vocation: that she was called to lead, not a contemplative life of prayer walled away in a convent, but an active one, translating

*41. St Catherine's Convent, 4 Lauriston Gardens, Edinburgh.
The place of Teresa's long retreat.*

the prayerful thoughts of her more retiring sisters into concrete deeds for God's good purpose in the hurly-burly of the sinful outside world.

Shortly after Teresa's advent at the convent, Reverend Mother wrote to her brother: "I am delighted with her and so are the community, and we are most grateful to you for sending her and allowing her to stay. She is so nice and homely that we quite take her into our confidence, and she lives with us almost as one of ourselves. One feels at once as if she could be so thoroughly trusted, and as if she sees everything in such a right light. Her judgment seems so sound, and her ideas and views so large, and she is very free from all those little narrownesses and cranky views which some pious people seem to have. I think that is the great

42. The Chapel at St Catherine's Convent, Edinburgh.

difference between 'pious people' and saints, or real sanctity."

Leaving her unnoticed was not so easy!

It has been historically observed that, following the enactment of the Mystical Marriage, agonies and ecstasies tend to diminish in both occurrence and intensity. So it was with Teresa, who told Father Snow: "Do you know that since the feast of St Raphael [October 24th] that agonising pain I used to have so *dreadfully* has gone, and I don't seem to have any great desires as I used to have, neither have I that extreme thirst for suffering and great desire for death – I seem to have no power to wish for anything … I think (which may be a great imperfection) I am becoming very much attached to the poor body and look to those things far more than ever I did which give it ease and comfort, for I feel a power from within (at least so it seems to me) which makes or inclines me to do anything and everything which would prolong my existence here, I think that so I may give Him greater service and a little more glory. This may be a temptation or a delusion, but so it is."

Subject to considerable anxiety on the score of this feeling that she should take more cognisance of the needs and demands of the body, she further wrote to Father Snow: "There arises in me at times a feeling that I must take care of the body as well as the soul, and little mortifications I used to practise, I feel they are better left undone. For example, I always made it a rule if the body wanted anything to give it the opposite – when I felt very worn and needed more rest I would take less, or none at all: if one part of the body called for more sympathy, through pain, etc., I always tried to make it bear the weight of the rest of the body. If my eyes ached and I wished to close them, I would do all I could to keep them open. ... But now I feel I should take more rest so that I may be better able to work with greater profit and be better fitted to do the things He intends me for. This feeling comes to me very forcibly at times; it seems to me that I pay little attention to mortifications, etc., though I have not as yet broken through anything I have been accustomed to do, thinking I was safe (even though a kind of reproof was given to me for not doing) I made up my mind not to change anything unless you told me to, fearing that the Devil might be trying to make me lose in one way what the dear good God, my divine Spouse Jesus, gave me in another."

Father Snow sent her reassurances.

In an explanatory epistle, which he wrote many years later after Teresa's death, he says, with regard to the subject of her abstinence from normal eating: "She was nourished by the blessed Sacrament and took no food whatever. She sat at the table with others and appeared to take simple food, but she was very

170

carefully watched, and nothing was seen to pass down her throat. But after the Mystical Marriage, there is a change, and souls feel that the body requires nourishment to enable them to do what God requires of them, and they have a doubt as to whether this feeling is a temptation to sensuality. Teresa had this doubt and consulted me. The whole question is treated by St John of the Cross. I told Teresa she might safely take what she thought necessary. Thenceforth she took food – a little tea and bread and butter, and, about midday, a plate of mashed potatoes."

In Lent and Advent, the old, familiar weakness surfaced again, often so severely and with such anguishes that Teresa had to be, literally, carried, albeit by willing hands, into and out of chapel. The stigmata still seasonally oozed and flowed, but it was only the sister deputed to tend her who shared these secret things, the knowledge of which was zealously guarded from the other nuns. Throughout Holy Week she lay for the most part in her little organ gallery bedroom, waxen and motionless as a corpse. The nun who looked after her saw the stigmata wounds, which she described as "purple swellings like small plums on the instep." And once, she went into Teresa's room to find her lying back unconscious in her chair, eyes cast up, mouth wide-open, and, lying upon her tongue, the sacred Host. Awestruck, she had softly closed the door, and glided straight off to tell Reverend Mother of the amazing spectacle she had just beheld.

Reverend Mother told Father Snow in a letter: "One of our sisters saw her receive Communion the other night, just before ten o'clock. I told her not to talk of it, but stamped it on her mind so that she *could* tell it if required to do so at any time. She, Miss H., is much the same as when you saw her, suffering a good deal at times, but always bright."

These Miraculous Communions were witnessed at St Catherine's on a number of occasions.

Teresa's culinary skills soon came to be recognised and

appreciated by the community. Consequently, much of her time was spent in a pantry, where meals were being constantly prepared for guests and visitors. Moving continually among the many and varied viands – boiling this, frying that, grilling the other – her personal absence of appetite was satisfyingly masked. She would lavish conventual hospitality upon others, even to the point of their embarrassment, as when she would pursue a parting guest down the passage to the very front-door, bearing for her, or him, a cup of steaming tea, or ply a small boy with cakes until, deferring to his groaning stomach, he would burst into tears, protesting, "Eh, Miss! Ah canna swallow ony mair."

It was generally known among the community that Teresa never ate, but the sister in the kitchen was most incredulous. There was a little room without a door which one was obliged to pass before entering the main kitchen. On this particular day, sister had, for some particular reason, left the chapel rather earlier than usual, and, as she passed the little room, she saw Teresa sitting in there with a large dinner spread out in front of her. Sister did not say anything to Teresa, but said to herself, "I've caught her at last!" At tea-time she went to Reverend Mother to tell her what she had seen. The Reverend Mother, seeming greatly astonished, asked sister at what time she had seen her eating her meal. And when she was told the hour, replied, "Well, it couldn't have been Miss Higginson, because at that time she was out with me." That particular afternoon Reverend Mother had been obliged to go out on business and the community had not known that she and Teresa were out together. It was, Reverend Mother felt sure, another instance of the Devil's impersonating Teresa.

When not occupied with kitchen or domestic duties, or waiting upon visitors, she would teach for the sisters in the schools, give religious instruction, go out and about in Edinburgh, visiting in charity the sick and the poor. Although she had her keep – that is to say a roof and a bed, she ate very little – from the good-hearted nuns, she earned no money from any of the tasks she carried out, and was herself entirely dependent on charity. Friends in Liverpool and Clitheroe sent her gifts of clothing, She always dressed in black, and as a rule wore a white scarf about her neck. She cared little about how she looked, and one of the sisters said that she was for ever running after her putting her straight. But it was to Father Snow that she was truly indebted. He was undoubtedly her main support. She would turn to him always for any of her real needs, and was, not without very good reason, forever thanking him for his unstinting help. In various endeavours at self-help, she wrote off a number of applications for teaching posts. None was successful.

Just after Easter, 1888, Father Powell wrote to Teresa offering her a position at his school in Lydiate, but in rather odd refusal she replied: "It was indeed good and kind of you to offer me it. But I should have been gaining in every way and would have had nothing to offer our dear b. Lord, my divine Spouse and only Treasure, and I have such a strong feeling that He wants me to remain in Scotland for the present, though not at the convent. I think He will very shortly find me a school. I have no doubt you may think it ungrateful of me, but you know I must do, as far as I can, His divine Will, and you can little think how hard it was for me to say *No*, for all my natural inclinations went with it, for besides having everything spiritual and temporal, I should be so near Rev. A. Snow, but I wish only His adorable Will – though I often feel exiled, as it were, and for the present I feel He does not wish me to have any settled place."

Over the years, there were intervals in, or respites from, her unremitting residence at St Catherine's. In response to an urgent cry for help at his school by Father Forbes Leith, S.J., she spent some weeks teaching at Selkirk. While serving at other outpost schools, she stayed several times in convents at Linlithgow and at Dalkeith – St Andrew's Convent, Eskbank. She went home to her sisters at Neston on three short holidays, and spent another staying with an old friend at Clacton-on-Sea.

In January, 1888, a Mission took place at St Patrick's Roman Catholic Church. [Situated on the east side of South Gray's Close, built in 1774 as an Episcopal chapel, where the last loyal Jacobites prayed silently for the King over the water, it became, in 1778, the Hanoverian Church, which was sold to the Roman Catholics in 1856.] Teresa attended, and felt the urge "to offer myself for them, that God would give grace and blessing to the work, and on Wednesday and Thursday nights the blessed Trinity seemed to withdraw (though I know they did not) yet They hid Themselves and inundated my poor trembling soul with fearful agony." Her sacrifice must have been acceptable. The Mission surpassed all expectations.

Teresa made another offering of herself on behalf of a wretched Edinburgh miscreant.

"There was a poor woman, Jessie King, in prison for the murder of nine children, and she was most impenitent, and I begged of our dear Lord, for the glory of His Name and for the sake of the agony His holy Soul had endured for her, to give her contrition and repentance, and I would willingly suffer more if possible and would take the punishment of her sins if He would only grant my prayer, and I told Him I would not leave Him till He heard me and granted her mercy – which He did."

In October, 1888, some boys playing football with a bundle that they had found lying on a green in Cheyne Street, in that part of Edinburgh known as Stockbridge, made the horrible discovery that their 'ball' was a dead baby parcelled up in an old waterproof coat. Subsequent investigation securely placed twenty-seven-year-old Jessie King in the dock of Court Number 3 at Edinburgh's High Court of Justiciary. Her elderly lover,

Thomas Pearson, who, by all rights, should have been standing at her side before the bar of Justice, was, instead, arraigned as a hostile witness, having been restored to liberty after his paramour's declaration of his ignorance and innocence of what she had been about. What she had been about was baby farming. Jessie was described by William Roughead, the celebrated Edinburgh lawyer who actually attended the trial, as a miserable little creature, crouched in the dock, mean, furtive, shabbily sinister, like a cornered rat. Her traitorous late partner in the baby farming enterprise was robust and of truculent mien, a dirty-grey-bearded face, a monstrous wen, big as a hen's egg, growing like an evil fungus on the vertex of the naked scalp of his grubby bald head. This engaging duo had been busily providing a very special social service, relieving distressed and awkwardly placed single mothers – maids in service and the like – of their new-born burdens. In return for a relative pittance, a few hard-scraped-together pounds, the babe would be taken care of, which phrase must not be ingenuously swallowed at its surface meaning, but in actuality signified economic short-term rearing and expeditious slaughter, usually strangling with a bootlace or something of the sort. The 'keep' money expended, mainly for its yield of drink, the advertisements would once again be scanned for another profitable 'adoption'.

Jessie was hanged. Tom toddled insouciantly off to female pastures new. But before her execution Jessie King handed to her confessor a written confession of her guilt.

Her plethora of sufferings notwithstanding, Teresa always managed to present a merry and bright countenance to the world. She was especially jolly with, and fond of, the hard-working, never complaining lay sisters, and was never so happy as when Reverend Mother said that she might go in with them during their recreation. She loved to tell them stories; she was a very good raconteur, and her particular delight was to dance for them, doing a jig to the tune of "Paddy on the Green". One of the lay sisters declared that she was "the merriest little soul I ever knew." She was very kind and considerate, too, to the novices and young sisters. They nicknamed her 'Johnny Love", because of her great fondness for a small boy who came to the convent, and whom she always addressed thus. It was well known that she used to squirrel away cakes and dainties for him.

Many tales about her have entered into convent lore. Old nuns at St Catherine's still remember hearing, from even older nuns, the cautionary tale of Reverend Mother's lunch. Wishing to entertain right royally some honoured guests who, though always welcome, had on this occasion materialised totally unexpectedly, and, its being a Friday, she had sent out for some salmon. The fish was an unconscionably long time in arriving, and had been on the fire only a matter of minutes, when the meal was called for. To make everything worse, time was veritably of the essence, as the guests had to catch a train. The appalled sister in charge looked at the salmon. It was virtually uncooked. Despairing eyes turned towards Teresa. She did not flinch. She made the sign of the cross over the cooking pot, and told the sister to go ahead and serve up. The guests pronounced the fish to be beautifully cooked and excellent fare.

Uncannily, she foretold the Great War of 1914-1918. Her eyes filled with pity, she would look at some of the wee laddies in the school in which she happened to be supplying, many of whom she *knew* to be destined to die in battles, which, she predicted, would take place in the air and under the sea – although at the time aeroplanes and submarines were uninvented.

She knew, too, of the deaths of people at a distance, and, eerily, would sometimes recount how, without ever bodily leaving the convent – bilocation making her transit possible – she had been present at a number of death-beds. Strangely, she did not always know the identity of the dying, but could often say if the decedent had been a priest. She confided to a friend that she had been with Bishop Roskell, who had been so fond of her when she was a child, when he passed away at Whitwell, in 1883.

Typically, in a letter which she wrote to Father Snow, she reported: "Rev. Fr. Pitter, S.J. has gone to reap the reward of his labours for souls. ... He died at about a quarter to six on Wednesday morning. I knew when he died, though I was not certain it was him. I told dear Sister Catherine when she came into my cell at five minutes past six, and we both said a prayer for him. Two other holy persons died that same morning, but I don't know who they were."

A Mrs Macpherson, who lived outside the town, would frequently come into Edinburgh to do her shopping, and she always stayed the night at the convent. Teresa, having charge of the visitors, usually attended Mrs Macpherson on those occasions. One morning, before Mass, Teresa went to the Mother Superior and told her that Mrs Macpherson had died during the night, even giving her the exact hour of the death. Two days later, Mr Macpherson wrote to Reverend Mother, thinking that she knew nothing of the death of his wife. The details in his letter corresponded precisely with those that Teresa had given to her. Reverend Mother afterwards said that she felt sure that Teresa had bilocated.

An old lay sister who was given the task of looking after Teresa during her Lenten and Holy Week 'illnesses', confided to Lady Anne Cecil Kerr how, often, she had virtually to carry Teresa back from the chapel, and how on one occasion, helping her to bed, she had begun to brush her hair, and found it full of blood. She had then noticed small round wounds, as of thorn pricks, on her head. She had seen, too, great purple weals in the palms of her hands. In October, 1888, the first anniversary of her Mystical Marriage, Teresa wrote to Father Snow:

"The feast of St Raphael was a real feast for me, and all the

43. Father (later Canon)
J. Constant Mussely.

week before the very thought of what took place on that day
seemed to fill me with an indescribable joy. At times, the flames
in the centre of the soul seem to rush upwards, and the divine
wisdom absorbs and enlightens, though so sweetly and calmly
(not with pain as it used to do), and teaches her (the soul), or at
least she sees, that her very desires are deeds, I mean are made
substantial in Him whom she loves and desires with so great a
desire." And a little later she wrote: " I don't think that if the
whole world calumniated me now that it would trouble me in
the least. I think I have been well taught that either praise or ill-
will of the world is but an empty bubble and not worth thinking
of. I am glad that I felt it at first, but I do trust it was but a
stepping-stone and not a stumbling-block, and, as you say, our

44. Margaret Murphy.
Father Mussely's housekeeper.

dear Lord in the least of His favours gave me more than all the reputation I have lost or may lose."

Teresa was still plagued by the notion that no real progress seemed to be being made in the cause of the Sacred Head, even though she claimed to have "seen rich graces and blessings untold descend upon those who practise the Devotion." The thought ever nearest to her heart, the subject of the spread of the Devotion, persistently recurs in her letters. There was a little shrine, paid for with monies collected from her friends, erected in the convent chapel, and a small booklet of prayers to the Sacred Head, which had been printed with the approval of the Bishop of Liverpool, had been translated into several languages and distributed far and wide. So progress *was* being made, albeit

45. Kitty Deady, aged 19.

slowly. But Teresa wrote in obvious, though uncomplaining, puzzlement: "Our dear Lord has not revealed to me the time when the Devotion will be acknowledged by the Church, nor when dear England will be brought back to the light of the true faith and the love of its saving doctrines."

There were breaks from life in Edinburgh. She had a summer holiday at Neston. In the Octobers of 1891 and 1892, Teresa spent some weeks there with her sisters. She also enjoyed a visit to Lizzie Dawson's at Clitheroe, staying once more in the room of sacred memory, where, as Cecil Kerr puts it, "heaven had come on earth to her."

Father Mussely, who was soon to be promoted Canon, was now rector of St Patrick's, Manchester, and, with his permission,

46. Sister Mary Evangelist.
The former Kitty Deady.

his housekeeper, Margaret Murphy, who had accompanied him from Rawtenstall, had invited Teresa to stay there. Margaret now had another servant to help her, Mary Jane, who long years afterwards remembered, not only the radiant atmosphere that seemed to fill the house whenever Teresa came to stay, but also how she loved to take her share in all the household work, cooking, washing-up, and dusting, singing all the while, as she came and went from room to room. And now and then the Canon would open the door and look in, then slip away without a word. Indeed, he seldom spoke of Teresa, but he had a deep veneration for her.

Also in the house was a little girl, Katherine Deady,[16] whom Father Mussely had brought over from Ireland, and Margaret

Murphy had adopted. Kitty Deady would afterwards recall the immense impression which Teresa had made upon her when she was a child. She loved to be with her, and would sit entranced, listening as she told her about heavenly things and stories of the little children that she used to teach. She would remember, too, how she had longed to be like her, feeling that it must be lovely to be so good.

Teresa was given an upper room, which, as usually seemed to be the case with her, looked out on to the church. Interestingly, we know the pattern of her day at St Patrick's. When her visit was in the summertime, she would rise at 5 a.m. In the winter, she would allow herself an extra half-hour in bed. Either way, she would be in church by 6 a.m., and remain there until nine o'clock. Breakfast, provided by Margaret, would consist of one small cup of tea, accompanied by wafer-thin bread and a scraping of butter. Often, she would have nothing else all day. After breakfast, she would busy herself helping Margaret to cook a dinner, ready for Kitty when she came in from school at half-past twelve. Many days they would go to benediction at the Church of the Holy Name, where Teresa, who had a sweet voice, would join whole-heartedly in the singing.

One day when Teresa was at Mass in St Patrick's a bird flew in and distracted the congregation. Between Masses one of the priests came to her and said: "You'd better get rid of that bird before the next Mass." Teresa always seems to have had a special affinity with birds. She called to it and it came to her. Stroking it lovingly, she said to it, "You nearly lost your life." Then she carried it in her hand to the door of the church and released it outside.

While Teresa was in Edinburgh, there was a child at the convent who was taken ill with diphtheria. The nuns had done everything in their power for the little girl, but the doctor had given up all hope of her recovery. Mother Superior turned to

Teresa in despair and asked her to pray that the child might get well, for she felt that in the event of her death she could not possibly face her father, who was an army officer in India. Teresa promised to do so. She also looked after the young patient with devoted care, not omitting to make use of any of the available natural means of cure. The little girl recovered, and the doctor, a non-Catholic, declared that the hand of God was visibly over the house, otherwise the child could not possibly have got well.

When Bishop O'Reilly, who had given her such short shrift back in the 1880s, fell mortally ill, and died on April 9th, 1894, Teresa wrote to Father Powell: "What a saintly man he has been and what a glorious work he has done in the Liverpool diocese since he came to it, and I am sure he will pray that someone may take his place who will be suited to fill it." Mary Jane came up to Edinburgh from Manchester on a visit. She was talking of Bishop O'Reilly's death and wondering who might succeed him. "It will be Dr Whiteside," said Teresa. A few months later, he was in fact elected.

The last quinquennium of the nineteenth century passed relatively uneventfully for Teresa. In October, 1895, she went for a short while to Selkirk, to help out at Father Forbes Leith's school. January, 1896, saw her briefly at home once more in Neston. During her Christmas break there, her sister had taken her for a sail, and also to an entertainment, its nature unspecified, called "Constantinople". If you go to Liverpool, see it, she advises Father Snow. It is very pretty, and she is sure he would enjoy it.

In the summer of 1897, she was at Neston again, and before returning to Edinburgh went to stay for a few weeks with some friends at Clacton-on-Sea, where a shrine was being set up to the Blessed Virgin Mary, under the designation of Our Lady of Light, Spouse of the Holy Ghost. The history of this statue was said to go back to the eighteenth century, when it was thought to have been brought over from Brittany by the two daughters of Sir Henry Trelawney, of Trelawney, in Cornwall. They had established a shrine near Looe, and named it 'Sclerder', which is Breton for 'Light'. The Catholic Trelawneys died out. The shrine fell into disuse. It was in 1860 that a Mrs De Barry and her husband discovered and renewed it. Mr De Barry having died, his widow was joined by a Mrs St John, and together they set to work on the Marian shrine.

In 1896, encountering difficulties which they believed to be the work of the Devil, they consulted Cardinal Vaughan, who advised them to move to Clacton-on-Sea, where the people had for some time been strongly urging upon him the need for a priest to be sent to serve in their area. Following the Cardinal's advice, Mrs De Barry and Mrs St John found a plot of land near the sea with a suitable house, which they immediately named Montfort, and there they installed the statue. They then travelled up to London, paid a visit to the Oblates of St Charles, in Bayswater, and succeeded in persuading them to assign a priest to Clacton, where Montfort became a Mass centre. Half a dozen years later, in 1903, a beautiful stone church, dedicated to Our Lady of Light and St Osyth, arose beside Montfort, and the old house became the presbytery.

All this had been accomplished before Teresa's arrival in July, 1897. She stayed for about two months. While there, she took a trip over to the Convent of the Canonesses of Holy Sepulchre, at Chelmsford, and was delighted to find that the priest and nuns there had been practising the Devotion to the Sacred Head for the past ten or twelve years.

Another, less pleasing, adventure at about this time, was when she went to Confession and was afraid that the priest was going to refuse her absolution. The trouble seems to have been that she had so little in the way of sin to confess. The priest told her that disobedience was not "sufficient matter". However, after asking her if the priest she went to usually gave her absolution, who that priest was, how long it was since she had committed the sin, and how old she was now, he eventually gave her absolution. Clearly, the sin in question was that childhood act of disobedience which Father Snow had once declared to be, in his opinion, the only true matter she can have had for absolution.

A reminiscence from 1897. One of the nuns at New Hall who, when she was a child, had known Teresa, recalls: "When Miss Higginson came here on July 22nd, 1897, I was still in the noviceship, so knew nothing about her coming till late on in the day, and I only received leave to see her about 5 o'clock. When I entered the room she was standing facing a large picture of Our Lady with her back to the window. She did not move when I entered (the door was on the side of the picture), so I said, 'I don't suppose you know me?' She answered, 'Of course I do … I knew you were coming in.' I said, 'How did you know?' (because only the portress knew beside the Mistress of Novices, and she had not told her). She replied, 'I have always honoured some people's guardian angels, and you are one of them. He told me you were coming in.'" The sister goes on to describe Teresa's appearance on this occasion. "She had black silk gloves on, though it was a very hot day, and she held my hands in hers very tightly all the time. Her hat was very much over her forehead, and her face was quite smooth and pale, just like a corpse."

Shortly after Christmas, 1898, Teresa wrote from Edinburgh to Father Snow: "As the year is drawing to a close, naturally we look back to see what we have done for Him who has done so much for us … And as usual I find my hands empty. … During our *Quarant Ore* when I was entreating our dear divine Lord to enlighten the minds of men by the Wisdom of His Sacred Head, and show Himself as He really is that all hearts might love Him, all tongues praise Him, and all minds bend in adoration and in

185

obedience to His teaching – I reminded Him, as I often do, of His expressed wish to have His Sacred Head honoured as the seat of Divine Wisdom. He brought before me very clearly how He had wished at the same time to have the mystery of the Incarnation preached and the Rosary said, as a means of teaching the people better the mysteries of the Incarnation, and that that was being done, and so the Church was preparing the world for the practice of the Devotion to the Sacred Head and Holy Soul. He showed me how His Word was an act, that what He says must be, and I have felt a great delight and secret joy when I think of it or say or hear of others saying the Holy Rosary. I am sure this is a very funny letter, but if you understand what I mean that is enough."

Archbishop Vaughan was at this time making an earnest appeal for volunteers to join the Foreign Missions. This was a work in which Teresa had long found fascination and interest. She would, as a matter of fact, gladly have devoted her life to it, and hoped to achieve the final crown of martyrdom. Many years before, she had confided to Father Powell the ardency of her desire, and how the Lord Himself had given to her the martyr's palm. Now, she wrote to her confessor: "Oh my Father, I have such a longing to do something for souls and to shed the last drop of my poor miserable life's blood for Him who is my only Treasure; and as I craved this favour from Him, He Himself appeared well pleased with my desire and presented me with that palm which I have so long desired, not only bearing leaves, but most fragrant and sweet-scented blossoms. May it not be His holy Will that I should go out to Africa, for there is little chance here, at least so far as I can see, to win the martyr's palm."

In July, 1899, an urgent summons came from her sisters asking Teresa to go home to Neston and help them. Fanny, who had always been an invalid, was now very ill, and Louisa was unable to cope with both nursing her and attending to her duties at the school. Before doing anything else, Teresa wrote at once to

Father Snow: "You know, dear Rev. Father, that I shall be quite glad to do whatever you think best, but where home is concerned I would never trust myself to decide, for naturally I have an intense love for my family and a deep sympathy for whatever concerns them."

Father Snow did not hesitate. Of course, she must go to help Louisa. Departing from the convent, taking her leave of the nuns, whom she loved and who loved her, she had no idea that this was to be a last farewell, that she would never again return to Scotland.

But her good Lord had other plans for His ever pliant bride.

NOTE

16 She subsequently became a nun, entering the order of the Sisters of Mercy, where she was known as Sister Mary Evangelist.

9

INTERREGNUM

Fanny, thank God, was better, back on her feet. Teresa felt immense relief. Relief mingled with anxiety as to what she herself was to do. Her mind turned to the idea of teaching. It was what she knew; what she did best. Should she take up full-time schoolmistressing again? She consulted, as, indeed, she always consulted, Father Snow.

"What I said about taking a school, of course I meant if you thought it would be for His greater honour and glory for me to do so. You know that I have all that I could wish for at dear St Catherine's, and far more than I deserve, and it would be very ungrateful of me not to acknowledge all the kindness and goodness I have received from the dear nuns, and I should be very sorry to leave, as I look upon the convent as home while I am here. My room [there] is next to the church, and I can get holy Mass every morning without going out; make a visit when I please, and am continually under one roof with Him, which I regard as, as it is, a real privilege and honour. But I think you understand me and know that, so far as I am concerned, I have no wish either one way or the other, but willing and waiting to do whatever you think is the best."

There was, in fact, no teaching post immediately visible, but it so happened that some mutual friends of Teresa's and Father Snow's, the Garnetts, two sisters, Margaret and Annie, and their younger brother, Alfred, were going through a very difficult period in their lives, owing to the illness of Margaret, and Father Snow suggested that Teresa, being at a loose end, should go and help them.

These three were the last survivors of the Garnett family. Their ancestors had been staunch supporters of the Old Faith during the great persecution at the time of the Reformation, and one of them, Father Henry Joseph Garnett, 51-year-old Jesuit superior, was executed in 1606, for his involvement in the Gun Powder Plot.

For many years Maggie Garnett had been the mistress at Father Snow's school at Aughton, but had now had to retire through illness. Annie and Alfred, who had from birth been handicapped by a very painfully diseased right leg, lived together at 21 Churchill Street, off Upper Warwick Street, in the Princes Park area of Liverpool, where Maggie had moved in with them. Annie worked in town as the manageress of a shoe shop.

Only too pleased to be able to be of use, Teresa packed her bags and went off to join the Garnetts. She was to spend the next three years living with them, doing everything she possibly could to help them materially, and working really hard at cheering them up. They came to love her dearly, called her 'Little Mother', and were to say afterwards that, because of her presence, they regarded those three trouble-veined years that she was with them as the happiest time of their lives.

We are afforded stray glimpses of her Garnett days. Every morning she would sally forth and attend two or three Masses. When she got back, she would settle down to read through the sizable bundle of letters that arrived for her each day. Methodically, she would sort them into piles, and would have read them all before breakfast. They were mostly from priests and other religious, seeking her advice.

Alfred was always to remember how one day when he and Teresa were out walking in the street, she had suddenly stopped in her tracks, turned to him, gazed full into his face with that penetrating look of hers, and said to him, "Alfie, what about your leg?" There were just so many domestic difficulties besetting them at the time, that Alfie replied, "Oh, my leg is

47. Margaret Garnett. The invalid in need.

nothing compared to all the troubles at home." But he had felt instinctively, then, and ever since, that "Little Mother would have cured my leg then, had I wished it so."

He remembered, too, Teresa's terrible ordeals in Passion Week. He would say: "She would come downstairs on Holy Saturday looking hundreds of years old, but on Easter Sunday morning she was herself again."

When Teresa first arrived at Churchill Street she was eating nothing at all, but later, in obedience to Father Snow, she began to take a little food, although she never seemed to want to eat anything. At breakfast time, Alfred would pour her a half-cup of tea while she was reading her post. As a rule, she would let it grow stone-cold. She would then pour hot water into it. It would

48. Alfred Garnett.

end up more like water than tea. Sometimes Alfred would stealthily try to pour some cream into her tea while she was occupied with her letters. He never succeeded. She would look up at him with her usual sweet smile and put her hand gently over her cup.

Maggie tells how one late afternoon she arrived home feeling very poorly, and, all through the bout of illness which subsequently developed, Teresa valiantly, and most conscientiously, attended her. During her convalescence, Teresa used to sing jolly songs to her, and, sometimes, intent on cheering her up, would pat her on the shoulder and say, "Now, my dear, if you are very good I will dance for you in my shorts!" and proceed to prance around executing a *pas seul* in her flannel petticoat.

Another day, noticing that Annie looked absolutely worn out after all the nursing of Maggie that she had been doing, Teresa seized her physically, pushed her into a chair, and said, "My dear, you are not to run up and down stairs any more. Sit there and I will tell you a story." The story was not of the cheeriest. She told how she had once come across a group of children who were making fun of an idiot boy known locally as Silly Billy. She had shooed off his tormentors and seen Billy safely home. It was quite a while afterwards that she heard that the little lad was dying, and she went round to his house. His mother took her in to see him. He was lying unconscious on his bed. His mother begged Teresa to pray for him. She had knelt down there and then and begun to do so, when, all of a sudden, the child, who had never spoken in his life, opened his eyes wide, sat up, and, loud and clear, cried out, "What does Silly Billy see? Three in One, and One in Three." And fell back on his pillow dead.

For her part, Teresa derived great spiritual satisfaction from her stay in the big city, with its multitudinous convenience of churches.

How can I thank our dear divine Lord for all His loving kindness to me. I get three holy sacrifices every morning and sometimes four, besides Benediction nearly every evening, and visits to the churches where the *Quarant Ore* is going on. You know as well as I, how little I deserve these favours and I wish you to join with me in thanking Him for them, and also for allowing me to drink of the drops that flow from His chalice of suffering and desolation. Though I mention suffering last, yet I know its precious worth and look upon it as a great grace and as a caress from our thorn-crowned and crucified Spouse. ... Though during the last few days and nights I have suffered much, *Deo gratias*, I am able to go about and do all the little kindnesses I came to do for dear Annie.

In September, 1900, there was a grand adventure. Mrs. Elizabeth Fleck, a wealthy widow who owned a modern hotel in Dunbar, had known Teresa for some years. In 1895, Mrs. Fleck had helped her to provide a daily meal for the needy priest in Selkirk, Father Forbes Leith.

Mrs. Fleck recalled: "During my intimacy with Miss Teresa Higginson, she was about to leave St Catherine's Convent, where she had been staying, and was sent to Selkirk, as he [Father Forbes Leith] had no teacher or housekeeper. He could not afford to pay either, as the woollen trade in Selkirk was at a standstill; it was made up principally of weaving. The town is situated in the Cheviot Hills and the inhabitants are engaged in sheep farming. When Teresa went there she found the poor father living on one meal a day, which consisted only of cabbage, so she set about seeing to his comfort. He would take no collection as the people were so poor, and she then came to me. We arranged that there was to be a substantial meal sent to him every day, on condition he was not told whence it came. Teresa gathered the children, and their daily prayers were for the return of the trade to Selkirk. In the course of time it slowly got better, and one day, as she was passing the Town Hall, she met a gentleman, who, she understood, was the provost or mayor. He spoke to her, as he evidently knew she was the teacher. There was a statue high above the entrance, and she asked him if he could tell her who it represented. He said he did not know any further then; he believed it had been there since before the Reformation. He asked her if she thought the trade would ever return to Selkirk. She told him she was certain it would all come back, for the children had been praying continually to God for it, day after day, and He never left children's prayers unanswered. ... She had several chance meetings with him, until one day she heard from the children

*49. William H. Smith, who took the portrait photograph
of Teresa in the Mantilla.*

that the looms were all at work. She again met him, and he was delighted to tell her of the turn things had taken. 'Well now,' she said, 'we must all do something for this, I would ask your permission to allow the children to have a procession through the streets of the town in thanks to God for so wonderful a favour.' He said he had no objection to that – 'but,' she said, 'there is something else I would beg of you to do. Could you have the statue taken down in order that we may clean it and carry it at the head of the procession. I must tell you, it represents the Mother of Our Dear Lord. He also consented to this. They had it placed on a shoulder barrow, and it was beautifully decorated with flowers. It was carried at the head of the procession with Father Forbes Leith and the Provost himself in front, with the children and Miss Higginson following on behind. When the procession was over, the statue of Our Lady was replaced in its former position, and Teresa told them it was now to be known as Our Lady of Selkirk."

Another bond between Teresa and Mrs. Fleck was that they were both Franciscan Tertiaries, and Mrs. Fleck had given her a full-length statue of St Francis for her room in the convent. Her daughter, Mary Fleck, was about to celebrate her twenty-first birthday, and her mother had asked which she would prefer as a special gift; a big party with all her friends invited, or a trip with her to Rome. Mary chose the party, and Mrs. Fleck invited Teresa to accompany her to Rome, all expenses paid.

They met in London and caught the ferry over to Dieppe. That first night of the journey they slept in an hotel in Paris. They spent the next day visiting some of the most famous of the Parisian churches, before boarding the night train for Genoa, where they had several hours wait, which they put to good use, attending Benediction in a church near the station. Arriving in Rome at nine o'clock in the morning, they made their way straight to the Scots College, only to find, to their great disappointment, that Mrs. Fleck's friend, the Rector, Monsignor Fraser, and all the students were away at the College's summer house at Marino, on the Alban Hills. Destiny directed them, however, to the Minerva Hotel, where they found not only agreeable accommodation, but a friendly and obliging gentleman with the comfortably familiar name of Smith. William Smith, an Edinburgh sculptor and artist, knew Rome like the back of his hand, and he volunteered to be their guide, and managed to secure tickets for them for a Papal audience. According to Mrs. Fleck, Teresa seemed to have a special guidance in all her actions. The vast crowds – there was an English pilgrimage in Rome at the time – and their inexperience notwithstanding, they got about splendidly and contrived to see quite a few places of interest which the official pilgrims did not see. On the day of the papal audience, when all around were struggling to find a place, they simply walked quietly up the stair, past the papal guard, and, moving calmly into a large chamber at the top, found themselves close to His Holiness, Leo XIII, to whom they were duly presented. Cecil Kerr observes: "No outward sign marked this meeting between the chosen Spouse of Christ and His aged Vicar." While in Rome, they visited all the main places of interest. They went into the famous basilicas, they heard Mass in the catacombs, they mounted the *Scala Santa*.

Leaving the Holy City, they travelled on to spend a few days in Florence, before going north to Venice, where they saw the Patriarch, who was afterwards to be elected Pius X, in his cathedral of San Marco. Thence, they made their way to Padua and Assisi, of particular interest to them as Franciscan Tertiaries. In St Francis' beautiful church, they knelt in prayer beside his body, they gazed in reverent wonder at the crucifix which was said to have miraculously spoken to him, they gathered a posy from the little garden where the saint sang his praises to Brother Sun. They saw, too, the tomb of St Clare, and the ancient convent of San Damiano, virtually unchanged since the days when she lived there. Filled with a great peace, they dawdled quietly among the olive trees on the hillside that hung high between the azure sky and the beautiful, sparkling plain stretching to infinity below.

Their last Italian weekend they spent in Milan, paying their respects to the shrines of St Ambrose and St Charles. Then it was the St Gotthard from Milan to Lucerne, and home, arriving in London in nice time to celebrate the feasts of All Souls and All Saints at Brompton Oratory. It was while they were in London that, by great good fortune, they met again the kind Mr. Smith of the Roman Minerva, who begged them to be permitted to take

50. Mrs Elizabeth Fleck. Teresa's benefactor.

their photographs in memory of their happy pilgrimage. After all his noble service how could they refuse? They went with him to his studio in Oxford Street, and it is to Mr. Smith and his felicitous impulse that posterity is indebted for the only real portrait extant of Teresa, resplendent in mantilla.

Mrs. Fleck and Teresa were never to meet again on this earth. Reminiscing later, describing Teresa's mien, Mrs. Fleck said that she spoke very little while they were on their travels, but made her admiration of, and gratitude for, everything abundantly obvious by her sweet smile, more eloquent than words. For her, daily Communion had been an absolute essential. The Blessed Sacrament had been throughout her only sustenance. She would sometimes accept a cup of tea, but never at any time partook of any food. This was remarked at the hotels, and Mrs. Fleck had to explain that her companion was rather delicate and somewhat of an invalid.

Before they parted, Teresa and Mrs. Fleck exchanged Franciscan Tertiary habits,[17] Teresa asking her to come to her if she were ever dying, and promising that she would perform the same office for her. It was not to be. Late in 1904, Teresa wrote telling Mrs. Fleck that the weather was so bad and her part of Devon so remote that she must not think of coming.

In later years the once wealthy Elizabeth Fleck lost her fortune – "The Lord took everything from me by degrees," she said. At the age of 77, she entered the Carmel, at Gillingham, in Dorset, and became an extern sister, taking the names Mary Teresa.

When she reached journey's end back in Liverpool, Teresa wrote to Father Snow: "Really I do not know what to say to you, my poor heart feels too full to speak when I think of all His tender care and kindness to this poor little worm." She could, perhaps, have added that, at a more mundane level, Mrs. Fleck was deserving of an iota of speechless gratitude for her tender care and kindness, too!

It was around November, 1900, that Father Powell was taken seriously ill and Teresa went off to Lydiate for a little while to help nurse him.

The following February, [1901], Teresa set out on another tranche of foreign travel; this time to escort the invalid Garnett sister to the ancient town of Bruges.

She seems to have thoroughly enjoyed the trip. She writes to Father Snow: "You will see from the above address – 12 Quai Des Teinturiers, Bruges – that I am in Belgium. I had a very nice journey the whole way, leaving Liverpool from Central Station and arriving at Bruges between three and four. I had to stay in the waiting room here at the station until five o'clock. I managed to hear holy Mass and receive Holy Communion at six, and assisted at two other Masses later on. There is a beautiful custom here of having exposition [of the Sacred Host] during seven o'clock Mass every Thursday and First Friday, then, as Saturday was the Purification, we had it during the last Mass, so I had a real little feast. Three Masses every morning, one of them a singing one with exposition and Benediction, then we have a Benediction every evening as well. On Friday, we visited the church and venerated the relic of the Precious Blood ... They always are venerating relics here of one saint or another, and have grand processions. There is to be one tonight or this afternoon. I believe the principal persons and acts in the life of the saint are gone through and represented."

Teresa was in her element with all the religious activity. She had also a sad human story with which to regale good Father Snow. "Here in this little old town of Bruges ... there is one dear old lady, the wife of the late governor, R.I.P., who has suffered desolation for the last twelve years without one little gleam of consolation, and who for the last seven years has had gangrene in her feet, one of which has fallen off and the other causes her such fearful pain that she writhes in agony. Yet she is so sweet and patient. This morning she received Holy Communion, and I followed the procession which left the church as a guard of honour to our chosen Lord and King. (She is to undergo an operation at ten o'clock to cut the nerve in the remaining foot, and it is to be done during the Mass that is being offered for her at the church of St Walburga.) She opened her heart, as it were, to me when I first saw her, and this seems to be a great consolation to her, for she says she is so reserved that she can speak to so few. I cannot tell you what a wretched little mite I feel beside her ..."

The visit to Belgium is said to have been connected with the saintly Belgian mystic, Louise Lateau, who, it is believed, made contact with Teresa when she was in ecstasy.

On March 24th, 1901, Teresa writes from Churchill Street to Sister Barbara:

Very dear Sister Barbara,

I wish you a really happy feast, one full of spiritual joys and blessings. If I do not write, do not think for a moment that I forget my promise of daily prayer for you. I do not. I always remember you after Holy Communion, and when I kneel before Him in the Adorable Sacrament of His Love.

I often think of you, and have made up my mind several times to write to you, but something has turned up for me to do, and I have put it off. If it were for God's greater Glory and our personal good, I should be delighted to see you, but He knows best ... What a long time it is since I saw you, dear; and how many things have happened since we last met.

For over twelve years I was living in the Convent of Mercy, Edinburgh, which I left twelve months last August. Since then I have travelled a good deal. I went to Rome last year for the Jubilee and had audience of the Pope. I visited also Assisi, Florence, Padua, Loreto, Venice, Bologna, Milan, Zug, Zurich, Lucerne, Bâle, Paris, Turin, Calais, Rouen, Genoa, Pisa, and many other places.

I left England the first Monday in September [3rd] and did not return until November 15th, returning by Dieppe. Then I was at home over the New Year and went to Belgium on the 7th of January [1901], where I remained until last Friday, 22nd March. So you see I have visited many holy persons and shrines and seen marvels of Nature and Grace. *Deo Gratias.*

You will have heard that dear, good Rev. E. Powell has had a stroke and though he is better I am afraid he will never be able to work as he used to do. He walks badly and speaks thickly and his heart is very weak. He has gone much stouter and quite ruddy in the face without getting any stronger, and gives one the impression that he might have another attack under the least excitement. I am sure you will pray for him and also get others to pray for him. Fanny is, I am pleased to say, much better than she has been for many years. Louey is as wiry as ever, and Percy[18] is quite well. I trust you are fairly well.

And now, dear Sister, I must draw to a conclusion, begging your most fervent prayers for all who have asked me for prayers, and also for myself. You know I need all the help I can get, at this time of the year specially.

Praying that the pure love of God may reign in our hearts for ever. With much love and every good and kind wish and begging God to bless you and yours always, remain, dear S.M. Barbara,

Yours very devotedly in the Sacred Head and Loving Heart, Teresa Higginson, *Enfant de Marie.*

Father Powell died on December 26th, 1901. Teresa wrote to Father Snow: "I trust I shall be able to prove my gratitude to our dear holy Father E.P., R.I.P., by all the indulgences and holy sacrifices I can procure for him now. His death will in many ways be a sorrow to you, yet I know you will gain a great merit through it, and give glory to our dear, kind and loving Spouse, who has taken him only a little while before us. He can now do a great deal more than he has ever done for the devotion and we shall soon have another dear advocate in Heaven to help and intercede for us now, and welcome us at the end of our journey home."

The following June [1902], Father Snow was created a canon of the Diocese. Teresa congratulated him: "I made a *triduum* of Masses for you, praying that the Holy Ghost would enlighten your mind and inflame your heart, and make you wise as a Solomon, and strong in goodwill as Samson was in natural strength, and humble as a real servant of God should be. For a canon without humility would be of little use. But I know how well you love humility and hate pride."

The year 1902 witnessed a most curious instance of the exercise of Teresa's alleged faculty of bilocation. Let Mr. Joseph Pope tell in his own words what happened.

"It was in 1902, on the fourth of January, that I met with a serious accident. I was driving my father's wagon, laden with manure and drawn by one horse. It was a young one, full of spirit. I was riding on the shafts of the wagon, and going under a railway bridge when an electric car passed. The noise frightened the horse and he set off at a gallop. I pulled at the reins till they broke. Then I fell under the wheels and was dragged for several hundred yards over the greasy road. The horse was stopped. I was then taken to Mill Road Hospital,[19] where it was found that my right knee was broken and the flesh all ground away. They dressed the wounds, but bloodpoisoning set in, and the doctors wanted to take my leg off. They sent for my father and mother to get their consent. My father asked if I would get better if my leg was amputated. The doctor said, 'No.' My father said, 'If he is to die, let him die with his leg on.' I was getting weaker every day until they gave me up and sent for my parents. They came and stayed until late in the evening. Miss Higginson, who was staying with Miss Garnett, my former teacher, had been to see me previous to this. She had visited me on several occasions in the daytime. Nothing extraordinary occurred during these visits. Meanwhile, I became worse, and there seemed to be no hope of recovery. Then she came in the dead of night. There was quite an uncanny feeling this time. The nurses could not make out how she got in. One nurse said that she must have been an old witch. It was a mystery. No one had seen her come, and the gates were closed. She told me to put my trust in God, and that

I would get better. She seemed to stay hours praying at my bedside, and from that night I gradually grew better, and, to the astonishment of the doctors, I slowly but surely recovered My right leg is a little shorter than the left, but I am able to walk and do all sorts of farm work. I am fully convinced that I owe my cure to the prayers of Teresa Higginson."

Mr. Garnett, in whose home Teresa was living at the time, was absolutely adamant that she could not by any normal means have got out of the house at night to visit Mill Road Hospital without his knowing it, for he always did a round, making sure that all the doors of the house were locked at night, and he personally kept the keys in his bedroom. Mr. Pope lived on until January, 1968.

Maggie Garnett, having recovered from her first bout of illness, fell sick again, and died on March 15th, 1903. She was forty-eight, having been born in 1855, at sea, in the Bay of Bengal, her father having been a master mariner.

Teresa wrote: "I often think what a joy it will be in Heaven, to see and be with those whom we love, and to feel that nothing can ever separate us. There will be no more parting."

Before Maggie's death, Teresa found for the Garnett trio a small grocery shop at the top of Mount Pleasant – Number 134 – near the corner of Chestnut Street, opposite the old workhouse. Teresa, incidentally, foretold that a Catholic cathedral would one day rise on the site of the workhouse. When Teresa took Alfie and Annie to see the shop that she had selected for them, Annie was not at all pleased; she had wanted a much grander shop. In a huff, she would not speak to Teresa all the way home. Asked how Teresa reacted to Annie's angry silence, Alfie said, "Oh, Little Mother took no notice. She could not be offended or hurt at anything that was done to her." However, the shop was rented, and Teresa saw to the stocking of it. Alfie and Annie used to go there and open it for business, during the daytime only.

51. The Garnetts' shop, at No.134
Mount Pleasant, Liverpool.

After Maggie's death, Teresa helped them to sell most of their furniture and move from Churchill Street into the living quarters above the shop, which now stayed open until far into the evening. "She came with us to be our support," said Alfie, "and when her work in the house was finished she would help to serve in the shop."

Somewhere about the year 1936, three decades after Teresa's death, the Abbé Billé, who had translated Lady Cecil Kerr's book into French, went to Mount Pleasant and enquired of a passer-by where he might find Mr. Alfred Garnett.

"'Oh, yes – go down there to that little shop on the corner.' I directed my steps to the door, which was open," wrote the Abbé in the French magazine, *Sagesse*, in the January-February,

1938, issue. "It was a little grocery store of most modest appearance, with the goods all jumbled together, common and uninviting. No one was there when I entered but presently an old man emerged from behind the counter. Before I had time to speak he looked at me and exclaimed, 'You are the Abbé Billé!' In spite of my surprise at being addressed by my own name, I admitted that he was right and told him I had come to speak to him about Teresa Higginson. He then led me into a little back room. Here everything was piled one on top of the other – clothes, papers, old kitchen utensils, etc. He looked round for a seat to offer me and drew one out from beneath a pile of old papers. It was leaning against the wall in a corner. He sat on an old chest, pushing aside various odds and ends. His voice was feeble and I had to lean towards him to catch what he said. 'I was the one who accompanied her to the station very late one night in 1904 when she left us to go to Chudleigh in Devonshire,' he said. 'She had a feeling that she would not return and gave me her last instructions: "If I do not return, give this case to Canon Snow," she said. This I did, although I did not know what was in it. She had a particular devotion to the souls in Purgatory and prayed continually for them – not those of her own family but for others, the most abandoned, for those Our Lord Himself wished to deliver. Her favours and care Teresa lavished on others rather than upon her friends.' What struck me particularly in talking to him was the strong conviction of the old man in the necessity of suffering – wretchedness truly seemed to him a mark of predilection, of the special protection of his friend. And in it he was happy, very happy. "Have confidence in her", he told me, "she will help you – but has a way of waiting until one gets into great difficulties!" At last I rose to take my leave. Mr. Garnett took my hands and looked at me with tears in his large eyes. Mine also moistened. He knelt for my blessing, and after losing myself in the noisy streets of the great city I still felt that he was following me with his affectionate gaze. In spite of his extreme poverty this good old man knows how to communicate to his friends a little of the happiness and joy that he has deep in his heart."

NOTES

17 This habit of Teresa's was in the Carmelite Convent, at Gillingham, in Dorset, where Sister Mary Teresa (Mrs. Fleck) died. The Reverend Mother of that convent subsequently sent it to Miss Arkwright, at Ormskirk. It was to remain in her custodial care until September, 1952, at which time Mrs. Cottriall (the former Ellen Nicholson) sent it on to St Catherine's Convent, Edinburgh.

18 Percy Jones, Teresa's nephew.

19 Mill Road Hospital, Liverpool, had been originally built by the West Derby Union Board of Guardians as a workhouse for the sick poor. By 1891, it had been renamed Mill Road Infirmary. It remained a general hospital until the Second World War, during which it was very badly damaged by air raids. It survived for another forty years, but was finally closed in 1995.

10

OBIT

The sufferings of Margaret Garnett were ended. She was laid to rest in her narrow earthen bed at Ford Cemetery. The moving finger of Fate – or God – had written and Teresa had to move on. But where? After Maggie's death she had returned to Neston, and embarked once again on the hunt for a school. On November 23rd, 1903, a letter arrived from Sister Mary Philip. Teresa went to see her at the Mount Pleasant convent.

"She told me," Teresa informed Canon Snow, "she had sent a letter to you, the copy of which she enclosed. It was from the chaplain at Chudleigh.[20] What shall I do? I told Sister I was grateful to her but that I should prefer a convent, but she said the nuns she had written to did not answer so she thinks they may perhaps have got someone. She also says there is no hurry and if in the meantime she is applied to by the nuns she will at once let me know. She talked for a long time and thinks that any teacher who can manage it at all ought to look upon it as a sacred duty, for protestant teachers have in several cases been installed in Catholic schools."

The enclosure Teresa referred to was dated December 6th, 1903, and read as follows:

The Rev. H.J. Dowsett has applied to Rev. Mother of Mount Pleasant Training College, Liverpool, respecting a mistress for the school of the Rt. Hon. Lord Clifford and has been advised to write to Miss Higginson.

The school is a small one, at present only 24 children on the books, but the number after Christmas should be close on 30, though it could not, for a long time at least, exceed that number. The children are clean, bright and exceedingly well-behaved. They are all children of the people employed on Lord Clifford's estate. A mistress is required, fully certificated, to take up the school after Christmas. The school has not yet been definitely accepted by the County Council, but there is no doubt that it will be. The buildings and other parts of the school are in good repair, but Lord Clifford is awaiting the report of the County Council when he will erect new schools as they may wish. At present the mistress, Article 50, is receiving £40 *per an*. With three furnished rooms (one sitting-room and two bedrooms) and firing.

The caretaker is required to make up the mistress's fire and do up the rooms each morning and the sum of £5 extra is given to the mistress to engage the caretaker or anyone she chooses to do her cooking or other work required. A fully certificated mistress would of course receive such a salary as her position demanded.

The school is not very far from the church and in future would probably be nearer. The country is very beautiful and the climate soft and healthy. If Miss Higginson would care to know more about the school Fr Dowsett will supply

information. He would like to know Miss Higginson's qualifications, past schools, and salary required *with or without* the arrangement made between the present mistress and caretaker. These are not necessary adjuncts of the position. ... The school-house adjoins the school. The fact of having three rooms allows the mistress the pleasure of having one of her friends to stay with her.

On receipt of the County Council's requirements the probability is that a new school and house will be begun as soon as possible. The rooms were furnished throughout in 1902.

Fr Dowsett would like an early reply to put before Lord Clifford.

With the consent of Canon Snow, Teresa, who seemed to feel that her divine Spouse was asking something special of her in going off to this lonely, far away spot, accepted the position.

She set off from Liverpool in January, 1904, and, having missed her connection at Exeter, she spent the night there, and took advantage the following day of the chance to visit the cathedral.

"I did go into the old cathedral at Exeter and prayed, and asked all in heaven to intercede, for the restoration of the Church, all who prayed and received the Sacraments there who had learnt the truths of our holy faith and enjoyed the peace and blessedness that can only be found in the Church of Peter."

She arrived at Chudleigh in pouring rain. Chill and misted, the place seemed desolate indeed. She wrote to the Canon: "Thank God I have been very sick all the week, but feel rather better tonight. We begin school on Monday, so I am sure you will make a special offering of me and my work to our dear divine Lord. ... I do not know how I am to get stamps here, as there is no post office nearer than Chudleigh, and no letter-box in the wall nearer than two and a half miles off. The house is between two hills, and no other house near that I can see. ... I am writing under difficulties – have no lamp and only a very thin candle." She asked him to send her some stamps.

But the mundane difficulties diminished beside the major practical disaster, the distance away of the church; attached to Lord Clifford's house, it was fully a mile of hilly road's hike. She did, however, discover a short cut across the fields, which, except in rainy weather – and there was plenty of that – when it became an impassable morass, was a help.

The school-house, which stood at the head of a coombe or

small valley, was approached by a steep path which led up from the road. The building was composite: two houses under a single roof, a wide stone passageway running between and separating them. The door of the house on the left-hand side led into the house of the caretaker, Mrs Bond, a widow, with a large family – six boys and three girls. The door of the house on the right, which was that allotted to the schoolmistress, opened directly into a sitting-room; low-ceilinged, two windows filled with lovely views of unspoiled meadows. A pleasant place. Upstairs, two bedrooms. Unfortunately, the building, which was in a bad state of repair, was terribly damp. It was also infested with rats. The school premises were situated on their own, at the rear. There was a delightful garden, access to which was through a back porch, covered in summer with a tracery of climbing roses. Idyllic. But not in winter, the time of Teresa's advent, when all the earth lay desolate, either drenched in downpouring Devon rain, or locked hard in frost beneath snow-threatening sky.

The country folk were, as country folk are, inquisitive. They wanted to know all about the new teacher. One of them, a Catholic, remembered her first sighting of her. Cecil Kerr records: "It was a Sunday morning and on her way to Mass she overtook a little shrunken woman looking far older than her years, creeping along the road in a tall old-fashioned hat, wearing galoshes and huddled up in no fewer than three shawls! The woman could not help wondering how one so frail and simple-looking would be able to deal with her own big, unruly children."

The communal reaction to Teresa was half amusement and half consternation. They need not have worried. The toughest children became lambs in her hands.

On the Monday after her arrival, Teresa was invited to Lady Clifford's Christmas party given to the Catholic children on the estate. There was a grand tea followed by a magic lantern show presented by one of the monks from Buckfast Abbey.

Teresa despatched her first 'school report' to Canon Snow:

Between the tea and lantern Lady Clifford played for the children to dance. It was a real farce for they had not the slightest notion of dancing. I think they can never have seen anyone dance. However they seemed to enjoy it and that was everything. Lady Clifford said she hoped I would be very comfortable and that I would stay with them for many years, to which I made no reply. I am afraid I shall not be able to manage the walk to and from the church. It is a great distance for me and up and down hill all the way, and no made road up to the highway, nothing but ruts and puddle mud over the shoe tops. It has rained every day since I came and rev. H. Dowsett says that this part of Devon is called the watering-can of England.

There are rats in the house and as soon as I put out the candle I can hear them at it, and they eat it all or take it away. Today Fr. Dowsett has sent up a lamp and a coal scuttle. There are only six geographical readers and Burns and Oates' *Catholic History of England* to read from and these all torn. A register recording three whole years' attendances and room for another. I have been busy adding the year's attendances as none had been added. There is *no* summary and an old admission book with record of baptisms in it. No time-table, conscience clause and hardly anything for the children to work with.

I gave Fr. Dowsett a list of books etc. required but have not heard anything about them. He came into school for a short time on Monday morning and said he would bring some charts of Lord Clifford's estates which they must learn for geography – he said that grammar, geography, and history was all bosh for that class of children, and too much reading was not good for them either. He said that he wished me to work up the prayers, catechism, and religious knowledge of the children as they had utterly failed at the religious examination. He said also he could not believe children could be so ignorant of the simplest truths. He blames the parents and teacher. I do not find them so bad as he makes them. They are very good children and above the average for intelligence in country children. Not having tools to work with, I have found it rather hard work to keep all the children well employed. When I get books it will be much easier.

Do pray very earnestly for me. Rev. H. Dowsett kindly gives me holy Communion before Mass and I leave the church at the post communion and am only back in time to open school, and I get a cup of tea at the play time. As soon as Lord and Lady Clifford go away Holy Mass will be at a quarter to eight so that I shall be better off. Last Sunday when I was going for holy Communion I fell in all the *slutch (sic)* and had to go back and change my dress, etc. and wash myself, so of course I was late, but Fr. Dowsett came to me as he came down from the altar and said he would come out again in about a quarter of an hour. He really is very kind in that way. I think I have now told you everything about the school, children, and other things.

Teresa posted off another report to Canon Snow:

It is a month tomorrow since I came south and no one has been to see me since I came. The pane of glass has not been put in nor the window frames mended, so each morning I have to wash up large pools of water both upstairs and down. Last week was the worst – on Monday it was freezing and bitterly cold, on Monday night there was a thaw and regular storm of rain and wind which has continued with more or less violence all the week and what is worse I have not been able to get to holy Mass except Monday and Saturday. The latter and today I really had to wade through the water ankle deep in some places. Fr. Dowsett said I was not to attempt to go down for Benediction as I have a very bad cold, stiff neck and swollen face, and black and inflamed eye.

In a rather curious note, she told Canon Snow:

I am quite convinced that this is the place I had to come to and that I saw some years ago. The school is what I thought was a little white church on a hillside – for as I came along the low road and looked up at it and saw the four windows and a door at each end on a line with the windows, and looked at the roof etc., I felt quite convinced that this was the place in which God wished me to do something for His glory and the good of souls. If it were not for this certainty I do not think that I should venture to stay here as Lent is approaching, and to be so far from the church and such a difficult road to go to it.

And as Eastertide drew near:

If we have all Easter week as a holiday I propose going to Lancashire on the Monday and returning on Friday, at least if you think I should. Of course it is a long time to look forward to and we do not know whether we shall be here or not at that time or what might happen between this and then. But if it is for the best I think I should like to go.

Canon Snow voiced no objection to her plan, and Teresa did indeed spend her Easter holiday, 1904, at home with her sisters in Neston. On Sunday, April 10th, 1904, returning to Devonshire after the Easter holiday, she sent a postcard off from Chudleigh

52. Postcard to Alfred Garnett. The Clock Tower, Newton Abbot.

to Mr Garnett. Written in pencil in small somewhat crabbed writing, it read:

Biddlecombe
10/4/04

Arrived safely. Had nice company all the way. Travelled with an old lady that I met in Florence and again in Lucerne. We were mutually pleased. Trust that you are both better. All sorts of good kind wishes from
Yours
T. Higginson

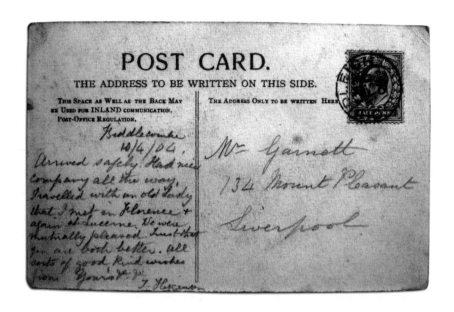

53. Postcard written by Teresa to Alfred Garnett
(in the author's posession).

On her return to Chudleigh, she was taken sick with a nasty attack of bronchitis.

> I have had a rather bad bronchial cold ever since I returned and had linseed and mustard poultices on day and night, and, as the congestion did not give way, I gave [them] a holiday and tried turpentine. I am a little better today, but very weak. I have not been out all week. I wrote and told Fr. Dowsett, but I have neither seen nor heard anything from him. No one ever comes near school or house. The place is so damp that a pair of slippers that I left in a cupboard near the fire had long blue and green hairs about half an inch long grown from them when I returned on Saturday.

54. The house and school-house at Chudleigh.

I do hope that you may have fine and warm weather all your holidays and that the change and rest may really do you both permanent good.

A week later Teresa could write more optimistically:

I am a great deal better today. I have been to holy Mass etc. and Benediction was immediately after Mass. It is the first time since last Sunday that I have been. I did not get to Benediction on Sunday for I could hardly get home from church in the morning, I was so faint and my heart was so bad. I sent for rev. H. Dowsett, and he came up yesterday, Friday, morning. He says he will see that the house is made airtight. The rat holes are made up and tarred and a shed is built up over the passage to the school. I succeeded in getting him into the house and I showed him the doors etc. and he says I shall have curtains also, and some other things.

Lord and Lady Clifford will be home for the first week in May, Sunday or Monday, Fr. Dowsett says, and I will then see Lady Clifford and know what is going to be done. I do not know that I have done whatever it is that our dear Lord wishes me to do here. If I did, I should leave at once, but under the circumstances, as I am somewhat better and the weather is more settled, with your prayers and blessing I shall wait a little longer.

She was still "on the sick list" at the beginning of May; she was feeling "so very weak and my heart is bad and cough also." But the weather was becoming pleasant and soon she began to pick up. It was one of her great joys to gather up boxfuls of roses and send them off – "a little message in each petal of every flower," as she used to say – to Canon Snow to decorate his church.

The summer holidays of 1904 she spent at Neston. When she returned to Chudleigh for the beginning of term, she found things much improved. The muddy road had been made up, the cottage repaired, the rat-holes blocked off, and oil lamps had been provided to replace the candles.

The children, her "dear chicks', she called them, all thought the world of her. There had been a time when some of the big boys had reckoned they were going to have it all their own way. They soon found that they were mistaken. Not only could Teresa be surprisingly severe if she considered it necessary, but the sight of her distress made the miscreants feel sorry.

Cecil Kerr writes: "She once caught one of the older boys playing the fool during prayers in order to make the others laugh. She at once punished him, but the rest of the children were so astonished to see that teacher herself was crying that they ran home to tell their mothers that the boy had done something terrible indeed. Teresa, fearing the mother would be seriously alarmed, sent for her to talk the matter over. The girls were devoted to her and she would often keep them after school hours to give them lessons in cooking, allowing them to take home the results of their efforts. In wet weather she was always careful to have something dry for each child to put on, and would give them hot cocoa and provide meals for the poorer ones, and when she came back from her holidays she brought each of them a nice present. For the rest, she kept very much to herself and never went into the neighbours' houses, unless they were ill or needed help, when she would be the first to go to them. She was always busy, and did a great deal of needlework, making vestments for the Canon or clothes for the children. Her sewing was most beautiful. She once made a baby's dress which was sent up for some competition of Queen Alexandra's and won the first prize. She hardly ever went anywhere except to church, and the impression grew that she wished to avoid attention. Accordingly little heed was paid to her and she got the name of being somewhat eccentric. Her chief companion was a little dog called Ruff which Fr. Dowsett had sent her to keep away the rats."

The year was winding down to its close. The school at Chudleigh broke up early and Teresa planned to spend Christmas back home at Neston. Her box packed, Ruff given his breakfast, on the morning of Wednesday, December 14th, 1904, she was waiting for the arrival of the cab to take her to the station. When it came, the cabby found her lying on the floor. Ruff, who had been given some rabbit bones in the corner for his breakfast, inconsolate, was doing his pathetic best to rouse her with a bone. He had carried it over and laid it down beside her in the hope that it might restore her. She had suffered a sudden

55. Teresa, taken at Chudleigh in 1904,
aged about sixty.

stroke. She was fully conscious, but totally helpless. Her mouth was drawn a little to one side, and her speech although not lost, was somewhat affected. Neighbours carried her up to bed.

Father Dowsett sent off telegrams to her sisters and to Canon Snow. Teresa was, he assured them, in no real danger. The doctor hoped that she might be well enough to travel up to Neston in a week or two's time. Since the school at Neston had not as yet broken up, Teresa's sisters decided to wait until she was declared fit enough to make the journey, when they would come and collect her, and take her home with them. Meanwhile, she was left for the first week in the well-intentioned, but not very skilful, nursing hands of her women neighbours. At the end of that week, Father Dowsett went into Newton Abbot in quest

56. The last known photograph of Teresa (fifth from the left, back row) with some of her pupils at Chudleigh. 1904.

of a properly qualified nurse. He found one, a Catholic, Miss Agnes Casey.

Nurse Casey has left a description of her feelings on being asked to go to Chudleigh. "There had," she says, "been a great epidemic of sickness everywhere, and after a long, strenuous time of nursing, I was feeling the need of a little relaxation. I was looking forward with pleasure to the Christmas festivities, in company with all the nursing staff, and in anticipation of this I was in the act of writing to a relative in London, asking her to send me a blouse for the occasion, when to my surprise Father Dowsett, Lord Clifford's chaplain, arrived." She had heard the patient whom she was being invited to nurse in a lonely cottage in the depths of a rural wilderness described as an "eccentric old frump", and was not at all keen to take the case. But her mother persuaded her that she had a Christian duty to do so, and, to what was to prove her lasting joy, she did. Nevertheless, "the prospect of spending my Christmas in an isolated lonely spot with a poor helpless patient, who was a complete stranger to me, was not alluring. A struggle arose within. However, as the carriage drew near to the house, I pulled myself together, for I knew that it would be unworthy of me to show the slightest sign of the interior conflict taking place. ... I knocked at the door of Teresa's room and a sweet voice said, 'Come in.' Holy Teresa received me most warmly, and at once we were friends. I felt quite at home. The first thing she insisted on was that I should have some tea, which I willingly accepted. Teresa partook of some also, to keep me company, after which I set to work to make my invalid as comfortable as possible."

The patient had not been washed, or had her bed made, for a week. Neither had the sitting-room, to which she had been carried down, been given even the most perfunctory of dustings. A rickety old towel-horse had been put by her bed to ward off the draughts. Nurse Casey concentrated all her endeavours on making the room as bright and cosy as could be. To this end, she borrowed several items, including a screen, from Lord Clifford's house, and covered the table with a dainty cloth which was the product of Teresa's own needle.

Dr William E. Tresidder decreed that his patient should have good nourishing food, and many a tempting delicacy was sent down to her from Lord Clifford's house. Obediently, Teresa ate whatever was put before her, but, unaccustomed as she was to eating, the result was alarmingly violent attacks of indigestion.

It did not, says Nurse Casey, take her long to realise that this was no ordinary patient "but a soul very near to God, and feelings of awe and reverence would come over me in my intercourse with her. Exteriorly there was nothing extraordinary about her but a wonderful child-like simplicity. Another point I observed was the great sweetness of her smile and the remarkable penetration of her eyes. One felt instinctively that she read one's very soul, so it was not surprising when she told me in one of our little evening talks together, that she knew of the struggle that had taken place in my heart and had begged our dear Lord to make it up to me, adding that although leaving herself entirely in God's hands to arrange for her as He knew best, she had asked Him to send her a Catholic nurse and one who knew Him and loved Him, and that the moment I entered her room she felt her prayer had been answered."

Father Dowsett was very good to Teresa, bringing her Communion as often as he could, but he was lame and could only manage the distance with difficulty.

Among Teresa's visitors was Nurse Casey's sister, Mrs Caroline Statt, who loved to come and sit and chat with her. One day Mrs Statt was talking about her house at 31 Queen Street, Newton Abbot, when Teresa suddenly told her of an occasion when she had been passing that very house and had felt a powerful compulsion to stand still in the street and pray for its inhabitants. As she stood there saying a decade of the rosary, she somehow *knew* that some time in the future she would be brought in touch with those who lived in that house.

She also told Mrs Statt that "Our Lord had shown her that little house and school [the school-house and school at Chudleigh] many years before, but she had no idea that it was one and the same place, until she had been there some time. One morning, returning from Mass across the meadow, she had looked up. She said the sun was very bright and she had at once recognised it, and she at once knelt down there in that spot and adored the Divine Will. She had, until then, been under the impression that the school of her vision was somewhere abroad, probably among little savages, and that she still had to go there to work and die.

222

Now she knew instead that she was already in her right place."

Teresa discovered that Mrs Statt was, like her, a Franciscan Tertiary, and when she mentioned that, in the event of her death, she had no brown habit in which to be buried, having already given away no less than three. Mrs Statt promptly promised to give her hers, should she be the first of them to require it.

Another caller was Father Dawson, the priest from Teignmouth, who had got to know Teresa when she took the Chudleigh schoolchildren there on a seaside outing. He had been deeply impressed by her saintliness. He sat for a long time at her bedside, talking of holy things, and he afterwards said that he had learnt many lessons from her, and had been loath to leave.

And Margaret Blacklock, the teacher who filled in for Teresa at Chudleigh after she had been taken ill, and used to see her every day, remembered: "She was a dear soul, so sweet and human, one to whom you could turn in any trouble. I often went to see her and she would walk with me just so far along the road, but she never went into anyone's house except in case of sickness. She was most charitable to the poor who lived near her. She was an excellent cook and a most beautiful needlewoman. After the school day was finished, she used to give cookery lessons to the older girls in her cottage. She was also a clever swimmer and held the medal of the Royal Humane Society for saving life." [Note: Enquiry at the Royal Humane Society has failed to disclose the presentation to Teresa of any medal. Neither has any evidence of her having been a swimmer emerged.]

"The beautiful feast of the Nativity was drawing very near," Agnes Casey continues, "and one afternoon I was sitting writing some of my Christmas letters to my family. From time to time I stopped to exchange some words with Miss Higginson in reference to the said letters. At last, when all was finished, Teresa, who had taken great interest in everything, said, 'Have you put the children's letters in separate envelopes addressed to each one individually?' I replied that I had put all the notes together in their mother's envelope. She said, 'Oh, my dear child, if you only knew the joy it gives a little child to receive a letter addressed to itself you would not, I am sure, deprive it of such a pleasure. The angels in heaven rejoice when we give happiness to a little child.' I did as Miss Higginson suggested, and later on I learned how the little extra trouble was the source of immense joy and excitement to the young folks.

Christmas Eve arrived and the hour for Midnight Mass drew near, but I was loath to leave Miss Higginson alone, as the caretaker had retired to rest, and in case of an emergency there would be no one to attend to her. I proffered to sacrifice the Midnight Mass in the cause of charity and go in the morning instead, but Miss Higginson assured me that she would be quite all right, that there was nothing to fear, adding, 'I shall be so happy, dear, if you go and bring "Dearest" back to me in your heart, and I will look forward with joy to your returning.' ... When I arrived at the little church several people were waiting for Confession. I asked Father Dowsett if he would kindly give me Holy Communion before the Mass, as I felt rather uneasy at leaving my patient so long alone. He asked the name of my patient. When I told him he replied, 'My dear child, do not have any scruple at leaving her, for Miss Higginson is a saint. You can stay for the Mass in peace. She will be quite all right.'

Christmas Day came, but, oh, how different from the one I had anticipated. We had Christmas fare, which was sent from Lord Clifford's house, in super-abundance, but Teresa's fare was the ordinary invalid's diet. ... I cannot possibly describe in words the perfect happiness of that privileged Christmas Day in 1904. It was a happiness not of earth, and I really felt I was in heaven. Of course, this was due to Teresa's prayers, for during the afternoon she asked me if I regretted the festivities I had given up, and I replied with great ardour of soul, 'Oh, Miss Higginson, I am too happy! I assure you I would not resign my post for all the pleasure and all the delights of the whole world.'"

On Boxing Day – December 26th – Nurse Casey informed Canon Snow: "*Deo gratias* she is getting much better and the doctor is very pleased at the rapid progress she is making. She wishes me to tell you that our Lord has sent her every comfort, screens, curtains, etc. everything to make her cosy and keep out the draughts. She is touched with the loving sympathy of the little children and their parents. Everyone has been so kind and considerate."

That night, however, the patient took a turn for the worse. – "7 a.m. There is a decided change in her since I wrote your letter. The use of her limbs is quite gone again for the present. She has had a very bad night. I don't wish to alarm you but she certainly appears worse than I have seen her yet. I am just sending a note to Fr. Dowsett asking him to come at once. If there is another change for the worse I will wire immediately."

Father Dowsett came, together with some of the older girls to assist at the ceremony, and gave Teresa the last Sacrament.

January 6th, 1905. Nurse Casey to Canon Snow: "It will comfort you to know that Miss Higginson is much better. There was a marvellous change in her since she received Extreme Unction and holy Viaticum, which Fr. Dowsett administered early on the Wednesday [January 4th] morning ... Our Lord has again restored the use of her limbs. She was able to use her hands almost immediately after the reception of the holy Sacraments. *Deo gratias*."

Canon Snow replied: "Your welcome letter with the good news came on Saturday night [January 8th] and I am very grateful to you for writing. I trust Miss Higginson will now speedily get better and be able to travel. You will be sorry to part from her, but you must comfort yourself with having made so good a friend, and thank our Lord for what He has done for you through her. She will not forget you. Tell her I both sympathise with her and congratulate her: sympathise with her because the going home day is deferred, and congratulate with her because she will have further time to do more for her Spouse and merit more for herself."

The improvement continued, slowly. Her sisters, Louey and Fanny, were exceedingly anxious to bring her home to Neston, but Dr Tresidder was not happy at the idea of her risking a long journey. He suggested that Nurse Casey should first take her for a little change to Teignmouth. But the best laid plans went again awry. All was ready for their departure the following morning, but that night, just as she was retiring to bed, Nurse Casey was taken ill, and with great regret she told Teresa she was afraid that their expedition would have to be postponed, the rooms they had booked cancelled. "My dear child, go quickly and knock up the caretaker and tell her to send her good husband into Chudleigh at once for the doctor. You are poisoned." The doctor came and stayed all night. He said it was a wonder Nurse Casey had not died. "Of course, I knew that it was entirely due to holy Teresa's prayers, for she seemed to know that I was in grave danger, even before the doctor came. The next day my two sisters arrived, one at eight o'clock in the morning, and the other later in the day. When I asked them why they came, both said that they felt something was wrong and had been impelled to come. On their departure I asked Teresa if she had had anything to do with their visit, and she smilingly replied, 'Well, yes dear, I sent my guardian angel to tell them that all was not well.'"

Nurse Casey soon recovered, but a great unease concerning Teresa settled upon her. "Is it not strange how our proposed visit to Teignmouth was so suddenly nipped in the bud?" Teresa replied rather gravely, "Yes, dear child, we shall not go to

Teignmouth now, nor to Scotland. Our dear Lord has evidently other designs and we must lovingly bow down and adore them." Those words struck dread into Nurse Casey. "I could not believe it meant that my beloved spiritual mother would never again travel in this world. Only a little while before we had made arrangements for a quiet time at the seaside, and then Miss Higginson proposed a visit to her dear friend, Mrs. Fleck, in Scotland. From there we were to have gone to Neston." But none of it came to pass.

January 16th, 1905. Nurse Casey to Canon Snow: "Miss Higginson is not nearly so well again. She has been suffering very acute pains in the head since last Thursday, 12th, and it affects her eyes so that I am obliged to keep the room almost in perpetual darkness. She cannot even bear the fire in at night, for the glare although shaded by a screen seems to make her as she says seasick. The doctor says the heart is much weaker and is the cause of these severe pains in the head. It prevents her from sleeping. She can neither sleep night nor day."

January 31st, 1905. Nurse Casey to Canon Snow: "She is still very up and down. One day the tiniest bit stronger and the next down at the lowest. She has had one or two very bad turns since I wrote before asking permission to move to Teignmouth, and at present her heart is in such a weak state and her nerves are so unstrung that I doubt we shall have to postpone our going to Teignmouth at least for a few days more. ... She cannot do anything for herself, but she is not helpless. She has recovered from the seizure, but it has left her nervous system in a frightfully weak state. She cannot bear now the least sound, and light is a torture to her. She suffers acute pain in the head, and flatulence is another great trouble to her."

Father Dowsett dropped Canon Snow a line on February 4th, 1905: "I do not think Miss Higginson is quite well enough for a day or two to take the journey to Teignmouth. Is there a possibility of your being able to come down here and see her within the next few days? I should be very pleased to put you up. I will let you know how things progress. Her heart is so very uncertain and I am consulting the doctor as to the possibility of Miss Higginson being removed without any danger of catching a chill, as the weather is not very propitious here. Please do not think I want to interfere with any arrangements made for Miss Higginson. The truth is that Lord Clifford and I are under a great obligation to Miss Higginson for all she has done, and I could not risk her being removed unless the doctor not only gave the permission, but really advised the removal. I am sending for the doctor to ask him to call and see me, then I will telegraph you the result. I think Miss Higginson would far prefer your opinion than even that of her sister. This is my reason for writing to you. I could not in a letter tell you all the circumstances of the case. I do not think there is any danger of death, but such a valuable life deserves all the care and consideration that those who know Miss Higginson can possibly give."

Another disappointment for Teresa, who had been looking forward immensely to an impending visit from Canon Snow. On the very day that she was expecting him, the sad news of his brother's death arrived. The Canon would not be coming.

Letters to Teresa still arrived in considerable numbers. She was by now no longer able to answer them herself, and she asked Nurse Casey to do so on her behalf. The nurse protested her incapacity. Teresa told her to go upstairs and ask her guardian angel; he would help her. And so he did, for Nurse Casey found herself perfectly capable of tirelessly rattling off replies non-stop until two or three in the morning. The odd thing is that she could never, on the morning after, remember anything of what she had written on the night before.

Even now, as Teresa's days on earth were drawing to a

close, her old enemy seems to have been unable to leave her unmolested. Nurse Casey remembers: "One night, in particular, I was called up several times, to find my holy invalid in a state of complete exhaustion and the coverings of the bed all wet. I was quite mystified until Teresa explained to me that it was only the Devil trying to annoy her. I replied, 'Oh, I do wish he would go to sleep and let us get a little sleep too.' 'My dear child, he never sleeps', said Teresa with a smile. It was quite evident that the Devil had been there, because Teresa had the appearance of one who had been struggling with someone and could scarcely get her breath."

In a letter written to me, Richard Whittington-Egan, on the eve of the 36th anniversary of the death of Teresa Higginson, Sister Mary Francis of Assisi, the *ci-devant* Nurse Agnes Casey, told me: "Oh yes, the Devil came often during her last illness, although I did not see him, but I knew he had been there, by the effect produced on Holy Teresa. She had the appearance of one who had been through some terrible conflict, and was completely exhausted. I used to give her some refreshment to renew her strength, which she always most gratefully accepted."

Teresa, says Nurse Casey, never neglected an opportunity of showing her how to profit spiritually from the most trifling occurrences. One morning they were expecting a visit from the doctor, and Nurse Casey was busy making everything ready. 'The little dog, Ruff, who had been Miss Higginson's companion on her walks, kept frisking about my feet. Poor little doggie, he was so delighted to be in the room near his mistress, but just then I found him a hindrance, and exclaimed a bit impatiently, 'Oh Ruff, do be quiet! Lie down!' Miss Higginson, with her usual sweetness and gentleness, said, 'Oh, my dear child, is it not just as easy to say. "Dear Lord, I thank Thee. Thou knowest what is best," as to say "Oh Ruff do be quiet." The act of love would have united your will to our dear Lord's and increased your merits for eternity. ... Whereas the act of natural impatience will not profit you anything.'"

The invalid had a keen sense of humour. She could always enjoy a joke. She recounted how one of the little girls in the school had come to her and said: "Miss Higginson, Mamma says I may stay to dinner if you invite me, but if you don't invite me, I mustn't ask to stay, but come home." Of course, Teresa promptly invited her, and the child was delighted. On another occasion, when she was living at St Catherine's Convent in Edinburgh, a six-year-old girl had come into her room and said: "Miss Higginson, dear, you are not very, very, very, are you? But you have a dear, good face," and then flung her arms around her neck and smothered her in kisses. "Of course, dear, the child meant to say I was not very pretty," Teresa told Nurse Casey, "but feared it would not be polite." She laughed heartily over this, remarking, "Children are so sweet and so confiding, and so charming in their simplicity."

One day Nurse Casey was giving her patient a blanket-bath, when Mrs. Bond, the caretaker, walked into the room without, as Nurse thought, knocking, as good manners dictated that she should. Nurse felt that she had every right to show her annoyance at this lapse, which she promptly did, reprimanding most severely, Mrs. Bond, who, it seems, actually *had* knocked, and who stumped angrily off. Teresa did not speak. She waited until Nurse Casey had recovered from her annoyance. Then she said: "That was not worthy of you, my dear. You were made for a nobler end; to make amends, do this act of kindness. Take these flowers to Mrs. Bond, and ask her if you may sponge her sick child." Nurse did as Teresa suggested. Mrs. Bond was delighted to see her little one looking so comfortable and refreshed after the sponging, and was most humble. That evening she came round, bearing with her a pot of home-made jam for them, and apologising for having been cross in the morning.

Teresa predicted that Nurse Casey would, as indeed she did, become a nun. "My dear child," she told her, "one day you will become a religious. It will not be for some years yet, for you will have some work to do in the world. In your vocation as a nurse you will minister to our dear Lord in His suffering humanity, but eventually you will be a religious. I, myself, wished to be a Poor Clare, because prayer, the divine office — day and night — mortification and penance form the chief part of the rule, but our dear Lord wished me to teach little children how to love Him instead."

Nurse Casey reports that during what were to prove to be Teresa's last days she endured great physical suffering, together with terrible desolation of soul. She was at times positively swamped in a suffocating blanket of sadness, and seemed quite changed. But there were also times of relative superficial calm. On one such day, Nurse Casey's two brothers-in-law called at the cottage to see her. "We must do all we can in honour of this visit of St John and St Paul, [Note: In her letter to me, Nurse Casey says, "St John and St Paul", not, as elsewhere reported, "St Peter and St Paul".] said Teresa, with her sweet smile, and she bade the nurse to lay the best cloth and provide the best meal possible for their unexpected guests. The two men were quite overcome, and went on their way full of awe and reverence for their hostess.

On the night of February 9th, 1905, Nurse Casey noticed a very special tenderness as Teresa said goodnight to her. "She always wished me goodnight affectionately, but on this particular night ... she thanked me most warmly for all my devoted care of her, and ... holding my hand in hers she [said] 'I want you now to promise me, dear, that in the event of my death at any time, I do not wish any hands but yours to touch my body.'" These were Teresa's last words to Agnes Casey. Embracing her, with tears rising in her eyes, her devoted nurse faithfully promised that she would perform the last sad offices for her alone, unaided.

At midnight, Nurse Casey observed that her patient's respiration had become very quick and laboured, and asked her if she was feeling ill. Teresa did not answer, so she went over to her, and found that she was unconscious and completely paralysed. The caretaker was called and the doctor sent for, but when he came he said that there was nothing more that could be done. At 10.21 a.m. the following morning Father Dowsett telegraphed Teresa's sisters and Canon Snow. "Patient unconscious. Sudden relapse. Can you come?"

The Canon, enmeshed in ecclesiastical duties, was unable to come. He was later to say that as soon as he received the telegram he went into the church and, standing in the sanctuary, said the *Te Deum* with great fervour and consolation, thanking God for all the marvellous graces He had bestowed upon her. "I have not," he afterwards wrote, "said one single prayer for her, being sure she is in heaven."

Writing, on March 8th, 1905, to Nurse Casey, he told her: "Miss Higginson desired that her death might as far as possible resemble Our Lord's. Hence the desolation she suffered. That she might endure this desolation He hid from her that she was going to die. Had she known that He was about to take her to Himself so great would have been her joy that the most intense bodily pain and any other suffering would have been as nothing. All during her life He permitted her to participate in His Passion and it was fitting for her own greater reward and for the good of the Church and of souls that her death should be in suffering and not in consolation. You say in one place that she clung to the hope she was going to get better and teach again. This was simply impossible. She had reached the highest degree of union it is possible for a soul to reach on earth and a soul in such a state cannot cling to anything but the Will of God. The Will of God and the will of the soul are one. But as I have said, Our Lord concealed from her that she was going to die, and when someone about her said she would get better, then no doubt she would consider it her duty to get better as soon as possible and if Teignmouth was to do her good to get there without delay, this was not undue eagerness. I am not in any sorrow about her death. ... Knowing all I do about her I should feel I was not doing right by Our Lord to imagine she was in Purgatory. Some here have told me that when they tried to pray for her they found themselves praying to her. Nor do I feel any sense of loss, for I feel her nearer to me now than when she was at Biddlecombe."

Louisa set off for Devon at once. She caught the night train and arrived between six and seven in the morning, to find Teresa so changed, face so livid and teeth clenched together, that she was almost unrecognisable.

She wrote at once to Canon Snow, telling him: 'Teresa is still unconscious in an uncertain heavy drowsy sleep and then apparently not breathing at all. God has been so good to her that I trust she may be spared to travel home. Unless the good God intervenes in some miraculous way she cannot last very long. The doctor shook his head this morning and said he was not looking for this new development. ... Teresa does not take any nourishment. Of course she cannot. I hope consciousness may return to her before I have to return. ... The nurse is a little body and so devoted. Fr. Dowsett honoured me as her sister by sending a groom to meet me for which I was very thankful although there was a bus at the station."

Louisa wrote again: "Tess is still unconscious although at times she seems to have lucid intervals and will press your hand although she has not known me yet."

57. The room in which Teresa died, at Chudleigh. The armchair is believed to have been there in Teresa's time.

Nurse Casey had made it her practice to anoint every night Teresa's five senses with holy water. After she had lapsed into unconsciousness the nurse continued to do this, and when it came to the anointing of the palms, the hands would open, and a sweet smile would spread over her face.

Louisa wrote and told Canon Snow not to come as there was absolutely nothing that he could do for Teresa in her present condition, and promising to wire him if she showed any sign of coming to.

February 14th. Louisa sent a card to the Canon: "No change; there was a slight improvement but not maintained today. Sleeps and breathes loudly and fitfully."

On Wednesday, February 15th, 1905, the end came. In the

afternoon Father Dowsett wired Canon Snow: "Patient dying. Cannot last long."

The last struggle began at about five o'clock in the evening – "her face had an expression of the most intense agony, pitiful to witness, and there were continual convulsive movements of the mouth. Her face would every now and then become livid and distorted, and her respiration was loud and laboured. Never before or since," said Nurse Casey, "have I seen a more heart-rending death agony or one that lasted so long. In this state she lingered on for six long hours, her sister and myself kneeling and sitting alternately by her side all the time, saying the rosary for her, litanies, and the prayers for the dying, and sprinkling her frequently with holy water. When we spoke to her she made no sign. At ten minutes past eleven her Beloved came to clasp His own faithful and devoted Spouse in His everlasting embrace. Her state of unconsciousness was best, as Divine Providence willed she should suffer so terribly. She was, indeed, the Spouse of the Crucified."

About this time, Kitty Deady, Margaret Murphy's adopted daughter was very ill. She was, in fact, said to have been lying at death's door for the last six months. Margaret wrote to Teresa asking her prayers. Teresa replied: "Kitty will not die yet. It is Our Blessed Lord's Will that she should still suffer and that she should get better when it shall please Our Lord that I should take her sufferings. I will ask Him in due time that I may take her sufferings and sickness." On February 15th (1905), Kitty was worse than ever. Then, suddenly, she felt all her pain leave her, and, although still pathetically weak, she found herself able to get up from her bed and put on her clothes. A few hours later a telegram arrived. It brought the news of Teresa's death. She had died of a cerebral haemorrhage.

Louisa wrote: "The end came unexpectedly, although we were looking for it all day. Sister never regained consciousness,

*58. Teresa's Grave. Pre-1930. No mention on the
stone that she is buried there.*

and it was God's almighty Providence that she was in that state,
for she suffered terribly."

True to her promise, refusing many kind offers of help,
Nurse Casey locked the door and set about the performance of
her last services to Teresa Higginson's corpse. She saw with
relief that the look of suffering had gone. In its place was an
expression of heavenly peace and happiness. "There was a
delicate tinge of colour in her cheeks and she looked so life-like
that I began to wonder if what we thought was death was only
ecstasy. There was an exquisite perfume coming from her,
filling the room with a sweet odour." The odour of sanctity. She
laid her out in the brown habit of St Francis.

Louisa said: "Sister is looking more like herself. She had

*59. Close-up of the original inscription at Teresa's burial place.
Note that little Freddie Hallifax's name is there.*

such a suffering look but now she is changing. ... The undertaker has brought the shell and Sister looks happy. I would like her to be left in the church over night and buried on Tuesday. As she is in a shell it will not matter. There is no smell of death about her and no discolouration."

They carried Teresa's body into the schoolroom, where the children and their parents came to pay their last sorrowful tributes to her and offer up their prayers. She was placed in a coffin, unexpectedly grand for one who had lived all her days in the voluntary shadow of Christ-like poverty, of polished oak, with a very beautiful thick brass cross, extending the entire length of the coffin, and upon which was inscribed her name and the date of her death.

60. Post-1930 additions to Teresa's grave.

The ground was white with snow when, at seven o'clock in the darkness of a winter's morning, Teresa's mortal remains, were driven, a modest cortége, the seven miles to Newton Abbot station. The body was placed in a private carriage on the train, Louisa accompanying it to Neston.

"We just had a hearse and one coach and a wagonette to take the seven carriers back.," she wrote. "Lady Clifford is abroad but she ordered a beautiful cross of arum lilies and bunches of violets and her card attached. His Lordship came home late on Sunday evening but he allowed us to travel through the park as it shortened the distance considerably. She was shown every mark of respect and kind, large-hearted Fr. Dowsett would have liked her to have lain amongst them.

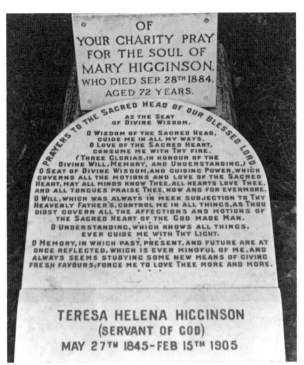

OF
YOUR CHARITY PRAY
FOR THE SOUL OF
MARY HIGGINSON,
WHO DIED SEP. 28TH 1884,
AGED 72 YEARS.

TO THE SACRED HEAD OF OUR BLESSED LORD
PRAYERS
AS THE SEAT
OF DIVINE WISDOM.
O WISDOM OF THE SACRED HEAD,
GUIDE ME IN ALL MY WAYS.
O LOVE OF THE SACRED HEART,
CONSUME ME WITH THY FIRE.
(THREE GLORIAS, IN HONOUR OF THE
DIVINE WILL, MEMORY, AND UNDERSTANDING,)
O SEAT OF DIVINE WISDOM, AND GUIDING POWER, WHICH
GOVERNS ALL THE MOTIONS AND LOVE OF THE SACRED
HEART, MAY ALL MINDS KNOW THEE, ALL HEARTS LOVE THEE,
AND ALL TONGUES PRAISE THEE, NOW AND FOR EVERMORE.
O WILL, WHICH WAS ALWAYS IN MEEK SUBJECTION TO THY
HEAVENLY FATHER'S, CONTROL ME IN ALL THINGS, AS THOU
DIDST GOVERN ALL THE AFFECTIONS AND MOTIONS OF
THE SACRED HEART OF THE GOD MADE MAN.
O UNDERSTANDING, WHICH KNOWS ALL THINGS,
EVER GUIDE ME WITH THY LIGHT.
O MEMORY, IN WHICH PAST, PRESENT, AND FUTURE ARE AT
ONCE REFLECTED, WHICH IS EVER MINDFUL OF ME, AND
ALWAYS SEEMS STUDYING SOME NEW MEANS OF GIVING
FRESH FAVOURS, FORCE ME TO LOVE THEE MORE AND MORE.

TERESA HELENA HIGGINSON
(SERVANT OF GOD)
MAY 27TH 1845-FEB 15TH 1905

61. Close-up of the newly affixed marble
inscriptions on Teresa's grave.

Mass was said for her every day and this week also. Sister and I at Newton Abbot were placed in a separate coach and we never left it till we reached Neston. We were several times hitched off and left for a short time. I had all her luggage placed in the carriage with me." A cab was waiting for Louisa at Neston. Teresa's coffin was conveyed the short distance to the church on a milk float "We had only a float and a cab at Neston as the distance is so short, and she was taken straight to the church."

At eight-thirty the following morning, Mass was celebrated at St Winefride's, Neston, by Father Bernard Thompson, and after he had breakfasted, he conducted the funeral service. Teresa was buried with her mother in the grave in St Winefride's churchyard which had been dug twenty-seven years before for little Freddie Hallifax.[22] She was laid to rest with, as she would have wished, no great fuss. Her only mourners were her sisters, Louisa and Fanny, and her faithful friend, Margaret Murphy, the trinity on earth who loved her best.

NOTES

20 In Devonshire.

22 The original monumental masonry cross and slab erected over the Higginson family grave bore the names of only Mary Higginson and little Freddie Hallifax. For many years there was no reference to the fact that Teresa had also been interred there with her mother and nephew. In the 1930s, however, as a result of the setting up of a fund by the family of Lady Kerr, a flat slab of York stone, suitably inscribed to commemorate Teresa, was set upon the grave. Misfortunately, a marble tablet, carved with Teresa's memorial details and bolted to the base of the cross, completely covered up the inscription recording the death of Freddie Hallifax. And in the late 1980s, a large, arched slab of marble, bearing upon it a more prominent inscription to Teresa, together with the full text of Prayers to the Sacred Head of Our Blessed Lord, was placed horizontally on the grave.

11

AFTERLIFE

True to her vows, Teresa Helena Higginson lived in the odour of sanctity and died in the grim stench of poverty. Earthly possessions she had few. The clothes she stood up in. Her best things, relics of her Continental tour of 1900, hanging moth-balled in the wardrobe. Effects to the penny-whistle-thin tune of £99. 10s. – doubtless, largely compounded of unspent teacher's salary, and earmarked for charity. All left to Louey.[23] Her shroud was the habit of a Franciscan Tertiary. It was given to her. Her coffin, too, was given to her. Louisa had first tried to get the joiner on the Chudleigh estate to make one, but she failed. She was then directed to a small town some distance away, where she found a cabinet-maker. When he heard her mission he said: "Now, that is strange! I have a coffin which I have laid aside for some considerable time, in the expectation it might be wanted some day." Having taken the measurements of the corpse, and found them similar to the dimensions of the already made coffin, and upon learning the name of the dead, he told Miss Louisa that he had heard much of the deceased lady from the little children, and that he would deem it a privilege to have the opportunity of making this offering to her of that which was to carry her to her last resting place.

And that last resting place remained for long unmarked. When Lady Anne Cecil Kerr and her mother made their first pilgrimage to Neston, they could not find Teresa's grave. Her name had not been added to the stone.

Teresa had not lain long in the Neston earth before the

whisperings began to stir the air. The tales, the mysteries and the memories were soon wreathing about her grave, thick as flights of wingèd seraphim. The worldly great and famed, among them high ones of the Church, hurried forth with their commendations.

The celebrated Dominican, Father Vincent McNabb (1868-1943), well-known preacher at Speakers' Corner, in London's Hyde Park, was firmly in favour of Teresa and her writings, and, indeed, admitted that he had sought her intercession for the success of a book on philosophy upon which he was engaged.

St Katharine Drexel, Mother Foundress of the American Order of the Sisters of the Blessed Sacrament, dedicated to the educating of the underprivileged – in the main negroes and Indians – thought that Teresa ought to be taken as the model for teachers, and urged her sisters to try to imitate her.

Similarly, Mère Guélin, foundress of the Servants of Jesus-Wisdom, at Cagnotte, in the Landes of France, inspired by the life and writings of Teresa, was without doubt her greatest exponent. In the course of forty years a constancy of articles about Teresa came from her pen, in addition to a short *Life* and a number of brochures. She edited the bi-monthly bulletin *Sagesse*.

The eminent French theologian and professor at Rome, Father Maurice de la Taille, S.J., wrote of her: "She is a saint – a great saint – because the love of God, neighbourly charity, amiability and effacement of self, startling humility, astounding mortification, perfect obedience, respect for superiors, all flow in full stream throughout the whole of this life, which, like a great river, broadens and deepens till it reaches the sea. If there is one thing beyond contradiction, it is the accent of the pure love of God in the hour of distress, sustained without a discordant note for years, the like of which has not appeared for ages. Most decisive of all is the perfect truth of the sudden transition from crucifying purification to the great day of the mystical marriage, which dawned seventeen years before her death."

And Canon Snow delivered himself of this rock solid testimony: "In any place in which she stayed many interesting and edifying incidents took place, such as what I may call little miracle and miraculous answers to prayer, and these would be known only to a few and they kept the knowledge to themselves. Such things would make interesting and devout reading, but would, as it were, be out of proportion to the greatness of her sanctity and the work she did for God, the Church and souls as a mystic and as revealed in her writings. I do not know that anything happened anywhere that attracted public attention. This seems to me to be according to the design of God in her regard acting in great part through her profound, and I may say *abject* humility."

The Canon made no effort to promote Teresa's claims to beatification. Never, even after her death, did he exhibit the smallest endeavour to vindicate her name when it was vilified. A man of God, he was content to leave the correction of the balance in God's hands, and a lesson he had long ago learnt, he said, was that "Almighty God is never in a hurry."

Those who knew the Canon remembered how, towards the end of his life, he loved to linger on Teresa's memory, and was scarce able to speak of her without tears welling in his eyes.

The laity, too, humble men and women, several of whom had been taught by Teresa as children, came eagerly forth with prized memories.

Some of these recorded memories go right back to the days when Teresa was teaching in Bootle. For instance, an old lady still living in Liverpool in the 1930s, and who simply signed her name M. Boyle, recollected: "Miss Teresa Higginson taught me in St Alexander's. I remember her as being very kind. On confession days Miss Higginson knew that if we went home for our tea at four o'clock, at least the majority of us would not have come back to go to confession, so she kept us in school. She had a big urn in her class-room, and she would make tea for us and give us a large bun. Then in due time she would take us to Church and we would all go to confession. This incident gave rise to doubts as to Miss Higginson's total abstinence from food. It was said that she had been seen buying buns and concluded without evidence that she had bought them for herself. This was taken as another proof of her hypocrisy. I remember seeing Miss Higginson at the dinner hour carrying cans of soup to school for poor children. The owner of the little grocer's shop where Miss Higginson previously lived told a friend that she begged ham-shanks, boiled them, and made the stock into pea-soup for the poor children at St Alexander's."

Another former St Alexander's pupil of Teresa's, signing himself B. McLoughlin, recalled: "Miss Teresa Higginson taught me in this school in 1883. I was in Standard IV at the time, and remember how the children preferred her class to another in the same room. She was very kindly disposed towards her pupils, and they were very happy and never wanted to leave her. She was always bright and cheerful, and taught some nice little songs. There was always a beautiful odour from her near presence. I used often to play truant in the days when I was in the lower classes, but when I reached Miss Higginson's, she made me a monitor, and I never stayed away from school again. In fact, I won a prize for regular attendance. I now realise that Miss Higginson knew of my weakness, and she knew, too, that, by promoting me to the position of monitor, she was providing an incentive for me to attend regularly." Significantly, Mr B. McLoughlin became headmaster of the Boys' Department of St Alexander's School.

One unnamed former pupil at St Alexander's steps briefly forth from out the clouds of witness to sketch for posterity how he or she "looking back can picture Teresa Higginson to myself as though it were today, with her stately walk, slightly bowed

244

head, and a smile for those she knew. 'To know God is to love Him,' was impressed on those who came under her influence. And all those who knew her would testify that to know her was to love her. There was her kindness to the poor children, ill-clad and barefoot. There was no P.A.C. in those days (probably refers to the Poor Law Public Assistance Committee), but she attended to their wants, and clothes and clogs were provided for them somehow. As a school teacher, she was unexcelled. Her earnest and persuasive methods before lessons gave you a sort of confidence in yourself that you could accomplish the task satisfactorily. That she was so thoroughly efficient, I can testify, for it is very evident to me that the average boy in her Standard III had a more solid education than those of the present day, after going through Standards VI and VII. She prepared us well for this world as well as the next. The Faith she had installed in us remains throughout life."

What is perhaps the fullest picture of Teresa in her St Alexander's days is provided by Miss Agnes Donnelly, whose father was headmaster and mother, a teacher, at St Alexander's in Teresa's time.

My parents, Mr J.J. Donnelly and Mrs Donnelly (*née* Jane Wood), always spoke of Miss Higginson as a saint. They knew her to be very holy and charitable, and often related to us the wonderful things that happened in her life. For instance, though my mother knew her for many years and spent many hours in her company, she never saw her take food or drink of any kind. Once, when my mother asked her how she lived without food, Teresa answered that the Blessed Sacrament was sufficient food for soul and body.

During her talks with my mother, Teresa once described the place where she, Teresa, would die – Ugbrook [*sic*], Devon. This must have been at least twenty or more years before her death. I well remember the day my mother, when reading one of the Catholic papers, saw the notice of Teresa's death and remarked, "Yes, that is where Teresa told me she would die.

Another time, Teresa, in conversation with my mother, remarked: "I see all Europe in great confusion, but you and Mr Donnelly will be saved the worry of that." True, both my parents died before the 1914-1918 War. When on her death-bed, my mother suddenly said: "I wonder when the Church will recognise Teresa's sanctity?" One thing stands out in my mind about my father, a remark he made when Teresa's name was under discussion. "If Teresa had belonged to a community of nuns, she would have been canonised long before this. The Order would have seen to that." At one time, Teresa, when praying in St Alexander's Church, was disturbed by Satan, who appeared before her, distracting her. She mentioned this to the parish priest who recommended her to use holy water. She did so. Satan disappeared. She was able to pray without interruption.

Then one day, appearing before her again, Satan remained tormenting her, even after her throwing the water at him. She went in to the priest and told him what had happened. He smiled and said: "Now we know it must be your imagination." Teresa was puzzled. "No, Father," she said. "There is something wrong." She asked if the water was blessed. The priest discovered on making enquiries that the curate had forgotten to bless it. Teresa was using that day *unblessed* water.

When my parents first went from Liverpool to Paisley, about 1895, there was a young German curate at St Mirren's, where my father was head teacher. After he had visited our house several times, my mother quickly saw that he was a very holy priest. He made great friends with our family. Having known Miss Higginson, and been in close touch with her and her friends, my mother soon realised that Father Grau was somewhat of a mystic. She began speaking to him of Teresa Higginson and told him many things relating to her. At first, Father Grau listened carefully, then after a bit he remarked that he would give no verdict on her, never having met her. He then said he would like very much to visit her in Edinburgh, if at all possible. My parents wrote to the Reverend Mother asking the favour of a visit. The nuns immediately arranged a time for Father Grau and my parents to spend the day there. They went and met `Teresa, chatted with her. She asked about all her old friends, especially Helen Nicholson (Mrs Lonsdale). The Sisters took my parents away to view the house and garden, while Father Grau was left with Teresa. No remark was was made when they returned. When Father Grau and my parents had left the convent and were walking along the road, he turned to mother and said: "Well, Mrs Donnelly, I believe everything about Teresa that you have told me. I have just been talking with a saint." Later he said that Teresa had read his soul.

After my parents' move to Paisley, and while I was still a pupil teacher at Mount Pleasant, I spent many short holidays at the home of Mrs Blackburn – The Turret, Keble Road, Bootle. She was a Lonsdale. Teresa Higginson often stayed with them during her years in Bootle. It was here that Aunt Teresa lived, acting as housekeeper. Aunt Teresa did not at all like Teresa Higginson. There was around that time much talk of Teresa Higginson's receiving holy communion miraculously, and Aunt Teresa's sister, and others who knew of this, kept blessed candles ready to be lit whenever it occurred. Aunt Teresa suddenly made up her mind to watch Teresa Higginson very keenly, and not to go down on her knees as the others did. Some little time after, while she was present in the room, a light appeared. They all knelt down. The candles were lit.

Aunt Teresa said to herself, "Now I will do it." But some unseen power brought her to her knees and her head was raised. She could not bend it down nor move. While in this position she saw the Sacred Host coming through the air and on to Teresa's tongue. "I was one of her enemies. I went about telling people Teresa Higginson was a hypocrite and a liar, and not to believe in her," she said. "Almighty God punished me in that way for my behaviour." I thought it was a beautiful punishment. Aunt Teresa wept over this, and did her best to make reparation to Teresas Higginson.

In Bootle, one of the staff, Miss Cullen told me the following incident, one of many occurring frequently. In school it was time for marking registers, very strictly supervised in those days. Miss Cullen, to her horror, found she had left the key of her desk at home. She rushed round to Teresa's room and told her to pray. Miss Higginson went with Miss Cullen into her class-room, asking if she had tried all the keys, etc. "Yes." "Well," replied Teresa, "if you have tried all *natural means* first, then it must be done in the Name of the Father, Son and Holy Ghost." So, making the sign of the cross over the desk, they saw the lock spring open. The trouble was averted.

On another occasion, Miss Winifred Donnellan, one of the staff at St Alexander's, related the following. Her mother had been taken suddenly ill – Winnie Donnellan had to leave her and go to school, very worried as to how she would get on in her absence. Again, as they always did, they asked Teresa to pray. Miss Higginson answered: "Don't worry, my dear, she is all right." Sure enough, at the dinner hour Miss Donnellan found her mother not only better, but downstairs getting the meal ready. She had become quite well suddenly – about the time Teresa prayed.

One Christmas holiday – I was home from Mount Pleasant Convent, Liverpool, where I was a pupil teacher – Father

Grau advised my mother to arrange a visit to Edinburgh for my sister, Gertie, and myself. She wrote to Reverend Mother, who very kindly asked for us to spend a day at the convent, and so see Teresa. We got a warm welcome from the community and Teresa. It was Christmastime, the table was loaded with Christmas fare. We were delighted and ate heartily, while Teresa herself waited upon us, but did not partake of the meal. She chatted about all our family and people she remembered in Bootle and Wigan, etc. Then advised us to go and see the sights of Edinburgh. We did. Then returned for another meal, later. As we were saying goodbye, I turned to Teresa and said quite earnestly: "Teresa, what do you think of Father Grau?" She gave me a beautiful smile and said: "My dear child, he is a very good and zealous priest." I was satisfied.

Father Grau had given us a letter to take to Miss Higginson. I asked her if there was an answer. She just looked at us and replied: "It is all right, my dear child." Secretly, I was glad, because we were suspicious that the letter referred to us. But on arriving back in Glasgow, we were met by Father Grau at the station. He said: "I got the answer to my letter when in church during the day." (In a vision.)

During that visit to the convent in Edinburgh, Teresa asked us about all her old friends in and around Liverpool. One of them was, of course, Mrs Lonsdale (the former Ellen Nicholson). We said that, so far as we knew, she was well. Teresa became serious. "Poor Ellen," she said, "she will have a lot of worry with one of her boys." I cannot recall whether she mentioned the name, but on returning home and relating this episode, my mother said, "Do not tell Ellen if you see her; she has enough trouble just now." Needless to say, we did not. But later, in the 1914-1918 War, her eldest son was wounded and had his leg amputated.

Ellen herself told me the following: "During the time Ellen was teaching with Miss Catterall in a small country school, Teresa, who was living with them, did much of the household work to help. One day Ellen, a young girl then, was first in the school home in the afternoon. She commenced making the fire, to boil the kettle. The coal was finished, not enough to start a fire. Ellen hurried to tell Teresa, who quietly asked: "Have you looked in the coal place?" Ellen answered: "Yes. It is empty." "Go back again, dear, and look," said Teresa. To Ellen's astonishment, there was enough coal to last a day or two. Teresa had prayed. Ellen said that often during the hard times of those teachers food was put on the table, even before their eyes, when Teresa prayed.

One early morning when Ellen met Teresa, she noticed blood on her white cravat. She mentioned it to Teresa. It disappeared at once.

Visiting Cologne, 35 years after Father Grau had returned there, I said to him: "I wonder if Teresa will be canonised?" Father Grau: "My child, *God knows she is a saint*, what does it matter what people here think?"

Teresa continually helped in strange ways her friends who invoked her aid. Here is one of the "Domestic Miracles", as we called them, small in their way, but very helpful to the people concerned at the time. Ellen Nicholson and Kate Catterall arranged a visit to Neston for a lady who was about to enter a religious order. I went with them from Liverpool across to Neston, in Cheshire. We paid a visit to the little church and to Teresa's grave. Afterwards, we had an interview with the parish priest. The talk lasted some time, and we all forgot about the return journey to Liverpool. So when Miss Catterall suddenly remarked that we had very little time to catch the train, we hurried out and along the road to the station. Poor Miss Catterall felt the journey very much, her heart was in a bad state. It was all she could do to arrive at the station, up a slope, just as the train came in. We sat down, all a bit out of breath, but Miss Catterall looking and feeling very bad. As she sat down, she remarked, "Now, Teresa, it's up to you to help me. I could never climb those stairs at the Junction. We were silent until the train drew up at the Junction platform. As we slowed down, a porter walked straight to our compartment, opened the door saying, "Come this way, Madam, you will never climb the stairs." Again, we were silent and amazed. He took Miss Catterall, we following, to the flat luggage lift, and pointed to us to join them. We were four together, holding on to each other while the lift passed over the line to the other side, near our train. We stepped off, followed the porter to a compartment, got in. Then Miss Catterall put her hand in her purse and turned to offer the man a tip. He had gone. Nor could we see him anywhere on the platform. Miss Catterall just sat down and said quite simply, "Thank you, Teresa."

One of the old staff of St Alexander's, Miss Cullen, was in great trouble about suitable accommodation. She could not find the kind that she wanted, and it was necessary to move that week. I suggested a trip to Neston. We went straight to the church. All the time while in the train Miss Cullen was praying, making it a real pilgrimage. We prayed in front of the Blessed Sacrament, then went to the grave of Teresa. After this, we returned to the church, to pray at the picture of the Sacred Head – since removed from public veneration while the Cause is shelved. Before this picture was a votive stand, with little red candles. A matchbox was attached, nailed by ribbon to the *prie-dieu*, but empty. I remarked: "Let us fill all the stand with candles and make a brilliant light." We placed candles in every container, then looked for a match to light them with. There was not a match anywhere. I tried the Lady altar. No. It was impossible to reach the sanctuary lamp! I was disappointed, wishing to light all the candles before leaving. Miss Cullen was kneeling, praying fervently, not listening to me (re. candles). I knelt down near her on the floor and said: "The only way is to ask at the presbytery." Then, looking down, we both saw a match at our knees. We had previously searched all around the stand and floor for any sign of a match, and found nothing. So astonished were we that neither of us would touch it at first. Then we struck the match on the empty box, lit all the candles, and said a prayer of thanksgiving. On returning to Liverpool, Miss Cullen was offered a most suitable and unlooked for room.

Hailing from Teresa's Scottish sojourn comes the recollection of Catherine Callaghan.

"My memory goes back to my early days as a teacher. I was just beginning at St Ignatius' School, in Edinburgh. At that time, Miss Teresa Higginson gave occasional help in school work. I fancy I see her now, with her slight form of medium height and her delicate face, which gave one the impression that she was a perpetual invalid. She would move gently in school and give an object lesson to the younger children. It was wonderful to watch the expression on the children's faces. Her quiet, low voice seemed to draw the attention of children as if they were spellbound. Not an eyelid would flicker, so rapt was their attention. It was the power that came from within. It seemed not to belong to this world. Whenever she gave a writing lesson, she began by drawing a cross at the top of the blackboard. Above the cross she wrote the words 'God sees me.' I took her good example, and always wrote on the head of the blackboard 'God sees me,' and also drew the cross. This is only one of the good acts she left behind as an example to others."

One of Teresa's last pupils was Tom Strowbridge. When Brian Honnor met him in 1958, he was 64 years of age. He was, he said, around twelve years old when he was being taught by Teresa at Chudleigh. The figures do not quite work out, but there is no reason to doubt his recollection. He had to walk four miles to school. At first, he brought a meal of sorts with him, but Teresa said not to bother. She would provide one for him. He said that as a teacher, she was good in all ways, although religion was her "special thing." He said that "she never used a cane, and didn't bully us, but had her own way of getting us to do what she wanted. You couldn't get out of it – you had to do it! She was a good teacher. Topping! All the children liked her. You couldn't help it. She was strict, but gentle."

He had been among the children invited to pay their last respects to her after she had been laid out. "She looked very peaceful," he said. "more like an angel than anything."

Miss Emily Ewing, a nurse friend of Nurse Casey's, who had visited Teresa once or twice as she lay on her sick-bed at Ugbrooke, wrote to Brian Honnor in 1957: "On standing in Teresa's room one felt one was on holy ground. I shall never forget her and her sanctity, she seemed to radiate happiness; there seemed to be a radiance around her as she was in bed."

And Father Dawson, who had first met Teresa during a school outing to Teignmouth, and came to know her rather better through paying visits to the school-house during the time that he was serving as *locum* to Lord Clifford's chaplain, Father Dowsett, had sought her advice on certain matters. According to Nurse Casey, Teresa had foretold things concerning him which later came to pass. So impressed had he been by her, that, after Teresa's death, he made a report to his Bishop, and travelled the length and breadth of Britain seeking information about her, thus becoming effectively a pioneer for her cause. In the course of his peregrinations, he called in at the presbytery at

Stonehaven, Aberdeenshire. Agnes Donnelly happened to be staying there at the time – "Father McLellan, the parish priest, asked me to prepare tea for a visitor. The visitor was a priest from the south of England. During the meal he remarked that he was travelling round gathering information re. Teresa Higginson. Father Dawson told us at the table that he had been called to the school-house, Ugbrooke, Devon, while the local priest was absent. The teacher, Teresa Higginson, was dying. He ended up by saying: 'I have had the honour of being present at the death-bed of a saint.'

That was the opinion, too, of Alfred Garnett, in whose home Teresa had dwelt for the better part of three years. His memories are fascinating. He recalls, for instance, the day when Teresa discovered that the small supply of linseed which was absolutely vital for poultices for his invalid sister, Maggie, whom Teresa was nursing, was exhausted. She asked him to go out and buy some at a nearby chemist's, but it was Sunday, and the shop was closed. After trying three chemists, and finding them all shut, he returned home empty handed. Teresa would have none of it, she insisted that he should go out again and have another try. Mr Garnett said that he never knew whether or not she sent her guardian angel with him, but, at the very first shop he tried, the door was opened to him, and he was served with the linseed.

Another of Mr Garnett's stories is of how the doctor attending Maggie Garnett, already impressed by the general efficiency of Teresa's home nursing, was astonished to find one morning that, off her own bat, she had, during the night, changed the medicine that she was, on his instructions, administering to Maggie, and, in so doing, had done exactly what he would have done, had he been there. "You have a wonderful woman staying in your house," he told Mr Garnett. "Your sister would have died long before she did if she had not had the care she got."

Teresa told Alfred Garnett that while she was staying with him and his sisters she was frequently visited by souls who came to her to ask for her prayers, and would return a second time to thank her. On their second visit she saw them as in a mist, but never knew if they were priests or laity, male or female. One night, however, a soul on its way to heaven that had come to thank her, turned towards her and bowed, and she recognised that it was a female. The same night, Mr Garnett was suddenly awakened by the vision of his dead mother's face, which he saw quite distinctly. He felt certain that the female soul that came to thank Teresa was that of his mother.

As time wore on, Mr Garnett's physical incapacity increased, making it almost impossible for him to go out, but he was able to cross the road and go to Mass and Holy Communion in the little chapel where, years before, services had been held for the Protestant inmates of the workhouse. "Little Mother," he was wont to say, "took our little shop because she knew, in 1903, that one day I would not be able to go to Mass, except across the road." One morning, his gammy leg was so bad that he could not get out of bed, much less put it to the floor. A quandary, for since Annie had died some years previously he had lived alone, and there was no one to help him. "I *had* to open the shop," he said. Then, suddenly, he knew what to do. "I tied Teresa's bodice, a precious relic which I always kept within reach of my bed, round my foot. Immediately, the wound healed up, and I was able to go down as usual,"

All through the decades, Alfred Garnett never forgot Teresa's birthday. Every May 27th, he used to ask a certain lady of his acquaintance to make the journey to Neston on his behalf. He would pay her fare and give her the money to buy flowers to be put upon her grave as a birthday present.

After Teresa's death, Mr Garnett had made it a regular practice each morning, before going downstairs and opening the shop, to go into Teresa's old room, kneel down, and pray to her. And each night, after closing the shop, his first act, no matter how tired he may have been or how much his leg aching, was to go again into Teresa's room, and, in spite of his painful lameness, to kneel down once more, and pray to her.

Alfred Leo Garnett died on April 16th, 1940. He was 77 years of age.

NOTE
23 Administration. Chester. 31st March, 1905.

12

SCRUTINY

"The claims made for this lady are not small. They rest wholly upon her own statements as conveyed for the most part in letters to her spiritual directors. These statements are not submitted to any critical examination by those who record them.[24] It is, indeed, indicated that during her life there were critics, both clerical and lay, who doubted Teresa's good faith, but we are given no means of assessing the value of their objections. In short, the critics get no hearing.

Nevertheless, even had there been no doubters, it is a pity that her biographers should have felt themselves under no obligation to submit some verification of the astonishing statements they were disseminating by their books.

In addition to the miracles and visions recorded in the life, one is struck by the frequency with which Teresa became the victim of severe and disabling illnesses, all of a mysterious character, and often as suddenly and mysteriously cured. None of these illnesses ever seems to have been identified with any of the ordinary ills from which humanity suffers. Even of greater medical interest is the statement – again wholly unsubstantiated – that for a period of years Teresa abstained from all food.

Despite the harrowing vicissitudes which punctuated many years of her life, Teresa is said to have displayed an edifying calmness in suffering, a calmness which her admirers advance as proof of her sanctity and as an argument against the suggestion – apparently made during her life – that she was an hysterical subject. Such a story necessarily interests the Catholic doctor, especially if his labours have covered the field of nervous disorders. Is it probable, is it possible, that this history may, wholly or in part, express the nervous instability of the subject rather than any inherent sanctity?

It has to be admitted that the obviously medical elements in the story, the mysterious illnesses, the swoons and trances, the romancings as to wounds said to have been caused by practices of mortification, and the alleged agonies of pain, all these are the constituents, clear and unequivocal, of an hysterical illness, nor is there any available medical alternative interpretation thereof.

What must be borne in mind in assessing these aspects of Teresa's life is that the form and content of an hysteric's disorders of conduct and of speech are determined by the circumstances of her training. If, from early infancy, she lives in a pietist atmosphere, it is inevitable that she should take the mode of life and feeling she knows as the material for her psycho-neurosis. Thus her conduct and utterances may take on a completely religious semblance. Every doctor with experience of the neuroses of young women must be familiar with this chameleon-like behaviour of the hysteric. It provides a key without which it is not possible to assess Teresa Higginson's story.

It is further significant that the characteristic emotional tone of such a subject is one of beatific calm in the face of what are alleged to be intolerable sufferings. This *belle indifférence*, as the French neurologists have called it, so far from excluding the presence of hysteria – as the uninitiated think – is one of its hallmarks.

With these considerations in his mind, the medical reader must derive the strongest impression that there are in this life we have been considering elements which call for the most careful study and interpretation."

So wrote Dr F.R.M. Walshe, O.B.E., D.Sc., M.D., F.R.C.P.[25] in *The Tablet* of May 8th, 1937.

Another doctor, Letitia Fairfield,[26] entered extremely fiercely into the fray.

There can be no gainsaying the brilliance of Dr Fairfield; I knew her well when we were fellow-members of the Medico-Legal Society, and can testify thereto. She edited two of the volumes in Hodge's classic *Notable British Trials* series – *Trial of Peter Barnes and Others (I.R.A. Coventry Explosion)*, (1953), and, with Eric P. Fullbrook, *Trial of John Thomas Straffen*, (1954). Her presence was not unknown at the odd meeting of the Society for Psychical Research, of which I was a member, and her interest in the supernatural, witchcraft, exorcism, and miracles was intense. I am sure that it was this aspect of Teresa Higginson's multifarious activities which particularly aroused her interest – and hostility.

'Sacerdos', writing in *The Harvest*, tartly observes, "Dr Letitia Fairfield has a profound respect for the opinion of Dr Letitia Fairfield." She is "convinced that Teresa was a mental neurotic, a fraud, and a cheat, a snare for the foolishly pious, and ... appalled that nobody seems to have realised it; that thousands of people, including Archbishops and a Diocesan Commission, have no medical knowledge to spot the dotty."

The Reverend J.C. Hardwick, M.A., B.Sc., writing in *The Modern Churchman*, in May, 1936, is in a similar state of undiluted opposition: "It is clear that this woman was a pathological case and, like so many religious neurotics, the victim of hallucinations. Persons of this 'mythomaniacal' constitution are characterized by credulity, exhibitionism and a tendency towards deceit. Teresa Higginson had clearly set herself to imitate two famous saints of the Roman Catholic Church – St Catherine of Siena and St Margaret Mary Alacoque. St Catherine had no food for years save the Blessed Sacrament, though she had no convenient guardian angel to take her form and place at table. Similarly, St Catherine is 'married' to Jesus;

and the present pamphlet {Note: *Teresa Helena Higginson*, by Cecil Kerr. Published by the Catholic Truth Society of Ireland. Price, twopence. 1933.] contains close parallels to the 'official' story of St Catherine's betrothal. St Margaret Mary was the foundress of the cult of the Sacred Heart. Teresa Higginson must, therefore seek to found a devotion to the 'Sacred Head'.

It is perhaps unnecessary to add that she could work miracles, or at least miracles were attributed to her. She could fan dead embers into flame by making the sign of the cross over them, and could get St Joseph to place firewood in an empty cupboard, while, like St Paul, she 'heard and saw things which it is not given to those who hear them to utter.' Teresa Higginson imitates the experiences of the saints, but instead of their spiritual wisdom she pours out trash worthy of a spiritualistic séance.

The Higginson pamphlet is the type of literature considered quite suitable by the Jesuits in Manchester as spiritual pabulum for the faithful. The stuff is nonsense, but it is the right kind of nonsense, and the Jesuit Fathers collect the public's tuppences by retailing it at the Church of the Holy Name."

Even that great and scholarly authority on mystical theology, Father Herbert Thurston, S.J., articulates unease. In *The Catholic Medical Guardian*, of July 3rd, 1937, he writes that with much of what Mr Hardwick says, "regarded merely as a statement of Teresa's mystical experiences, I should be inclined to express agreement."

He continues: "One or two other points which I confess impress me unfavourably are connected with the devotion to the Sacred Head. She prophesies that in the immediate future it is to work wonderful effects. The 'time is not far distant' when 'poor dear England will bow her understanding to the obedience of Faith' and the devotion to the Sacred Head will be 'the greatest means of her conversion.' This was written 50 years ago, but neither has the devotion spread nor has England been converted. Secondly, the threats pronounced against those who oppose this devotion are unpleasantly reminiscent of similar maledictions in certain forms of the 'snowball' prayer [Note: This is the pious version of the chain letter, though executed verbally, not by the written word.]

'Those who shall try by word or means to hinder or neglect it (devotion to the Sacred Head) shall be as glass that is cast down or as an egg that is thrown to the wall, that is, they shall be shattered and become as nought and shall be dried and wither as grass on the house-top. Our Beloved Spouse also let me know that it was in this church (St Alexander's, Bootle, where she then lived) that He would manifest to the world, the manner, etc., in which He wished to be honoured, and the time and everything concerning this most wonderful and excellent devotion.'

To anyone who reads attentively it is quite clear that in Teresa's idea the Sacred Heart devotion was incomplete and subsidiary beside that to the Sacred Head of which she was the chosen apostle. The promises, so she declared, made to those who practise the former 'shall be multiplied a hundredfold' to those who adopt the latter. In spite of Teresa's mortified life and protestations of unworthiness there is a latent element of self-absorption which seems to me to point more in the direction of hysteria than of true sanctity; and I venture to think it regrettable that a Memoir [Note: Cecil Kerr's biography.] so crowded with entirely unverified marvels should have been presented to the Catholic public, without a word of caution, as a trustworthy record of heroic virtue."

Without question the most spectacular of the phenomena connected with Teresa were the alleged attacks mounted upon her by the Devil – frightful crashing noises, thunderous booms that seem to rock the house, unearthly screams and screeches of fiendish laughter, foul stenches, and slaps in the face from invisible hands, all testified to by independent witnesses And, whatever your point of view, *these* manifestations cannot by any stretch of the psychiatric imagination be written off as subjective.

What *could* be suggested, although upon closer examination it does not really seem to fit the bill, is that the disturbances were of poltergeistic origin. They began when Teresa was a schoolgirl at the Nottingham Convent of Mercy, and such an onset would square with the widely accepted view that the phenomena very frequently centre upon a young girl about the time of puberty, when her sexual awareness is beginning to flicker to life.

Teresa was, we know, it is testified to from all sides, a strong character. She might be expected to present a readily available reservoir of sexual energy – albeit strictly suppressed *and* repressed – to be drawn upon by the poltergeistic entity. A contra-indication of a poltergeistic source is the fact that Teresa had reached the age of forty-two when the attacks were persisting in Bootle. The poltergeist generally deserts its victim a couple of decades before that.

Father Thurston confesses his faith in the reality of poltergeists, but also confesses that he has not the remotest idea of what they are – "They may be devils, or you may call them elementals if you like." But he also says, [*Ghosts and Poltergeists.* Herbert Thurston, S.J. Burns Oates, London, 1953. p.VI.] "That there may be something diabolical, or at any rate evil, in them I do not deny, but, on the other hand, it is just possible that there may be natural forces involved which are so far as little known to us as the latent forces of electricity were known to the Greeks. It is possibly the complication of these two elements which forms the heart of the mystery."

In further elucidation, let us postulate the case of a young man who travelled many years ago to some remote jungle locality, taking with him a film camera, and there recorded for anthropological purposes various scenes and features of native life – primitive rituals of song and dance, the manners and customs of the people. Let us suppose that, twenty or thirty years later, that man's son returns to the locus, and that he takes with him the film shot by his father all those years before. He decides to show it to the natives, sets up a screen, and projects the film on it. Watching is the son of the chieftain who sang and danced. He is terrified. Cannot believe what his eyes are seeing. His father, the chieftain, lies, has lain these many years past, under the hump of earth over there. Dead. Yet here he is, dancing, singing, capering as of old. Alive again. This is magic. Devil's work. Of course, the chieftain's young son is quite right. It *is* magic – to him. But when you know the workings of the 'science' of moving picture photography, the supernatural magic dissolves. May it not be so with regard to the still puzzling phenomena we call poltergeists – or assaults by the Devil?

Father Thurston maintains that the dismissal of the poltergeist-like phenomena which beset St Jean-Marie Baptist Vianney, the Curé D'Ars, and the age-long series of energumens as variant types of hystero-epilepsy, is not acceptable. In any event, the Congregation of Sacred Rites does not pronounce upon the supernatural character of the mystical phenomena ascribed to holy people.

In illustration, Father Thurston refers to the then beatified – since canonised, in 1940 – St Gemma Galgani, and a decree issued on November 29th, 1931, by the Congregation of Sacred Rites. Pronouncing judgment on the heroic character of this young Tuscan woman, Pius XI decreed the heroicity of her virtues fully established *constare de virtutibus theologalibus, Fide, Spe, Charitate, et in grado heroico,* with the significant added clause: *nullo tamen per praesens decretum (quod quidem nunquam fieri solet) prolato judicio de præternaturalibus Servae Dei charismatibus;* that is to say, "Without any judgment being expressed regarding the preternatural endowments of the said servant of God, for this is a thing which is never done." In his

62. Father Bertram Wilberforce, O.P.

great treatise, Benedict XIV bears similar testimony.

We are thus at liberty to discuss and to question the supernatural status of bizarre occurrences recorded in the lives of even the canonised saints. Taking advantage of this dispensation, Father Thurston refers to instances in which faith is strained almost to breaking point, and admits that he "counts the case of Teresa Higginson as belonging to that class."

Responding to Father Powell's request for his opinion regarding a volume of Teresa Higginson's letters sent to him, Father Bertram Wilberforce, O.P.,[27] of Holy Cross Priory, Leicester, wrote a lengthy memorandum, dated November 9th, 1882. In it, among other things, he commented upon the proposed Devotion to the Sacred Head.

"There would appear to be no theological objection to a devotion in honour of the Sacred Head as the Shrine of the intellectual faculties and powers of the soul of our Lord Jesus Christ. For the soul is the *Form* of the whole body, and therefore of the head, the principal organ of the body.

We may therefore conclude that the devotion to the Sacred Head, as the Shrine of the divine Wisdom, can be defended theologically and is in harmony with the teaching of the Catholic Church.

The next question which arises may thus be put: Is the Devotion a congruous one? Is there any special fitness in it? 1. In itself? 2. At this particular time?

1. If we consider the Devotion in itself, it will be acknowledged that there is a certain special fitness in it as a Devotion to the Eternal Wisdom. In support of this view the teaching of St Thomas [Aquinas] can be adduced.

2. It will not be difficult in the second place to show that there is a peculiar fitness in this devotion to the age in which we live. In order to suit a particular time, a devotion ought to meet the special dangers of the day, supplying the antidote to prevalent spiritual diseases. Now the spirit of this age is evidently one of spiritual rebellion. The human mind, intoxicated by modern scientific discoveries, is inclined to cast off all restraint and to refuse any longer to remain subject to the sweet yoke of Faith. Rationalism, pure and simple, is the prevailing spirit of the day. This spirit is at once more injurious to God and especially to the Wisdom of God on high ... because it causes man to love and value the foolishness of human wisdom, despising what they consider to be the folly, but which truly is the eternal Wisdom of God. Moreover, this spirit is more destructive to souls who are induced by it to love the darkness rather than the light.

Against this pernicious spirit of evil and its consequences the devotion to the Sacred Head is especially directed. Just as the devotion to the Sacred Heart met the error of Jansenism, so destructive of the spirit of Love, so the devotion to the Sacred Head will oppose the blighting errors of rationalism and infidelity, so insulting to the infinite Wisdom of God incarnate.

We may then conclude that this devotion is thoroughly theological, in strict harmony with the devotion already so solemnly and frequently approved, of the Sacred Heart, most congruous in itself, and lastly peculiarly suited to the special needs of the age in which we live.

What ought to be thought of the writer of these letters, her spirit and the truth of her visions? I feel that in attempting to answer this question I am treading on delicate grounds, and it would be presumptuous to assume too much certainty in a matter of such gravity, without personal knowledge of the writer.

Still, however, this much I can assert with confidence, that everything that has come to my knowledge, through her letters and accounts given me by her confessor of her acts and dispositions, all lead me to conclude, not only that she is in a high degree of holiness, but also that her mind is wonderfully illuminated by the Light of God.

In order to judge of the holiness of a soul, in other words of the degree of divine Charity with which that soul is endowed, we should examine the four test virtues of humility, patience, obedience and mortification. A soul pretending to very exalted gifts of contemplation and yet failing to practise these virtues in corresponding perfection, would almost certainly be in a state of delusion.

Of her *Humility*. To judge from her writings, taking for granted that they reflect the true dispositions of her soul, the person in question would appear to possess this fundamental virtue in high perfection. It would seem that she thoroughly despises herself, is truly anxious to be despised by others, is free from that self-will which would make her desirous to guide herself instead of submitting to others, has a fear of delusion, yet with confidence in God: is anxious that divine favours should remain hidden, yet mentions them with simplicity under obedience. Of course the grand point is to prove that these written sentiments are genuine by the test of practical trial. This, I am told, has already been done, and that her calmness under sudden and violent reproof and even abuse remains unruffled. Her conduct under the trial of desolation of spirit also proves her humility.

Her *patience* under the pressure of extreme mental and bodily suffering, to judge from her writings corroborated by particulars I have heard, is shown to be heroic, because, not only does she endure these things without repining, but she displays an ardent thirst for more numerous and more painful afflictions, in order to unite her soul to Christ crucified.

Obedience is proved by the promptitude and simplicity with which she lays bare her secret soul under authority in spite of all repugnance, and gives up at once any penance or exercise without agitation of mind when commanded.

As to her spirit of *mortification* and *penance*, it would appear to be universal in extent and extraordinary in degree. Her penances from childhood have been extreme, and she has never shown any disposition to persevere in them against the advice of her confessor. Her abstinence and fasting and the generosity with which she has mortified her sense of taste is, to judge from her letters, heroic, and by the testimony of her confessor, miraculous, but this she has ever striven to conceal.

The Visions about the devotion to the Sacred Head. Is there solid reason to place confidence in those visions as described in the letters under consideration? I will make three preliminary remarks suggested by the case.

1. The person has read no books of mystical theology, even the ordinary spiritual books common among the faithful, yet she describes most accurately and in most striking

terms how a vision which is neither imaginary nor even intellectual is infused by the action of the Holy Spirit in the centre of the soul itself.[28] It is impossible to avoid the impression that she is speaking from personal experience. This description is decidedly in favour of the belief that the vision was from the Holy Spirit, whereas if she had described a vision seen by the bodily eyes or by mental images, the case would be more doubtful and she might mistake her own imagination for the working of God's grace.

2. The theological way in which this simple and unlearned person explains the doctrine of the Trinity and Incarnation and speaks of the devotion to the Sacred Head is a decided indication of superior illumination.

3. The fact that this person is unlearned, has read no books, and has ever lived secluded, makes it unlikely that she should have invented herself a devotion so admirably suited to the times in which we live.

Lastly, to apply the rules laid down by theology for distinguishing between true and false visions.

I. As to the vision itself (the ones instructing her as to the Devotion):

1. As above proved, the vision contains nothing contrary to faith, but is entirely conformable to the traditions of the Church.

2. Nothing unbecoming, trivial or irreverent can be detected in it. We may therefore conclude that there is nothing in the vision itself to prove that it could not be from God, but all the circumstances are such as are found in approved visions.

II. As to the person to whom the vision is made.

1. She is an orthodox thoroughly obedient Catholic.

2. She is fervent and holy in life.

3. Her humility, obedience, patience and mortification are heroic.

4. Does she desire visions and favours? I have seen no indication of this desire. On the contrary, she often humbly and lovingly expostulates with our Lord, reminding Him that by favouring so great a sinner in so extraordinary a way He may cause His gifts to be despised.

5. She is no novice in spiritual life for she began very early to serve God and has persevered with the utmost fidelity in spite of all difficulties, desolation, etc. Moreover, a favourable sign is that in early life she was led to the solid virtues of penance, humility, obedience and hatred of sin and had no extraordinary favour till after these had become habitual in a high degree.

6. Visions are certainly to be more cautiously received in the case of a woman, but manifestly, when other signs are satisfactory, the fact they have been vouchsafed to a woman is no sign of delusion. This soul has had diabolical visions and has detected them.

III. The effect of the vision.

1. The visions seem to render the soul more humble by revealing to her the abyss of her own nothingness etc.

2. She has always been directed by the vision to reveal all to her spiritual guide and to follow exactly what obedience prescribes, even when contrary to the vision itself.

3. In this message to the confessor, if terms too flattering to himself personally had been employed there might be grounds for suspicion, but in this case all that is said is simply 'tell my servant.' Now as all priests are God's servants there is here nothing excessive coming from the human spirit of a devout woman. Some soul is spoken of

who is to help the devotion and in this case terms of the highest praise are employed, but the name is not given. We may think it most probable that the soul is T.H. herself though she does not seem to suspect it.

4. Another favourable sign is that these visions seem to excite a genuine and fervent desire to suffer for and with Christ and thus nourish the spirit of mortification.

5. As to whether they promote the peace of the soul at least substantially, I do nor know, but if divine, this ought to be their effect.

Finally, I might mention that I was deeply impressed by the application of the texts of the *Apocalypse* to the devotion. (*Vide* Letter 48). It struck me as extraordinary as coming from the mind of so simple a person.[29]

Two points in conclusion I would suggest.

1. That the confessor would do well to try this soul by the test of mental obedience while she is in an ecstatic state.

2. That the matter of the Communions received by her from our Lord Himself should be carefully examined. Were these sacramental or only spiritual? Once or often in the day?"

A great deal of curiosity – and incredulity – has been expressed regarding Teresa's experience of what psychics define as a 'Double' or "etheric counterpart of the physical body which, when out of coincidence, may temporarily move about in space in comparative freedom and appear in various degrees of density to others." [*Encyclopædia of Psychic Science*. Nandor Fodor. Arthurs Press, London, *c.* 1933.] The Church admits this phenomenon under the name of bilocation and it is quite often met with in the lives of the saints; St Anthony of Padua, St Severus, St Ambrose, St Clement, and St Alphonsus de Liguori are all said to have presented this strange faculty of being in two places at the same time.

270

Father Thurston accepts that there can be no possible doubt that Teresa wrote the description of what she believed to have been nocturnal bilocationary transportations, and sent them as a matter of duty to her confessor.

On Saturday, January 1st, 1881, she told Father Powell:

I will relate that which you desire concerning Africa (at least so I suppose it to be, but I am not certain). Well, for some length of time I have from time to time found myself among the negroes, but how I am transported thither I really cannot say; I mean that I do not feel myself going. Just as people might close their eyes, and when they open them again they find themselves in a different place (not in spirit, but personally present) I find myself with them whom it pleases our dear Divine Lord I shall assist, and yet I am able to continue where I was and go on with the duties I was performing here. I have all along tried to persuade myself I was deceived, and yet I felt so positive of what I did, for our Divine Lord would instruct me very clearly about all He wishes me to perform in this way, and He impresses upon me that I must not take of the productions of this soil nor of their industry. It is not always the same place that I visit, nor the same people, though I am most of the time with a tribe whose chief is lately deceased, and whose name was Ja-am-pu-da, and his people were savages, and lived by hunting, I should imagine, by the furs and ivory which they possess in great abundance. It is now over four years (1887) since I first visited these people, and they were stricken down by sickness which turned their bodies purple and black, and of which many of them died; then I did all I could to relieve their bodily sufferings, and I was instructed to gather some bark off a tree which grew commonly there and make a beverage for them, and which I understood they called bitter waters and waters of life. This has astonished me a little, that I perfectly understand all that they wished to communicate to me and they comprehend all I say to them of the dear good God. I have told them all the necessary truths, and they were very much moved at the history of the Incarnation and death of our Divine Lord, and most of them I have baptised (though they were not in danger of death), they besought me so imploringly, and they and their good Angels have raised hymns of praise, thanks-giving and admiration of that Infinite Wisdom, power and love which arranges and directs all things to give glory to the adorable Three in One and the salvation of souls. ... It is about three weeks since the chief, of whom I have spoken, died, and I felt that he needed help, and I asked my dear good Angel to comfort him in my name, and on the Monday evening, I said a special prayer for him, for I felt he was dying or in great need, and I presently found myself by his side. I heard him distinctly call me and beg of God through that Infinite Wisdom enshrined in His adorable Head to guide me to his side, and when I took out the crucifix, he took hold of it and pressed it with reverential love to his heart, and then, the tears streaming down his cheeks, he devoutly kissed the Seven Wounds ... and he asked me to leave him the sign of man's redemption till he should stand before that Jesus Whom it represents dying in ignominy and shame, and then I hardly knew what to do; I mean I did not like to refuse him, and still I felt I had only the use of it and I should ask you before I did so; then the thought came that this would be some kind of proof to me whether it was a reality or if I was deceived, for although things that happened seemed to me to be so strange, yet I could not but believe them to be realities – so I left him the crucifix; on Wednesday, at about 12.30, I again found myself with Ja-am-pu-da, and I stayed with him till he died. I found,

272

too, that nearly all the holy water was used out of the bottle I had, and I have to refill it. These people burned the body of their dead and after the Wednesday I had the crucifix the same as usual, but from Monday night till Wednesday I was without; then I thought I should ask you whether persons could be in two places or more at the same time or not."

Apropos this crucifix of Teresa's: she regarded it as being of especial value, as it proved to her that she really had been bilocated, whereas, on previous occasions when what had appeared to be bilocations had taken place, she had thought that she had been deluded. But the visit to Ja-am-pu-da proved different. She was, she said, with the chief when he died, and after his death took possession again of her crucifix. When she came to herself back in her room, she found that her crucifix was there with her. The circumstances of its disappearance and subsequent reappearance convinced her of the reality of her journey.

After Teresa's death this crucifix passed into the keeping of Canon Snow, and when he died, his executor, Canon Dennett, gave it into the care of the late Canon's housekeeper, Miss Elizabeth Arkwright. When a dying woman, Mrs John Banks, of Ormskirk, begged Miss Arkwright to leave Teresa's crucifix with her on her death-bed, the request was not refused. One of Mrs Banks' children promised faithfully to see that it was returned. It was not. The person who laid Mrs Banks out (a Mrs Molloy) and the undertakers (Chisnall Brothers) vouched for the fact that the crucifix was buried with her, in Ormskirk graveyard. The name on the grave is Ratcliffe. Archbishop Keating discussed the matter with Canon Dennett and they decided that it was wiser to leave it there, as long as it was known where it was. It is still in that grave.

On Monday, January 2nd, 1882, Teresa addressed another letter on the subject of bilocation to Father Powell:

I will continue about the little missions of which it has pleased dear good God to send me. The people of whom I have already written are certainly the darkest in complexion, but by no means the lowest in intelligence. I have been five or six times among a people who make beds for themselves in the low brushwood (almost like birds' nests) and they climb up the rocky crags and from one projection to another like animals. These are certainly the most degraded people I have been among, and could never imagine human nature to be able to sink so low, for they live upon insects and crawling reptiles, and in form they are very diminutive and in features the least beautiful (I should imagine) of any of the nations of the earth. These people have not that brave and noble spirit of self-sacrifice which struck me very much in the people of whom I have written, these appear indolent and self-indulgent people, though confiding and friendly, and they lay much store upon bright and shining and useless baubles, which they will fasten in their hair, ears, and around their necks and arms, and they paint themselves different with coloured dyes on different occasions. They are not black like the negroes. I hardly know what colour they are, and rather fancy that they do not wear any clothing, at least, if they do, I have not noticed it. They also dig up a kind of earth nut, of which they are very fond, with their long, claw-like fingers.

They are timid and very slave-like in their service of any one in power. I noticed when I have spoken to them, they have crawled towards me many times, rolling their heads in the dust, so as to prove to me that they were as slaves waiting to do whatever I should wish them, and I have baptised many young children here, and have tried to instruct the older ones, but I do not think as yet they have at all a proper idea of God. Though they are anxious to learn, yet they are not naturally bright and intelligent and everything I have to explain by comparison; they have no idea of anything spiritual. Though they have an idol to which they offer human sacrifice, and in whom they place all their hope and trust.

I really believe that at first they would have almost worshipped me, though through a sense of fear they fancied I had some magic power over them, for they brought a number of children whom they had decorated beautifully with flowers (different kinds, cactus and primulas) and holding in their hands some of the earth nuts I have before mentioned, and I saw them wind round their children a garland of flowers, and this bound them very closely together, and I saw them place a quantity of beautiful blooming bushes and arrange the children upon it, three or four young girls followed, and I noticed in the hands of one a small cross made of twisted twigs, and I noticed she held it up in her hand. I hoped for an instant that she knew something of the Love and Wisdom of our Dear Blessed Lord, but I was mistaken.

Taking out the crucifix to my use, I held it up and said three times: "In the Name of the Father," etc., and all the people again rolled their heads in the dust, and I hardly understood what to do. Then I heard a most unearthly noise which they made with their voices, and I saw them carrying off an old man, whom it turned out was their chief, and he was covered all over with fearful holes, ulcers. Poor thing, he tried to crawl upon the ground, but he was not strong enough to do as he would wish, and his brother crawled behind him.

The old chief, too, was to be sacrificed at least as soon as this brushwood was burning amid the cries of the dying children and clapping and singing and shouting of the whole tribe, he was to throw himself on his own funeral pile and his brother would succeed him as chief.

It pleased our dear Lord I should see these things, that so I might understand in what way to deal with them and so as to make these people feel and know that I was their friend. God allowed the cure of the chief as soon as the shadow of the crucifix fell upon him, making the sign of the cross over him, and then I asked him, in the name of God, what all these things meant, and told him also to arise and be healed, and he was cured at once and rose and explained all to me.

Another people I have been among are copper-coloured. They are quick and intelligent, brave and noble-spirited, and I found that two of the oldest could make the sign of the cross, and I knew at once they had been baptised and by the hands of a priest. They knew many truths and have partly instructed their people. ... The elders of the tribe brought me waters from a neighbouring stream, and I baptised nearly all, for they seemed to have a wonderful faith. These people paint their bodies and wear clothing of skins, and feathers in their hair, standing straight up, and I think they live by hunting principally. ... I think now I have told you about the different missions on which the all-powerful God has sent me, and know you will return thanks with me for the souls whom He has thus chosen for His service ...

In a letter written on January 11th, 1881, Teresa informs Father Powell:

I have on several occasions taken the most Holy Sacrament to the dying, twice to nuns and once to a poor priest who communicated himself, and twice to young people. I have taken the ciborium from churches where the Sacred Particles were consecrated by sacrilegious hands (I think in Germany) and taken it where I have been instructed. I do not know how the others received, I mean by whose hands, but in each case I stayed with them till they died, and I have always been careful about replacing the sacred vessel. I have been often at death-beds and joined with the good Angels in helping the struggling soul to defeat its arch enemy. And God sent me once by night into a prison to a young man who was praying that his innocence might be proved, and that he might be restored to his friends, and God told me to tell him that He had heard his prayer and He would graciously grant his petition.

Citing another instance, Father Thurston writes: ["Georges Marasco and Some Others." [*alias* of Bertha Mrazek] *The Month.* January 1925. Vol. CXLV, pp.53-64.]

"She [Teresa] lay in a trance for three weeks. All save the doctor believed her dead. When she recovered, she told her confessor that she had been nursing a dying man in America. She described the house, etc., and gave the name of the street and full particulars. She found she had left her crucifix behind. The priest told her to return and get it. She fell into a trance again and recovered with the crucifix in her hand. The confessor communicated with the priest of the American parish in question and found all she said was correct. The American description of the 'mysterious lady' who nursed the dying man exactly fitted Teresa. To make certain, her photo was sent, and it was found to have been she. In addition the American said that the stranger had left her crucifix behind her, but it had since disappeared."

One would have liked to have had a few names and addresses supplied.

Another, less exotic, account of a Teresian bilocation is supplied by Kitty Deady. Father Mussely was hosting a large clergy luncheon at St Patrick's, and Margaret Murphy was cooking a huge joint for the occasion when she suddenly stumbled, fell, and burnt herself very severely. For several weeks after the accident she lay in bed in great pain. One evening as

Kitty came into her room Margaret said to her, "I hope you are making Teresa comfortable." Kitty, knowing that Teresa was at Neston, thought that Margaret must be wandering, but, seeing this, Margaret said, "No, my dear, I am quite clear in my head. Teresa has been with me. She put her hand on my head and blessed me." (As she always loved Teresa to do.) Some time later, when Teresa did actually come over from Neston to see her, Margaret asked her if it was not true that she had been to see her previously. Teresa's only answer was a smile.

The sisters at St Catherine's Convent in Edinburgh attested to several cases of bilocation while Teresa was with them. Cecil Kerr retails: "One day two of them went to visit a poor woman who lived quite alone and they found her very ill. They asked how she had managed during the night with no one to help her. 'Oh,' she said, 'that kind Miss Higginson was here and she boiled the kettle and made me comfortable.' It was afterwards found that Teresa had never left her room."

Teresa herself made reference to her bilocative activities in letters to Sister Barbara. In one, she says: "I have often stood by death-beds to help the dying to fight the Devil." And in another, she reports of Father Damien of the lepers (*vide post*) that "It went well for him." Presumably referring to her witnessing of his exit from life.

A species of psychic phenomenon straight from the séance room, levitation, figured in Teresa's mystic assemblage. Although she is said to have experienced it frequently, the only one among her friends to have claimed to have actually *seen* her raised in the air was Father Mussely.

In a letter to her confessor, Father Powell, dated September 20th, 1879, Teresa told him: "I was much terrified at finding myself raised up ... I mean that at first I knew I was being raised up and I was greatly humbled when I felt His infinite power ... He seemed to draw me up entirely into Himself as a drop of rain is lost in the waters of the mighty ocean, so does it seem here with the soul etc. Our Lord also takes away all the strength of the body and I remained very weak and hardly myself for two whole days."

Another letter to Father Powell, of April 27th, 1880, contains Teresa's own account of being raised in mid-air: "Our Lord surprised me, as it were, by drawing me up into Himself as a little bit of paper carried up by a mighty wind, so at times He carries me up by drawing my poor soul into His very essence ... and the body, too, is raised, and I know at the time that it is being raised, and I used to dread this immensely, but I see now so clearly that it is folly to resist ... It seemed to me at these times that the soul really left the body, she was in such agony though filled with delight and sweetness, though it remained cold, stiff and unable to move for so long afterwards."

And "We are as a kite in the air or matchwood in the torrent. Today it has pleased our dear b. Lord to confer one of those great favours on me. He filled me with such a love and desire of Himself that my body was raised: I could perceive it though I tried not to resist it yet I always have such an unspeakable fear at these times."

"Personally," says Father Thurston "I am quite prepared to believe that some, even many, holy people have been raised from the ground and have hung suspended in the air during their ecstatic prayer. The evidence, for example, in the case of St Teresa and of St Catherine of Siena, seems to me very strong. But there are other instances in which our faith is strained almost to breaking point, and I count the case now before us [that of Teresa Higginson] as belonging to this class." ["The Case of Teresa Higginson." A paper read by the Rev. Herbert Thurston, S.J. to the London Branch of the Guild, April 25th, 1937. Reprinted in *The Catholic Medical Guardian*. Vol. XV. No.3, July, 1937.]

Some of her friends, speaking of Teresa's being thus raised

in ecstasy, casually dropped into the conversation a question as to how it must have felt. Teresa, caught off her guard, replied, "Yes, it is a most strange sensation." Then, suddenly realising how she had been led into doing what she never did – talking about these supernatural favours – she put an instant figurative scold's bridle upon her tongue.

Teresa cherished a great fondness for, and devotion to, angels, especially guardian angels: she loved her own, and it grieved her that they were so little thought of. As regards guardian angels, Teresa's entire stance is difficult to cope with. Father Thurston observes: "It is not easy to be sure that they [her brothers and sisters] were serious when they told Miss Ryland that their sister Tess could ... get her guardian angel to carry upstairs a tray which was too heavy for her to struggle with herself." ["The Case of Teresa Higginson." *The Catholic Medical Guardian*, Vol. XV. No.3, July, 1937. pp.66-67.] And how about the occasion when, Father Snow having forbidden her to pretend to eat – as she sometimes did so as to avoid being noticed – told her that, instead, she should stay away from meals. She did so, found that her absence had not been noticed, and concluded that her guardian angel must have replaced her at the table! Teresa also claimed, in all seriousness, that she often despatched her guardian angel with messages to her confessor and others at a distance, and sent him on all sorts of errands for her.

St Gemma Galgani is said to have had the privilege of frequent visitations from her guardian angel, who, with wings outstretched, or else kneeling beside her, would reveal to her the most sublime insights into the Passion of Christ.

Equally controversial is the question of Teresa's self-claimed total abstinence from food. It was one which had the sceptical medical brigade holding up their hands in disbelieving horror. *Of course* it's impossible – unless, that is, you believe in the miraculous. In her later years, Teresa did eat and drink –

moderately. Thurston points out in his *The Physical Phenomena of Mysticism* that in the cases of almost all visionaries – and he specifies as exemplars Anne Catherine Emmerich, Domenica Lazzari, Louise Lateau, and Theresa Neumann, and many canonised saints – it is difficult to affirm with confidence that their inedia is necessarily of supernatural origin. Moreover, we know that convulsive contractions of the oesophagus, stomachic rejection of swallowed food, abortion of natural appetite (anorexia), are not symptomatic of heroic moral virtue; they are more likely to flag-up certain well-documented hysterical disorders. In the case of "those holy people who are reported to have lived for long periods with no other nourishment but the Blessed Sacrament, one looks," says Thurston, "but looks in vain, for the name of one who was free from strange previous inhibitions in the matter of diet and whom the neuropath specialist would have pronounced to be perfectly sound and normal. No competent physician could possibly have said this of Louise Lateau or Teresa Higginson." [*The Physical Phenomena of Mysticism*, pp.364-365.]

In this context, Teresa's suggestion that the only possible answer to many of the false charges, which were brought against her in all good faith, was that the Devil must have been impersonating her – as he is said to have done in the life of St Margaret Mary Alacoque, where the nuns were scandalised by seeing her, as they thought, devouring food in the pantry! – must be accorded an unprejudiced hearing.

Teresa was quiet and self-effacing, but, to her passionate belief, her visions were indubitable revelations of God's particular favour. Interestingly, asked point-blank if she had ever actually *seen* Our Lord, she answered, "Yes". She said that in former years she used to see Him with her corporeal eyes, but that such visions were lower in kind and far more subject to illusion than the intellectual ones that she was granted later. She

281

had indeed been seeing phantasmagoric angels since before she was twelve years old, and the visions continued all through her life – Our Lady, St Michael, and Our Lord Himself appearing to her – but, except to her spiritual directors, she was always reluctant to speak of what, with the eye of spirit, she saw, for the flame that burnt within her was not that of the Freudian motive of fame.

NOTES

24 The Reverend A.M. O'Sullivan and Cecil Kerr.

25 Sir Francis Martin Rouse Walsh (1885-1973). Neurologist. Born: London. Educated: Prior Park College, near Bath, and University College School, London. B.Sc. (1908), M.B. Bs. (1910), M.D. (1912), M.R.C.P. (1913), D.Sc. (1924). 1915: Joined R.A.M.C. and became consulting neurologist to the British Forces in Egypt and the Middle East. 1916: Married Bertha Marie Dennehy. Two sons. 1919: OBE. 1921: Appointed to the staff of the National Hospital. 1924: Department of Neurology founded for him at University College Hospital, London. 1946: Elected F.R.S. 1953: Knighted. 1973: Died at Brampton, near Huntingdon, February 21st.

26 Josephine Letitia Denny Fairfield, C.B.E., M.D., Barrister-at-Law. (1885-1978). Born in Melbourne, Australia, of Irish extraction. Family returned to Britain c. 1888. Educated Richmond High School for Girls, Surrey, George Watson's Ladies' College, Edinburgh, and Edinburgh University. 1907: Graduated M.B., Ch.b., with honours in all subjects and several medals. Worked in Birmingham City Asylum and Manchester Memorial Jewish Hospital. 1911: Settled in London. Active supporter of Women's Suffrage Movement. Member of the Fabian Society. 1911: Began work in public health for London County Council. 1920: Sent on medical mission to West Indies. 1922: Converted to Roman Catholicism. 1923: Called to the Bar at the Middle Temple. 1938: Went to Malta to advise on venereal diseases in women. 1939-42: Chief Medical Officer of the A.T.S. Her sister, Rebecca West, with whom her relations were somewhat strained, used her as the model for Cordelia in her novel, The Fountain Overflows (1957). 1965: Awarded the papal medal, Pro ecclesis et pontifice. Ill for fifteen months following a stroke, she died in St Mary Abbots Hospital, London, on February 1st, 1978, just one month short of her 93rd birthday.

27 Arthur Henry Bertram Wilberforce (1839-1904). Grandson of the anti-slavery reformer, William Wilberforce (1759-1833). Widely known as a missioner and a writer on spiritual matters. One of his last undertakings was when, already a very sick man, he officiated at a three-day retreat for the nuns of St Scholastica's Abbey, Teignmouth, in December, 1904, at which time Teresa was only a few miles away at Chudleigh. He died at Chiswick, on December 14th, 1904, which, by strange coincidence, was the same day that Teresa suffered her fatal stroke.

28 We are referred to Teresa's letter, numbered 34, of April, 1880, in which she writes to Father Powell, who has questioned her as to the way in which our Lord instructed her: "Our b. Lord places in the very centre of the soul those things which He wishes her to know, without any words or image being formed, and this comparison will make clear, I think, what I mean – that as one looking-glass casts those things that are reflected in it to another, so the soul being entirely in God, He impresses, infuses, or reflects in her what He desires she should learn. And sometimes He does this without the powers of the soul being suspended or the senses of the body being lost, certainly they are riveted

so to speak and made to drink in whatever He desires. But of my Father, who shall find words to express the delight and glory the whole being enjoys at being thus instructed by so heavenly a tutor!"

29 In the letter (No. 48) to Father Powell, dated May 27th, 1880, Teresa had written an explanation of the words of St John in the Apocalypse: "While making a short visit to our dear Blessed Lord in the most holy Sacrament of His Love, those things which I asked you to read for me this morning were represented in the soul and impressed very clearly in my mind, and I saw how admirably they corresponded and how beautifully the comparison described the Sacred Head as the 'Seat of Divine Wisdom', for, if you call to mind those things I have written regarding what our dear b. Lord has shown me and helped to narrate respecting His sacred Head, you will see how He Himself represented to me in the S. Head (as the mind) a transparent sea of light, in which were twelve beautiful precious stones in which sparkled and reflected all the splendour of that sun which overshadowed it and in which too were twelve other crystal stones all of unspeakable beauty and magnificence and in which gleamed all the colours of the rainbow. And I think I mentioned a resplendent light of greenish hue I see 'having the glory of God and the light thereof like unto a precious stone, as it were a jasper, as crystal.' And He gave me to understand that this Wisdom and Light was the seal that marked the number of His elect ('and they shall see His Face and His Name shall be on their foreheads.') And is not the Seat of Divine Wisdom 'as it were a new heaven and a new earth.' The soul and intellectual faculties and the dwelling place of the Most High, and the earth or human head the shrine and centre of the senses of the body by virtue of the hypostatic union a new earth. – And in another place it says: 'And I saw no temple in it, for the Lord God almighty is the Temple thereof and the Lamb,' showing distinctly the union of the two natures in the one Person of Jesus Christ."

13

MEMORIÆ

Exploding like a delayed action time bomb, came, somewhat late on the scene, the recollections of Mrs Bridget McVey, *neé* McCluskey, of Lawfield Tower, Dalkeith, near Edinburgh. It was, she recalled, at the end of November, 1887, that Miss Higginson had come to Scotland. "She then taught in our school, St David's, Dalkeith, near Edinburgh."

Looking back, Bridget McVey now saw, she said, that she had been silenced as a girl. "Sometimes everything vanished from my mind, or an overpowering fear or awe at my own unworthiness would prevent me speaking. Conscious of something supernatural, but beyond me to understand, I was always anxious to banish the thoughts of these incidents, which I called 'dreams'. Knowing the different places I had been to at the time, made everything mysterious. But now, giving my evidence re. Teresa Higginson, I can confidently say that I have been guided by Almighty God all through."

Mrs McVey recollected as best she could that it was in about October, 1932, that "thoughts of Miss Higginson came to my mind continually, until I made enquiries and found I had evidence. Gradually, every incident and detail connected with it, came to my mind like flashes, and remained there."

She would, she calculated, have been about twelve years of age, and the month would have been about June, when, "going down from the house at St David's Church, at Dalkeith, towards the gate, a face appeared looking into mine, and then vanished. Just outside the gate, a figure appeared with the same face, looking at something down the way, and smiling beautifully. I saw two tall nuns gliding up the way, and then stop as the lady went forward to them. All three turned to the right, and vanished. I did not see the nuns' faces. I went on. I had just reached the end of the church, exactly opposite the altar. I saw a semicircle of bright light in the sky. I seemed then to step into darkness, and sounds [were] coming into my ears.

I was going to school about one o'clock. The schools had just reopened, about the middle of July. As I got to the same place at the gates, the same lady, with two others dressed in black, the same build as herself, appeared at the other side of the road. They stopped when they saw me, and said goodbye. It seemed to be a sad parting for this lady. She was making her way to come across the road, looking sadly after them. All seemed to end here.

What seemed to me like winter time, Miss Higginson gave us instruction at Sunday School. I knew the face immediately, and while pondering over it and listening at the same time to her, just as she came towards me she turned up both her hands with the stigmata marks, and then put them up to her eyes, as though something had been too much for her, and went into an ecstasy for a short time. I learned afterwards that she was not living in Scotland at the time she appeared to me."

Bridget's mother had the pious habit of going to Mass every morning. Just occasionally, she would not be able to do so, and when that happened she would send her daughter along to the 7.30 a.m. Mass in her place, with instructions that she was to remain until a certain part of the second – eight o'clock – Mass, so as to hear two Masses.

"Holy Communion was always given before Mass. Miss Higginson was always the last to come from the altar rails. She went into the seat opposite me. After kneeling, she fell into a flat position over the bench, and lay motionless until after Mass. A nun came and shook her, and called to another nun, 'She is clean away.' Father Lea, S.J. came, laid his hands on her and blessed her, making the sign of the cross over her, saying twice, 'Teresa arise, be about thy Father's business.' She sprang straight up, took her shawl, and walked out of the church with the nuns. The nuns had knelt down facing Miss Higginson during that part. Miss Higginson looked dazed, her face set like marble. Father Lea came out again with an altar boy. He sprinkled the place with holy water, and prayed from his breviary.

Father Lea (the same Father Lea who knew Miss Higginson in Wigan) came into school next day and asked me rather sternly why I did not go home after the first Mass. I explained. After school that afternoon, I met Father Lea at our own door. I heard him say to my mother, 'I meant to be here before her.' I was sent out, but I overheard my mother say, 'Oh, yes, she did exactly as I told her.' He said, 'Then she was meant to be there.' I realised then I was being brought into something connected with Miss Higginson. I felt too unworthy to have anything to do with it, as everything savoured of great sanctity and heroic sacrifice. The stigmata marks and what that one flash revealed as she was clasping her eyes in church, always came back to my mind. I felt a shrinking fear and horror at having anything to do with the case.

About a fortnight later, I was sent to Mass and told always to go in front of a nun. The communicants were all at the rails except one nun. I had to go up to the fourth seat in front. The nun got up then and went to the rails, turning the last gas out as she was going up. Miss Higginson was the last to come back from the rails. As she reached the second bench on her right side, the roof creaked, a golden light in the shape of a dart coming from the roof, struck her eyes, she caught the bench with her hand. Another light from the left side, and then another from the centre struck her face. She stood gasping. I seemed to be in the aisle looking up in her face on my knees. I heard a slight noise. Miss Higginson turned her head to the left. I turned to the right, we both turned round again at the same time. A large white Host appeared in the air away from us at her right side. It went floating up gently until it got to Miss Higginson's mouth. It went into a flat position and remained in front of her mouth. Her lips were parted. As it reached Miss Higginson, a great beautiful light burst from the Host, illuminating Miss Higginson's face. It was too beautiful to describe. Miss Higginson seemed to be raised from the ground, staring and gasping as though her heart would break. She then stood motionless, the pupils of her eyes looked up to the roof at the back of the church, then followed something coming down until it reached the Host. By this time the light from the Host had ceased. I saw two dark shadows, one on each side of the Host. They waited a second, then carried the Host in the same direction.

What seemed to me months afterwards, I went to her convent for sewing. This particular day she seemed to be suffering. While I was standing near her, she clasped her side slightly. Sister Mary came to her and asked her if He was giving her an extra press. She gave her face a little twitch with pain and said: 'He wants reparation.' Then turning again she said: 'He wants atonement for the bad Communions that are being made today.' (I think she said in Spain.) Sister Mary asked her when it was made known to her. She said: 'Early this morning, at meditation time.'

Next time we went to the convent we kissed her ring. It was a black ring, like a crown of thorns. It was the stone with the Sacred Head we saw. The glass seemed to disappear and natural black hair with a forehead and two spokes standing up. It seemed to magnify as I looked at it.

The day she was suffering much, I saw the stigmata marks on her forehead, like a mass of tack marks from the eyebrows to the scalp of the head. They looked ugly. The day we kissed her ring, I saw a big gash in the centre of her left hand. The gash was black.

A few years afterwards, when speaking to the Reverend Mother Snow in Dalkeith, Canon Snow came along the passage where we were standing. I heard him say twice: 'You have the greatest saint in your house that ever stood on land.' Reverend Mother told me afterwards that he had come to settle the case of Teresa Higginson, and those were his words.

It was in the year 1887, that I suddenly found myself standing beside Miss Higginson. She was standing in front of a white cradle in which was a figure of a little elderly man in a sitting position. He waved his two hands to her and then to a crowd of little faces, all clamouring together. I then saw a second lot of faces and Miss Higginson was bending down just in front of me. Then everything vanished.

In January, 1888, she allowed we five children to see the insignia and ring of the chieftain of the pigmy tribe, which I, with Miss Higginson, had visited in the previous year. She said these were of great importance and had been sent on to her after the death of the little pigmy chieftain. She had baptised the whole tribe. A nun standing beside me said, 'What facilities had you there for baptising?' Miss Higginson said, 'They were baptised by the Holy Ghost, which embraces everything. It was a baptism of desire.' The insignia was a little animal's bone head and the ring had a large round setting of small stones inserted with seven vacant spaces at one side. Miss Higginson said these spaces will be filled up according to how the devotion to the Sacred Head progresses in the world. I took this to be a message from the chieftain. The colours were those to be used for the painting of the picture of the Sacred Head when the devotion is sanctioned by the Church. She said, 'Some of you ...', and then stopped. The nun asked, 'What period?' She said, 'Just a short time ago.'

'Dream' sequence Number 3.

It was early dawn. I seemed to be on the top of a very high

green mountain, large trees growing around. I alighted just in front of a pile of logs, laid cross-ways as though for drying. At the side, there was a passage, which took me to a three-cornered hut, covered with brown branches and thickets. As I got to the entrance, I saw a figure lying on a low bed covered with sacking, the head, black hair, lying or resting on the shoulder, the face tanned. I said, 'Oh, Father Kerr, here.' A dirty, filthy wretch was bending over him in a soothing, coaxing manner. It looked up as I spoke.

I then heard a clear, shrill voice call, 'By the power of God, Father of the Holy Trinity, clear out of the place for the Blessed Sacrament.' As I looked round, I saw the Host pass, golden flames bursting from it in a circle. Miss Higginson was at the back of it, but she stood still at the entrance, just opposite me. The wretch rushed past me like a blast of wind, blinding me from seeing more. It got into form again and stood at the edge of the hill, looking back into the hut. Miss Higginson alighted just at the back of the wretch, but it disappeared. She stood looking back into the hut (she had her hat and shawl on), her arms outstretched, her hands clenched, her face set, as though a great victory had been gained. I looked back into the hut, the whole atmosphere was entirely changed, all was calm and peaceful. Miss Higginson turned down the hill; I followed her. As she was going down, she turned her head in the direction the wretch had gone. We seemed to sail on clouds.

I came to myself standing in the bench, the priest at the Offertory. Everything vanished from my mind. Miss Higginson was standing raised from the ground, her hands joined, and looking upwards. She glided past me, a rustle of silk or leaves beneath her. I heard an "ahem" from some of the nuns at the back. I did not look round.

The following morning, after I had been with Miss Higginson to Father Kerr's death-bed, I was aroused out of sleep with a noise

63. Father Joseph Damien, the Leper priest.

and a tap, and a voice saying, 'Come', and then someone flying off in haste. I knew it was the same kind of errand I had before. I did not want to go. Miss Higginson came forward, dressed in her hat and shawl, saying, 'It is to give testimony'.

She raised me and carried me cross-ways, like a young infant. We landed on a rough, sandy, grassy entrance. Just as we entered, a figure came out of a side place, saying, '*Vobiscum*'. Miss Higginson answered, '*Et cum es*'. Teresa left us down on the ground in charge of the figure that had just come out (It was like a shadow, cassock, the head dress something three-cornered or pointed at the front – a biretta.) As she put me down, she said, 'It is to give testimony'.

She went into the side door. As she came out again, she

looked up, saying, 'It is well for him'. She took me by the right shoulder, the figure took me by the left, and carried me back again. As we were nearing the bed, Teresa said again, 'It is to give testimony'.

Next day or so, Father Lea, S.J. came into the school in a terrible state, saying that the great missioner was dead.

My mother met me coming home from school and told me if I knew anything about that death and Miss Higginson, to go and tell the nuns and priests. I said, 'No'. I had been in a dread. I could not understand, it was all beyond me. To this day, I remember the feeling of being lifted and laid down in bed.

The second part must have come to me to me twice, but I know for certain that I was in front of Miss Higginson at the hut. I knew that I had left her down in the church aisle. I knew that it was Father Kerr. (Father Kerr said goodbye to us before he went to the Foreign Missions)."

The 'great missioner' was held to be Father Joseph Damien. Born at Louvain, in Belgium, in 1841, he was sent out in 1873 as a missionary to the lepers in the isles of Molokai, Hawaii. In 1885, he caught leprosy, and died in 1889.

"About two or three days later, Father Lea came into the school. Throwing the door open, he called to the nuns, 'Father Kerr is dead. You have something in this place. This accounts for the happenings in the church the other morning.'

After school, I met my mother in a state about Father Kerr. She said, 'If you know anything about Father Kerr's death and Miss Higginson, go up and tell them.' I said, 'No.'

Everything vanished for the time. That night, everything in the second part came back to me very clearly. I remember in the morning thinking how I was being brought into more connections with Miss Higginson, in spite of my objections. That day Father Lea came into the school again saying another priest in the Foreign Mission is dead. He was speaking to the nuns. I knew I was being discussed. I heard him mention 'hut'. I could think of the awful sight I saw. If he had spoken to me I would have told him. I met my mother again, and she asked me again to tell them anything I knew. I said, 'No'. (I could only think of the wretch)."

Mrs McVey noted: "The whole came back to me about 1899. A priest advised me to go and see Father Snow, but I had the usual objections. When my mother was dying in 1912, she told me they had not been allowed to speak, but I would give evidence for Miss Higginson, and the nuns had been very anxious for me to speak, to confirm some happenings in the church about the time of Father Kerr's death."

The year 1905 was the last in which Mrs McVey claims to have experienced one of her extraordinary 'dreams'.

"I was at home. I don't know what time of day, but looking up I saw Miss Higginson standing, looking out of an open doorway, a porch, a bleak looking place, a window at the right-hand side, in a corner. She had a heavy, three-quarter, furry-looking coat on, a hat, and she was putting on gloves.

I next heard a call. I saw a workman with his shirt-sleeves rolled up, two women, the tallest in the centre, with a high-crowned hat on, a much smaller person, with a flat hat on, at the side, raising Miss Higginson from the ground in the passage beside the window. She was unconscious. There was a golden ray of light coming through the window, shining on Miss Higginson.

I next saw Miss Higginson in bed. The top of the bed was in front of a window. Miss Higginson had a dark grey jacket on and a light scarf or muffler round her neck. The bedclothes were over her left shoulder. The tallest of the two women who carried in Miss Higginson made an ugly grab at some article on top of the bedcover. She pressed her fingers into the cover to get it, making a sneer at Miss Higginson as she did so. Miss Higginson made a half-bound up in bed, throwing her head back and trying to speak. She seemed greatly annoyed, and was only able to make an ugly noise from her throat. She then lay back on the pillows dazed and exhausted-looking, but pondering-looking and quite conscious. The small woman or girl was a witness to that. She was at the foot of the bed.

I seem to have seen one thing and another in that house. The last thing was a woman exactly like the tallest woman who carried Miss Higginson in, but in a working garb. She was a well-built, fair-haired woman. She came dashing into the room throwing the door wide open and giving a great jeering laugh. She dashed forward to the bed and grabbed the blankets. As she threw the door open I caught sight of someone running down the passage and out by the outer doorway. There was commotion as though they had been having great sport. As the woman was going forward to the bed, the same workman put his head through the outer door and called to her to stop, but it was more of a warning. She paid no attention. The small person was following this woman. She had a sad, sombre look, and kept her eyes fixed on the woman. I next saw the tall woman outside, holding the blankets up and having a good, hearty laugh at what she had done. No one was with her.

Some time after, I heard a call. Looking up, I saw the same workman running from the end of a garden to catch the end of a coffin. The coffin was tippling over. A man with a black coat and collar, hat on, holding the top of the coffin, and two ladies with them, holding it up at the sides. The ground was covered with snow, a small stream was running down by the side of the garden. They seemed to be trying to carry the coffin to a car waiting at an opening at the right side. I saw only half the car. I heard a voice say 'Miss Higginson is dead'.

A little later on in the afternoon, looking up at the same place, I saw a coffin being lowered, three ladies going forward to the grave. I heard a voice say, 'That is the hole filled up now'. It was the same grave I saw when I kissed Miss Higginson's ring.

A few days later, my mother, coming from Mass, brought word of Miss Higginson's death. Unconsciously, I told her how she had been dead some time, and how she had been treated. That drew attention, as word had only just come to St David's. When I was questioned, I seemed powerless to understand or answer. The school-house at Chudleigh would occasionally come to my mind, but I could not recollect what it meant.

When I arrived home after visiting for the first time Teresa's grave, in June, 1937, I was suddenly able to distinguish the different people in the house at Chudleigh. It all came in three different flashes. It was a repetition of before, but, as one woman left the bed with something in her hands, suddenly, a wall with a coping-stone on the top, came along in front of the bed, only showing the end of Miss Higginson's right hand. The woman with a masterful smile on her face did something at the bottom of the wall with her hands. The wall moved along further. The woman's head with her hat on was placed like a statue on top of the coping-stone facing Miss Higginson, who was lying in a pleading position with outstretched hands, showing the Stigmata marks, her eyes piercing and watching me. She was dressed in red and golden colours. She was too beautiful for words."

So startling in many respects was this unexpected and late testimony, that it was received in several quarters with some incredulity.

In the course of a letter which she wrote on October 5th, 1927, to Miss Arkwright, Mrs McVey says:

I drew my breath yesterday when I got Lady C.'s[30] letter. She got a letter from Mgr. O'Brien saying they cannot be too careful of my evidence. (Whether he said it or not, I don't know.) I am to ask Miss Arkwright to type my evidence to make it easier for him, but no one else must see it without his permission. You will see the predicament I was in. Father Cullen said I did right to write at once to the postulator but he could not help me. As usual I got no answer. I was in a proper fix. Lady C. wrote to him then. I couldn't keep this last to myself, people will be alive now who can throw light on what I have said. You can rely on my word, everything is the God's truth. There is not a spark of illusion. I may have to suffer, but like Teresa, it will be for a purpose.

An interesting addendum. On September 1st, 1944, Mrs Marie Farron Smith wrote, from Weir Cottage, Marlow, Buckinghamshire, to Monsignor John O'Brien:

Since seeing you last, I have been to Scotland and found it a very profitable visit. I called to see you on my return as I wanted to talk to you about Mrs McVey. I was very impressed with her – a hard-headed, tough woman, she has still all her faculties, and owing to wartime conditions has to work very hard.

Mrs McVey has asked me to see you on her behalf, and to bring the case strongly before you. As you know, she withheld her evidence, and since 1933 has been regretting it. As time goes on, she feels more and more remorseful about it, and says she cannot die in peace until her evidence is given. Moreover, she is anxious to be examined whilst she has all her faculties. She was 70 last birthday (June).

She says that in 1933, Our Lord made it all so clear to her, it was as though a curtain was drawn back and everything became vivid in her mind; events, days, and dates coming back as fresh as ever. The matter is weighing so heavily on her that about a month ago she had approached her own Archbishop in Edinburgh, and made known her evidence, and asked if she could be examined by Liverpool, and could be helped in the matter. The Archbishop advised her to put this request in writing and register the letter. Mgr. Adamson acknowledged it, saying the letter would receive attention in due course.

Incidentally, the Archbishop of Edinburgh said he could not understand how it was that Liverpool had not done anything about it – Mrs McVey having told him that you already had much of her written evidence.

On a previous visit to Ormskirk, in either 1938 or 1939, Miss Arkwright showed me Mrs McVey's written evidence about Chudleigh and the ring. Mrs McVey had sent her this to be passed on to the proper authorities, and was under the impression that this had been carried out. On my return from Scotland I stayed last weekend with Miss Arkwright, telling her of my interview with Mrs McVey, and putting it very forcibly to her that she had very serious obligations in this matter.

Miss Arkwright has the evidence but cannot be sure whether she sent you a copy; she rather thinks so, but I remember at the time she thought it was too fantastic and far-fetched. Granted, the evidence is obscure – the composition difficult to follow, but I did not find any of this when questioning Mrs McVey. Miss Arkwright said she was getting in touch with Mgr. Adamson as a result of my visit to Dalkeith. I thought the matter should be brought to your notice.

Another point. Mrs McVey sent to Miss Arkwright by me her written evidence of bilocation, with Teresa Higginson at Father Damien's death-bed. This has not been written before. I carried out my trust in delivering it to Miss Arkwright, but once again made it very clear to her that it would be wrong to withhold it from authority. Besides this, I have in mind a conversation with Mrs McVey about an encounter she had with Cardinal Merry del Val in Lourdes. Apparently, he questioned her about Teresa, and she claimed to have had an ecstasy there and then. Cardinal Merry del Val told her that she *must* give her evidence about Teresa Higginson. She refused, saying she had been so afraid of all her supernatural experiences, discouraged them, and wanted to keep it all at bay. The Cardinal replied: "If you refuse now, you will still be called, even if it is at the end, and your evidence will prove the most important, and weigh heavily." (My quotation is not verbatim: I give you the gist of it.)

A further point that I want to bring out: Mrs McVey asserts most emphatically that she has never been to Chudleigh. As you know, I was evacuated there in 1940 with my husband, and have repeatedly been invited by Miss Hart, the teacher at Lord Clifford's school, to have tea and supper with her at the school-house. Not only does Mrs McVey describe very accurately the interior of the room where Teresa died, also the top landing (I have never been upstairs), but she made a remark to me about the queer planning of the place at the back. What she described she could not possibly have seen on a postcard, nor would a photo be taken of it – the long passage which runs from one house to the other, and which, I think, if I remember rightly, Miss Hart gave me to understand was used as a wash-house, and three doors off Miss Hart's kitchen, across the yard, happen to be three lavatories – i.e. school's and the two houses. It was I told Mrs McVey what these three doors really were.

Finally, I want to make it quite clear to you that Mrs McVey was exceedingly chary of giving me any evidence. I spent the day with her and it was only by very careful questioning – by bringing up false statements, and by revealing the fact that already I knew much of her evidence, that I was able to arrive at what I did. You see, she told me she had been advised not to speak of it before she had been examined by the ecclesiastical authority.

Scottish reminiscences of a rather different kind were provided, in 1950, by Mrs Margaret McKeon.

"There may be others as well as myself who, when visiting St Francis's Church, Edinburgh, see in their mind's eye saintly souls long gone to their reward, and who, while on earth, worked in St Mary's School. When an infant, I entered St Mary's School about the year 1883. Mother Bernard of St Catherine's Convent was the first teacher I remember. She was at that time infant-schoolmistress. She was a very clever and cultured lady. The infant school was on the ground floor, now used as a hall for parochial purposes.

On leaving the infant school we proceeded upstairs to what was designated the 'big school', and is now the church. Where the sanctuary is, there stood a large desk. Over this there was a crucifix, almost life-size. To the left was an altar of Our Lady, and on the right one of St Joseph. There was also a beautiful picture and altar of the Sacred Heart, between what is now the sacristy and the confessionals. These altars were at all times beautifully kept. It was a privilege to get the altar-cloth to launder.

The sister of the senior school was Sister Mary Alphonsus of the Sacred Heart. I cannot proceed without making special mention of the wonderful nun who was schoolmistress at that time. Sister Mary Alphonsus was one of the pioneer nuns of Edinburgh. She was a native of Limerick and was in her teens when she came from Ireland to take up work in Edinburgh. She was a very holy woman and did an immense amount of good among the very poor. Leaving St Catherine's Convent on Sunday, she would pass through Lauriston Street, down West Port, Grassmarket, and Cowgate, bringing with her all the Catholic girls she could muster, to St Anne's School, at the foot of the Cowgate, where she instructed and helped them in every way she could.

I was a young child at the time, but I remember that there was no Education Authority in those days. Sister begged, clothed, and cooked for the poor children in Lothian Street. She also possessed a stock of white frocks which she laundered for the poorer girls for examination days. It would be difficult to enumerate all the good she did in those days, when there was no 'dole' for the fathers, and winter was a most trying time.

Another nun who taught at the same time in St Mary's School was the late Reverend Mother De Sales. She was a model religious, saintly and of profound humility; a most accomplished lady, and a finished musician. She was sister of the late Lord Campbell of Skerrington. The old Irish people were very much attached to the members of this distinguished and holy family.

Now I come to a few of the things I can relate of one, not a nun, but no other than the saintly Servant of God, Teresa Higginson. I was ten years of age when, in 1888, Teresa's voice first fell upon my ears. I am now [in 1952] seventy-four. It's a long time to remember one outstandingly saintly, gentle, kind person. I was in Standard IV when I first saw Teresa. She used to come to teach us fine sewing and other lessons. Particularly I remember her religious instructions. In fact, 'word for word.' I can repeat part of an instruction she gave the class when I was about eleven years of age. I distinctly remember an instruction Teresa gave us in the top class-room of the school in 1889. The lesson was on the Incarnation, and at the end she asked us all to kneel and honour Our Lord's Sacred Heart, beating beneath the heart of Our Lady before He was born into the world. The children (all girls) were listening intently on this occasion. One girl, perhaps through nervousness, giggled. Teresa stopped and looked at her so very sadly that she at once stopped. She did not reprimand her. I remember feeling glad that I was not the girl who had laughed, to find Teresa looking at me with such a sad look.

One day before she came into the class Sister M. Adolphus told us to behave well and I remember distinctly her saying: 'There are forty nuns in St Catherine's Convent and not one of them is as good as Miss Higginson.' Indeed, Sister's advice was unnecessary, as I don't think I ever noticed a girl misbehaving while the holy Teresa was with us.

About the year 1890, when I would have been twelve, I attended St Catherine's Convent for fine sewing. There was an apple-tree in the garden with a surrounding seat where Miss Higginson placed my work. I've seen birds coming down on to her hands. She used to turn away and I would hear a faint whistle, then, turning back, she would show me the bird. When I found out that she was the one who whistled (not the bird) I said: 'Miss Higginson, you're the one who's whistling!' and she laughed joyously. Before leaving I was sure of a cup of tea with buns.

At one time there was an epidemic of scarlet fever raging. Teresa secured us little badges of the Sacred Heart with the words 'Cease, for the Heart of Jesus is with me.' We wore the badges round the neck outside and said the prayer often during the day. The chief devotion that Teresa tried to instil into our young minds was to 'The Wisdom of Our Lord's Sacred Head', combined with Love of the Sacred Heart.

That was over sixty years ago, and I never forgot that prayer of Teresa's. At various times I have met old friends, scattered here and there, who remember Teresa and her teaching of devotion to the Wisdom of the Sacred Head; one even told me that, although she forgot who taught it to her, she always said the prayer. One day she saw a paragraph about Teresa in one of the Catholic papers, and everything came back to her.

There must still be living a number who remember the sweet lady, shabbily dressed in black, ever gentle, with dark arresting eyes that seemed to read one's very soul. One dear old friend of Teresa's, Sister Mary Baptist, of St Catherine's Convent, promoted the devotion so much loved by the holy Servant of God. The late Father Humphrey, S.J., Sacred Heart Church, Lauriston, Edinburgh, blessed the picture of the Sacred Head in the convent chapel of St Catherine's, and also Teresa's work. She spent eleven years of her life in St Catherine's, Edinburgh. She taught for short periods in St Mary's, Lothian Street; St Ignatius, Glen Street; and St David's, Dalkeith. She supplied for a short time at Selkirk, where her holiness is still remembered, and in the Convent, Linlithgow, when the Sisters of Mercy had charge."

In 1925, Mrs McKeon received, she confided to Mother De Sales, a great favour after praying to Teresa, and she asked Mother De Sales if she thought Teresa was a saint. "When Teresa is honoured by the Church," the nun replied, "it will be as a very great saint."

Margaret McKeon died at Bathgate, West Lothian, in 1966, aged eighty-eight. Her faith was staunchly with Teresa to the end.

NOTE
30 Lady Cecil Kerr.

14

CAUSA

Taking up his pen and determinedly dipping it in the ink of cynicism, the sceptical Dr F.R.M. Walshe observed in the Higginsonian context, [In the Catholic weekly paper, *The Tablet*, of Tuesday, May 8th, 1938] in line with his personal caution and professional prejudices, "All that glisters is not gold," and remonstrated most insistently upon the great desirability of the case of Teresa Higginson being scrupulously investigated from the psycho-pathological point of view before being submitted to those canonical processes which lead to beatification.

That Process had been officially promoted in the early 1930s, by two Archbishops of Liverpool, the Most Reverend Frederick William Keating (1859-1928), who inaugurated the Process, and his successor, the Most Reverend Richard Downey (1881-1953), who, after Keating's death, continued it, and, in due course, despatched the findings of the Diocesan Commission to the Sacred Congregation of Rites, in Rome. There, for months, more likely years, all that is germane to the issue is examined, re-examined, argued, and debated, before arrival at a final decision is achieved.

The Diocesan Process is merely informative; that is to say its mandate is solely for the collection of facts; it has no duty to seek out medical or other technical advice upon the evidence gathered, neither should there be any formulation of commissional opinions.

Before a Cause can be initiated, it is necessary for at least five years to have passed since the death of the candidate. The purpose of this delay is to provide for greater balance and objectivity in the evaluation of a case, and to permit of the cooling and dissipation of the primal emotions. In the case of Teresa Higginson, some twenty-five years had passed since her death.

The Canon Law of the Church requires that there shall be a minimum of ten witnesses – eight of whom should be eye-witnesses – to the candidate's reputation for sanctity. And the Devil's Advocate is bound to summon for examination "all who were intimately acquainted with the Servant of God."

Those officially engaged in the Liverpool Archdiocese Informative Process included a Doctor of Divinity, a Doctor of Philosophy, a Doctor of Canon Law, and a Doctor of Science, in addition to others learned in theological, ascetic, and variegated scientific disciplines. They duly examined on oath every obtainable witness of Teresa's life, both for and against her, all of whose sworn statements were forwarded to Rome, where the Sacred Congregation of Rites would establish whether or not a *prima facie* case existed in her favour as a suitable subject for beatification. The Diocesan Court made no official examination of Teresa's voluminous writings; that was a duty undertaken in Rome.

The work of collecting, sifting, and assessing evidence, extended unceasingly over a period of more than seven years. The Devil's Advocate is the *Promotor Fidei*. An eminent, well-experienced theologian, it is his duty to collect and examine all allegations hostile to the candidate's sanity and sanctity. A Process of Beatification, as opposed to that of canonisation, is not litigious or contentious; the *Advocatus diaboli* does not here hold a brief for the opposition. His charge is simply to work impartially through the evidence, in order to ascertain that the Diocesan Commission has not, in its natural enthusiasm for its Cause, applied colour a shade too highly. The Pope is not held to be infallibly inspired in the matter of a beatification, as he is in a canonisation, but depends upon the information submitted to him.

"Hagiography: Past and Present", was the title of an article, contributed by an anonymity-preserving correspondent to the Tuesday, November 20th, 1937, issue of *The Tablet*. It was to be the precipitant of an avalanche of correspondence which, week after week, would blow up like dancing showers of dazzling snowflakes, and continue for months and months to come. The writer had, he informed his readers, had the opportunity of reading in the original some letters written about the late Miss Teresa Higginson by two of her fellow-teachers. One of the letters dealt with that period of its subject's life when she was a teacher in Wigan, living with Susan Ryland, whose letters and opinions are referred to in Cecil Kerr's biography as important sources of evidence. A passage quoted in the biography reads: "Such was Miss Higginson as I remember her. ... From the first day I met her until we parted, I could never find fault with her in any way."

"But," objects our anonymous correspondent, "reference to the original letter provides some of the missing passages, and the last sentence quoted above is preceded as follows: 'She often annoyed me, though. I used to think she ought to exert her will more and not be such a burden on poor Miss Ryland, who got quite worn out, and of course, while she was attending and waiting on her (Miss H.) she was absent from her own school which was then left solely to me: consequently we got into disrepute with the Inspector and I thought this unfair to Miss Ryland. *Otherwise*, from the first day I met her until we parted, I could never find fault with her in any way.' The omission of this additional material not only deprives the reader of vital evidence as to the subject's character, but the omission of the word 'otherwise' (not italicized in the original) lends a definitely misleading sense to the matter actually quoted in the 'Life.'

Another passage of the letter missing from the 'Life,' reads as follows: 'There were days when she literally lived on the Holy Communion and poor Miss Ryland had to half carry her to the

304

altar rails every day. I used to pity the latter, she was a real slave to her but she looked upon Miss H. as a saint, ' and again, 'I remember one Good Friday when very prostrate and in bed, she spent the day crying and craving for the Holy Communion. Of course the confessor paid no attention to her that day but the next day she received and was alright (*sic*) again on the Sunday. Some priests did not believe in her and said it was all hysteria.'"

Commenting on all this information, Cecil Kerr avers that Teresa Higginson was "calm and self-controlled, she was never known to cry or make a scene. ... Her very illnesses gave way before the call of duty and, except towards the end of Lent, she was seldom absent from her place in school."

But *The Tablet's* correspondent maintains that, "Passages in this and other letters of the series reveal other instances of that strong egotism which is so integral a part of the symptom-complex of hysteria: a symptom-complex which figures so largely and so intimately in the life of Miss Higginson, and lends this life so pathological a complexion in the eyes of any informed and critical reader. Who can contend that the passages quoted in the 'Life' and the cited comment upon them really give a balanced or reliable picture of the life and character of its subject? Biographers of the holy, and protagonists of causes for beatification bear a heavy burden of responsibility to the Faithful, and nothing less than a fastidious regard for accuracy and candour is due from them to their trusting audience. A cause that goes to Rome from this country carries with it, in a sense, the good name of English Catholics."

This drew, in the issue of Tuesday, November 27th, 1937, the following from Dr Letitia Fairfield, writing from 1 Raymond Buildings, Gray's Inn, London, W.C.1.

Sir, – The communication on Hagiography: Past and Present, has interested me greatly as a careful study of the large *Life* of Teresa Higginson had already aroused my suspicion that much had been suppressed. There are important gaps in her story, explanations are given which do not "hang together", and grave accusations, evidently believed by her neighbours and contemporaries, are lightly dismissed. Your correspondent's evidence goes further than this. He is entitled to ask what has been omitted from other letters. Further, it would be interesting to know whether Miss Higginson's own letters may not have been subjected to over-kindly editing. I venture to suggest that if examined in full they would show even more definite evidence of those mental aberrations – and, I might add, of those moral peculiarities which the documents already published reveal to the critical eye.

For the sake of the good name of English Catholicism which, as your correspondent points out, is seriously involved, I sincerely trust that the matter will not be allowed to rest here. Cannot the body of material be examined in the original by some competent theological expert before the cause is allowed to proceed further?

In case your readers may think that any unduly harsh view is being taken of Teresa Higginson's claims to sanctity, I would like to remind you of a few salient facts. Miss Higginson solemnly asserted in letters to her confessor that she was transported to savage parts, and there, under the direct instructions of Our Lord, she taught and converted and even baptized the inhabitants in large numbers. "It is not always the same place I visit, nor the same people, though I have been most of all with a tribe whose chief is lately deceased, and whose name is Jampooda."[31]

There are pages of this stuff in the official *Life*, appendices obviously drawn from old geography and travel books. She further claims that she took the ciborium from churches where the sacred particles were consecrated by sacrilegious hands (I think in Germany), and carried it miraculously to the dying, into prisons, etc. (p.363). Miss Higginson further claimed that she rarely, if ever, ate after her first Communion; that though she put food in her mouth she did not swallow it, and if other persons (including her sisters) saw her joining in the family meals, it was really her guardian angel taking her place (p.181). Of the many miraculous and diabolical encounters she relates, there is no real confirmatory evidence whatever, even in the official *Life*.

Comment should be needless, but apparently, so anxious are certain of the Faithful for signs and wonders, it is badly required.

Yours faithfully,

Letitia Fairfield.

Canon E. Campana, Professor of Dogma in the Seminary of Lugano, was tempted to break cover and hastened to beleaguered Teresa's defence in the very next issue of *The Tablet*, on December 4th, 1937. He deplores: "It seems the fate of Teresa Higginson to be, even after death, the sign which shall be contradicted." He confesses to being one of those of her admirers who is devoutly praying that the halo of the Blessed shall be soon placed upon her head. He will have no truck with those who deprecate her glorification as compromising religion. "If anyone finds me impertinent in interfering (as I am a stranger) in a question so delicate to the English Catholics, let me apologize on the ground that the sentiment of gratitude moves me to write these few lines, because I feel myself in debt of my poor life to Teresa Higginson, who saved me from a danger, whose remembrance always awakes in me the profoundest emotion. Just eight years ago, during my summer vacation in the mountains, one sunny morning I was sitting in the open air, under a magnificent Virginian tree, intent in the

307

recitation of my Breviary. Before starting my prayer I was seized by a great fear, thinking that maybe this was a good place for the vipers. But my fear lasted just a moment, because I put my heart in peace, telling to myself: 'Don't be afraid, my old fellow; let the snakes come if they want to; Teresa Higginson will help you.' And she did, in fact. At the end of my Breviary, putting aside the book, I saw coiled in my breast, and with the head already inside my suit, between the buttons of it, a viper of the most dangerous kind. With a sufficient presence of spirit, but not with a sufficient skill, I threw the snake up in the air with my cane, thus creating for me another danger, that of having the reptile fall upon my face. But the viper had been wise and descended obliquely. Should I have been bitten by the viper, far as I was from town and doctors, there would not have been other remedy for me to apply but the oil of Extreme Unction. Thanks to Teresa Higginson, I had been spared it. So I am not surprised that Teresa Higginson should have delivered many poor Africans from the jaws of the infernal serpents."

Father Herbert Thurston, S.J. entered the *Tablet* fray in its December 11th, 1937, issue. He felt the obligation to call attention to one feature in the story of Teresa which seemed to him suggestive. "She wrote that when she was not quite four years old God brought her 'to the full use of reason.' She had at that age a revelation of the mystery of the Blessed Trinity which affected her so powerfully that prostrating herself on the ground she said over and over again: 'Blessed be the holy and undivided Trinity now and forever more. Amen.' Still it is plain from her own statements that this spiritually precocious child was not 'prepared for the Sacrament of Penance' before she was eleven years old. She longed to make her first Communion, but, as she explains, 'I was several times put back on account of my age,' and the favour was only granted her when she was within a few weeks of thirteen. It was common, no doubt, in those days to postpone first Communion, but not first Confession. She belonged to an exceptionally pious family and she happens to mention that her sister made her first Confession when she was seven. Although supernaturally enlightened about the Trinity, Teresa would, presumably, not have been exempted from learning her Catechism, and from that she might have ascertained that children were bound to go to Confession when they came to the use of reason. Is it rash to draw the conclusion that there must have been something not quite normal about the child? Did she appear to her parents and others, unbalanced and over-excitable? Was age the real reason why her first Communion was delayed?"

And below, on the same page, is a letter from that distinguished Catholic convert novelist, Evelyn Waugh. He says: "I have a keen appetite for marvels and do not doubt that we constantly fail in gratitude by attributing providential interpositions to chance or to natural causes, but I must confess to being somewhat nonplussed by the tale, in your issue of today, of Canon Campana and the viper. Where, precisely, did the late Miss Higginson come to the Canon's assistance? As I understand his story, he began his office in the confidence of supernatural protection from vipers; sometime later he found one coiled in his breast with its head already inside his suit. I do not know how common these reptiles may be in his district, nor how high the local rate of mortality from snake bite, but we have the Canon's assurance that this particular viper was of the most dangerous kind, and it seems clear that, so far from being protected, he had been subjected to more than ordinary annoyance. He rid himself of the snake by tossing it in the air with a cane and, in falling, it 'descended obliquely and missed his head.' He certainly had a narrow shave; of the two dangers – that of the snake nestling in his bosom and of its falling on his face – the former, which he averted by his own dexterity, seems far more grave. Is it not possible that, in his natural agitation, he 'trembled for fear where there was no fear'; that he had thrown the snake further and truer than he knew and that when it seemed to be poised immediately overhead, it was in reality proceeding in a narrow parabola to a safe distance? Should stories such as these be allowed to discourage critical and precise investigation in a question of first importance?"

The Tablet. December 18th, 1937. Dr Letitia Fairfield lets fly!

Father Thurston's interesting letter raises several points of importance in regard to the life of this lady:-

(1). There is no evidence whatever concerning the childhood and early life of Teresa, except her own account, written at the age of forty-four on the instructions of her confessor, Father Lunn.[32]

(2). The portion of this autobiography dealing with her adolescence is very strange. Teresa states that at fifteen or sixteen, while still at her Nottingham convent, she was "taken very ill and given up by the doctors." The nature of the illness is unspecified, but she was in bed for nine months, unconscious for several days, and then got better. Yet not only did her loving and pious parents leave her at school during this prolonged and dangerous illness, [This is not correct. She was taken home.] but she remained at the Convent until she was twenty-one. What was she doing there? Her fluent pen fails her at this point and Father Lunn excused her from writing any more as she found it too painful. She was not being trained for any occupation as later events showed. Although her family fell into dire financial straits, she did not (unlike her sisters) begin to earn her own living at teaching till twenty-seven. The whole story suggests some definite abnormality (other than extreme holiness) in early life.

310

(3). Although Teresa had four sisters and three brothers, there is no evidence whatsoever from any of them supporting her claims to sanctity. In her list of "Sources of Information" Lady Cecil Kerr mentions "written and verbal statements from her sister," among others, but quotes nothing that can be identified. Yet her family must have had personal knowledge of many of the facts alleged, e.g. of her precocious piety, her austerities and self-mutilations (which *could not* have remained hidden in bedrooms shared by lively girls), of her supernatural visitations and her miraculous power of doing without food. Not only did they fail to testify to the wonders in their midst, but they almost behaved as though they did not believe in them.

"Dearly as they loved her they were often distressed and puzzled by her utter disregard of appearances and the strange stories that were beginning to be told about her ... she used to wonder sometimes at the things that passed unnoticed ..." (p.89). Her friend, Miss Ryland, records that in her presence her brother and sister (presumably sane adults) "teased her" because she lit a fire without coal or wood, by making the sign of the cross, and got her guardian angel to carry a heavy tray upstairs for her (p.54). This I submit is nonsense, if it is intended to mean that they really believed their sister to be the possessor of supernatural powers, Careful reading of this passage suggests they were trying to chaff her out of absurd claims.

(4). Finally I would beg to draw attention to an anecdote on p.321 of the "Life."

"A poor prisoner was awaiting execution. He was utterly hardened and unrepentant and rejected all the efforts of those who tried to soften him. Teresa had a method of her own. She bought a bunch of grapes and went to the prison. The wretched man was sitting on his bed in sullen despair, but she gently put her arms around his neck, saying: 'Look, dear father, what a beautiful bunch of grapes I have brought you.' Even the hardened sinner was not proof against such an appeal." Now this story is important, for I submit again that it is nonsense and cannot be true. At no time during Teresa's lifetime were visitors allowed into condemned cells under such conditions. Even if Teresa had known of the spiritual state of a man under sentence of death, she could not have got into the prison without an official order, and no reason is suggested why one should have been granted to her. Did Teresa tell this story about herself? If so, the inference is painful but obvious ...

Canon Thomas S. Kelly, whose brother was the current (1937) parish priest of St Alexander's, Bootle, in a letter to the Editor, published in *The Tablet* of December 25th, 1937, describes it as "where Teresa lived, taught and worshipped, and where many 'diabolical manifestations' undoubtedly took place. The sworn testimony of witnesses proves that happenings of a mysterious nature actually did take place. There is in existence superabundant 'real confirmatory evidence' of many unusual things relating to Teresa, and all documents have rightly been forwarded to the proper tribunal in Rome for final investigation, without details being previously divulged to all interested individuals, including the sceptically curious. To my mind, over-emphasis has been laid upon the unusual incidents, and not sufficient prominence given to the everyday saintly practices of this Servant of God. A psychologist is, of course, quite at liberty to look upon the mystic experiences of Teresa as 'mental aberrations,' but directly opposed to this is her life-long reputation for perfect truthfulness and remarkable commonsense with all who knew her intimately. In particular, Canon Snow, her spiritual director, was a man of great solidity of character and judgment, who made a minute study of the whole course of mystical theology and of Teresa's life for over twenty years. Was [Teresa] deluded? Anyone who wishes is quite free to think so. On the other hand, those who think she was not deluded have a strong case, founded on the overwhelming testimony of many competent and credible witnesses to her very great sanctity, her profound humility, and her thoroughly genuine virtues of every kind. Though it would be doubtless difficult to prove that these incidents of bilocation occurred, it would equally be difficult to prove that they did not."

In the January 1st, 1938, *Tablet* Dr Fairfield complains that, "one could not believe that much reliance could have been placed on half-century-old recollections of those who were either mere children then, or very old people now. The contemporary documents printed in the 'Life' state that the two sister teachers [the Misses Catterall] who shared Miss Higginson's lodgings, her landlady and Father Powell (the Parish priest) were alarmed by loud bangs, shrieks and sounds of slapping, etc., occurring on three consecutive nights in 1883. But nothing is described which Teresa could not have produced herself, as indeed other persons of her temperament have been known to do, to my own knowledge. It was not without significance that she was at this time reading the life of the Curé D'Ars. The priest who was asked to investigate Teresa's case on behalf of the Bishop of Liverpool, evidently came to this conclusion, for he disregarded the evidence of the witnesses and forbade Father Powell to act any longer as Teresa's director (p.169). The evidence given in support of alleged diabolical manifestations at Wigan is even less convincing. ... Canon Kelly further seeks to burke criticism by pleading Teresa's 'life-long reputation for perfect truthfulness and common sense,' but that is exactly the reputation she did *not* acquire – if again our only source of information is correct. At Wigan she had already gained a reputation for hysteria. At Sabden in 1879 she was accused by her landlady of stealing £100, and although the charge was not substantiated the episode evidently caused considerable scandal. At Bootle, the enquiries made in 1883 and already referred to, certainly did not establish her reliability, and from that date to 1886, when she was asked to leave the school by Father Powell's successor, the accusation grew more and more serious.

Lady Cecil Kerr admits 'many of the accusations brought against her seemed impossible of solution at the time ... Her own suggestion as to the Devil's impersonation of her is supported by some of her friends who are convinced that this did actually happen on more than one occasion (p.196) ... Many who had been her friends now turned away from her, and the greater had been their former devotion so much the more intense was their indignation against one they had come to look upon as a "lying hypocrite." Some of the priests were among the most active of her opponents.' Only two specific examples of these charges of untruthfulness and fraud are given, but one at least might leave the gravest doubts in the reader's mind (pp.187-190). Teresa's landlady at Bootle for some unexplained reason forbade her to return to her house and wrote grimly 'I think home is the best place for you.' Teresa could not get another permanent teaching post and Father Snow found her a refuge in his sister's convent in Edinburgh, where she remained for twelve years. Now it is very strange that these judgments of her contemporaries should fit in so exactly with the present day estimate of Teresa as a fantasy-building neurotic, passionately devoted to Our Lord but unable at times to distinguish between imaginative and objective reality. May I add that it is no lack of reverence for the mystics, or failure in gratitude for the favours shown by God to His creatures, which dictates this persistence in criticism. It is rather the belief that if there is one fact certainly established by psychological medicine it is this – the hysterical neurotic is a dangerous type of worship. Their faults are as infectious as

314

smallpox. If they can give their thoughts to God, so much the better, but that is no reason why we should be asked to admire and imitate their personalities or why we should be invited to regard pathological symptoms as evidence of sanctity."

Actually, even if it were proved that the startling mystical phenomena in Teresa's life were due to some form of hysteria, this would by no means necessarily prove a bar to beatification,

The Jesuit father, J.S. Cammack, writing from Heythrop College, Chipping Norton, Oxon, authoritatively pronounced, in January 22nd, 1938's *Tablet*: "The correspondence on this subject, has produced only two important points, and they are now in danger of being obscured by irrelevant matter. (1). It has been objected that Teresa Higginson was a psycho-neurotic, and consequently not a fit subject for beatification. (2). That the evidence to support this contention is being disregarded or minimized by the Diocesan Commission.

(1) Your correspondents who make the first objection seem to be confusing essential sanctity and the accidental phenomena which may accompany it. That this distinction must be made is clear from the Decree of Beatification of Blessed Gemma Galgani, which stated that the heroicity of her virtue was fully proved, but added: 'without any judgment being given as to the preternatural endowments of the said Servant of God' (*Acta Apostolicæ Sedis*, Vol.24, p.57). Therefore, even if it were proved that the startling mystical phenomena in Teresa's life were due to some form of hysteria, this would be no obstacle to her beatification if it were proved that her life showed the practice of the theological and moral virtues in an heroic degree.

(2) The question whether she did so practise these virtues is purely a matter of human testimony which must be judged by the ordinary rules of evidence, and we are told that this evidence has been collected and sifted by a commission which has been at work for some years. It is sufficient to indicate the articles in

The Month, January, 1925, and September, 1933; *Nouvelle Révue Théologique*, November, 1936 (p.1088); *Révue d'Histoire Ecclésiastique*, 1936, (p.447, sqq); *Etudes*, 1927 (p.474, sqq). This last article contains a masterly analysis of the problem, by Fr. De La Taille. He admits that the Devil's advocate has 'a strong hand to play'; but he decides that there are many illusions in the life, and some mysteries; but he decides that the theology is orthodox and that there is abundant evidence of heroic virtue. His conclusion restates the essential distinction made in the second paragraph of this letter, namely, that this life shows us *"le spectacle de ce que peut la grâce de Jésus-Christ dans une nature non soustraite aux effets, même pathologiques du péché originel.'*

Father C.C. Martindale, S.J., of Mount Street, London, W.1., observes in that same number of *The Tablet*,[33] "In the discussion about Miss Higginson, has there not been a tendency to suggest that she was *either* a neurotic *or* a saint: and, if a saint, that *therefore* all her alleged mystical experiences were supernatural or at least directly connected with her sanctity? Words like 'neurotic', 'hysterical' have not yet found a definition in which all agree: but none of them (I think) need connote anything 'moral' at all. We can, then, imagine a neurotic, anæmic, or hysterical Saint. Indeed, would not a man who heroically controlled a neurotic physique, be more of a hero than one whose stolid temperament provided him with no special material for control? I cannot remember that this discussion has distinguished accurately between ecstasy; the 'penumbra' of ecstasy; and, what happens when the ecstasy is definitely over and when its subject (its 'victim' St John of the Cross would hardly have hesitated to say) has to explain his memories: (1) to himself, (2) to others. By 'penumbra,' I mean the state in which the supernatural onslaught is over, and in which the normal consciousness is endeavouring to reassert itself: in such an hour, the Gift of God and the *voyant's* ideas about it, are apt to fuse, and mistakes are easily made. St Teresa said that sometimes she could so little recapture her ecstasies that it seemed to her that she had not even had one: still less could she state to herself by means of ideas, let alone of words, what had been its contents. But when an ecstatic *must* try to explain to *others* what has happened, words of some sort *must* be used."

Letitia Fairfield in *The Tablet* of February 12th, 1938: "We now have the important admission [in Mgr. O'Brien's information about the Process in the Cause of Teresa Higginson printed in *The Tablet* of February 5th, 1938] that no medical opinion was sought by those engaged in the Process. The reason why it was not sought is even more important, namely: 'As the Diocesan Process is only *informative*, that is, for the collection of facts, it is no part of the Commission's work to formulate opinion or to seek medical or technical advice on the evidence submitted.'"

Back in the January 29th, 1938, issue of *The Tablet*, Father Thurston had revealed himself as an enemy to the Cause, when he wrote: "There is a general and ever-growing desire to see Teresa Higginson beatified. No doubt Catholic schoolteachers as a body, and the people of Bootle, and a considerable number of good Lancashire folk are very keen about her cause. They would like to have a canonized saint of their very own, and they have made their voices heard. But the present discussion has, at least, done one thing. It has shown that among neurologists in particular, as well as among the *pars major et sanior* of the medical profession, not to speak of many other educated Catholics, the type of mystic represented by Teresa Higginson is regarded with grave distrust. Few of those who have now come for the first time to acquaint themselves with the alleged facts of her life, have been favourably impressed, and this adverse judgment is a matter of some importance. ... A decree of beatification is in its essence a concession made in response to a popular appeal, which is usually reinforced by renewed

317

allegations that the fame of the Servant of God is every day spreading, and that all are eagerly awaiting a favourable verdict. I submit that, in the light of the present correspondence, petitions cannot any longer be drafted in this sense without misrepresenting the facts."

Screened behind the, literally, *nom de guerre*, "A Vice-Postulator," and explaining – or excusing – the virulence of his attack, in *The Tablet*, February 19th, 1938, by the prefatory statement that it was in "accordance with Canon 2023, which requires that all Christians, whether asked or not, are bound to bring to the notice of the Church those things which seem to them to tell against the virtue or miracles of the Servant of God," that he wished to "add my protest to that of Fr. H. Thurston, S.J., against the Cause of Teresa Higginson."

It is "A Vice-Postulator's" opinion that the whole structure of Teresa Higginson's spiritual life "seems to be based on imagination. We are told on page 17 of the larger life: [Cecil Kerr's *Teresa Helena Higginson.*] 'One of the lessons their mother (a convert) impressed most deeply upon their young minds was the practice of the presence of God. She would *bid them picture Our Lord as standing always at their side*, and Teresa told a priest in her last illness what consolation this had brought her throughout her life. '*I had but to put out my hand to find it ever in His,*' she said." Coupling this statement with what she says of herself on pages 18 and 19: 'I was very headstrong, and almost always contrived to get my own way. … I would not rest until I had achieved my point … and invariably I got what I wanted," shows us how her habitual strong effort to imagine Our Lord near her, produced the 'image,' with its consolation, and that image was taken to be the truth. Whence, also, probably flowed her supposed visions, ecstasies, bilocations and the rest; for, had she not been told by various priests that she was a child of promise, a little apostle, to become a great saint or a great sinner; and had not her father and

318

mother sighed and wept over her? (pp.17,18)."

He sees as theologically questionable the devotion to the Sacred Head as "Seat of Divine Wisdom", and what strikes him as worse is her ascription of that devotion to Our Lord Himself. He quotes: "On page 105 we read: 'I understood that our dear Blessed Lord wished His Sacred Head to be specially worshipped as the "Seat of Divine Wisdom" *and* the powers of His Human Soul adored therein, as it is the seat of the intellectual powers of man.' The "Vice-Postulator" comments: "The 'Seat of Divine Wisdom' is *not* the human head of the God-Man, but His Divine Nature which is the Godhead. The human head of Our Lord may be the seat of His human soul, for all we know, with its intellectual powers. A decree of the Holy Office, May 4th-5th, 1892 (A.S.S. 25, 749), forbids the direct and special cult of the Holy Face, except indirectly as a reminder of the Sacred Passion."

Similarly to Father Thurston, our "Vice-Postulator" deplores the curses which Teresa "fulminates against those who do not accept her devotion," and observes that they are "certainly in violent contrast with Our Lord's gentle ways in dealing with obdurate Jews and hot-headed disciples: 'You know not whose Spirit you are of.' See St John ch. vi, vv. 52-65, when they strove against His promise of the Eucharist."

Neither is he impressed by the accounts of her "so-called bilocations." They have "no trace of that 'local colouring' and those 'minute details' of which we make so much in proving the genuineness of the Holy Gospels: which shows that they are the product of Teresa's effort to imagine. They also show her low grade or deficiency, for our school children, were they asked to imagine themselves missioners among blacks, would produce something better than, for example, this: 'It is now four years since I first visited these people and they were stricken down by a sickness which turned their bodies purple and black, and of which many of them died; then did I all I could to relieve their bodily suffering, and I was instructed to gather some bark off a tree which grew commonly there, and make a beverage for them, and which I understand they call bitter waters and waters of life.'"

Finally, with regard to Teresa's miracles: "The following incident narrated to me seventeen years ago by the nun herself, who is still alive, is instructive. There was a trunk on the ground floor of the convent at X, and the nun begged Teresa to get the key from upstairs. Teresa started making signs of the Cross over the trunk and shaking it to see if it would open; when she had made the sixth sign of the Cross in vain, the nun got impatient and bade her go and fetch the key at once."

The Vice-Postulator's last point is that beatifications and canonisations are not intended to elicit an infallible utterance as to whether that person is in heaven or otherwise; but to set up a model of some particular virtue specially needed at the time, and a patron to some particular class of people. What, he demands, is Teresa supposed to be the model of, and for whom?

Another destructive voice of sound and fury (*The Tablet*, February 26th, 1938) was that of Dr F.M.R. Walshe: "It appears that the Diocesan Commission, though composed of men of judgment, in fact exercised no judicial functions. It produced neither 'findings' nor 'a case.' It merely passed to Rome the raw material of both, leaving it to the relevant authority there to make what sense it can of this. There is still no evidence to show that any judicial enquiry has ever been made of a kind necessary to establish a '*prima facie* case' for the reference of the Cause to Rome. Now Teresa was a school teacher, and it cannot be said she was a model one. She was thoroughly undependable, was frequently absent from her class, forced others to be absent also, and was a hindrance to her colleagues in the discharge of their high responsibilities to the children committed to their care. In a letter which did not appear in the 'Life', the lady who deputised for Teresa at Chudleigh writes: 'One thing I could never understand, she used so often to whip the children, and as for the report of the Religious Inspector, it was so bad that Fr. Dowsett told me he stuck it in the fire, they just knew scarce anything of their catechism.'

The lady whose letter did not appear in Cecil Kerr's *Life*, and who claimed to have "deputised for Teresa at Chudleigh", casts the only such aspersions in Teresa Higginson, and in this context, Sister Mary Francis of Assisi, the estwhile Nurse Casey, wrote, on March 11th, 1938, to Sister Albania: "During Teresa's last illness, no teacher replaced her. The school was closed. I can assure you from what I know from personal observations of Teresa Higginson, whipping was not her method of correction. It was so foreign to her nature. I could not imagine her doing such a thing. It is a base lie, and whoever said it resmbles their father, the Devil, who is the father of lies. She could be very firm with the children, and I have heard her. She could correct their faults with a look. I remember there was a mother who had three unruly boys; and seeing Miss Higginson so frail and delicate, she wondered how she would be able to manage them. A look sufficed! Regarding what has been said about her harsh treatment of children, I answer that it was not in her nature to be harsh to anyone, and especially to little children, whom she loved as a tender mother. Also, she was too humble to be harsh, and I never saw the least shadow of harshness in her."

In brief, Teresa was a teacher whom no Catholic school manager would today dare to employ. Of her writings we know that she was the frequent recipient from Canon Snow of letters in which, as he tells us, he was preparing her for the Mystic Union. It is clear also, despite unfounded statements to the contrary, that she had read religious works of various kinds. Passages from these are scattered freely and inconsequently through her letters, and fragments of St Teresa, of Bossuet[34] and of the Bible have been identified, though they appear ostensibly as her own composition. In short, her letters are a patchwork quilt of passages 'cribbed' from different sources, fictions of her own – often flatly contradictory of one another, and of passages of pure jargon devoid of sense. In such a rigmarole it would indeed be remarkable if here and there we did not find scraps of 'sound theology', but what is true in her letters is not new, and what's new isn't true. In short, nothing remains upon which a claim to sanctity can be based."

Walshe believed that in writing thus, he was fulfilling a duty, fighting for rational religion as against miraculism, for faith as against credulity.

It is perhaps legitimate to set against this the testimony of one who knew Teresa, spiritually, better than anyone else in the world – Canon Snow, who had, for more than twenty years, been her spiritual adviser. His opinion, forthright, unshakeable, and, to the last, unshaken, was: "I think it right to say that I have the firm conviction that Teresa was not only a saint but also one of the greatest saints almighty God has ever raised up in His Church."

This is what the Canon had to say: " I became her director in September, 1883, hearing her confession for the first time on the 14th day of that month. At this time she was in that degree of union known as the Mystical Espousal. This took place, as she describes in Letter No.39, on the feast of the Sacred Heart, 1874. In this degree the soul is being prepared for the Mystical Marriage and this took place on 24th October, 1887. Teresa lived 17 years and nearly four months after the Mystical Marriage."

The Canon points out that she was essentially a contemplative and not an active saint. She never did any great outward work. She was always weak and feeble and suffered without ceasing. Both he and Father Powell had expected that great miracles would take place in proof of the Devotion (to the Sacred Head) and her own sanctity. "In any place in which she stayed many interesting and edifying incidents took place, such as what I may call little miracles and miraculous answers to prayer, and these would be known only to a few, and they kept the knowledge to themselves."

As her years mounted, so did this aspect of her life diminish. The little miracles became less and less frequent. The ecstasies, which at one time seemed to be almost continuous, grew progressively fewer. Towards the end of her life, the visible marvels had to all intents and purposes practically ceased. What remained were the wonderful revelations of her soul, preserved for all time in the letters which she wrote in obedience to her spiritual directors – Fathers Powell and Snow. These, Canon Snow conscientiously treasured, and squirrelled away for posterity most carefully. Often ill-spelt, not infrequently grammatically dubious, erratically punctuated, scrawled in a hurried chierography resembling the scutterings of a demented spider across the paper, the letters are, so far as their form is concerned, scarcely cultural icons, but their content is quite amazing. Examined and studied by priests and scholars learned in mystical theology, they have been almost unanimously hailed as exhibiting a knowledge and understanding of the most abstruse theological subjects that lay well beyond the bounds of her religious education and must surely be the gift of divine inspiration.

A Jesuitical death knell was sounded by the Reverend Herbert Thurston writing in the pages of *The Tablet* on March 12th, 1938.

"Teresa, as I hold, did suffer from delusions. There are a few rare cases of alleged bilocation in the approved *Lives of the Saints.* But, so far as my knowledge of hagiography serves me, there is not one which compares for a moment with Teresa's visits to Africa, continued for four years together, during which she baptized the people of Ja-am-pu-da and healed their diseases, etc. … But if Teresa was deluded in this way, why may she not have been deluded in the revelations concerning the Sacred Head, which occur as a kind of refrain in almost all her later letters? This new cult, she tells us, is to be 'the one great means of the conversion of poor dear England at a time not far distant.' This was in 1881. If Teresa's champions were content to claim for her such phenomena as stigmata, levitation, etc., I quite agree that the report of such occurrences, even if explainable by her pathological condition, do not prejudice the evidence presented that she was a woman of saintly life. But if her veracity is in question, we do not know where we stand; and I, for one, think that even if her personal holiness were ten times as clearly established as it is, she labours under a suspicion of delusion which, in view of the anti-Catholic prejudice rampant in a country like ours, renders her canonization inexpedient and undesirable."

NOTES

31 Dr Fairfield's own accuracy comes under fire here. The name given by Teresa is "Jaaampuda."

32 An unfortunate inaccuracy! This should surely be Father Powell.

33 January 22nd, 1938.

34 Jacques-Bénigne Bossuet (1627-1704). French theologian. Made his reputation as a pulpit-orator: 1669, consecrated Bishop of Condom and became tutor to the dauphin: 1681, appointed Bishop of Meaux. Author of Discours sur l'histoire universelle (1681), interpreting human history in the light of divine providence.

15

SUMMARIUM

In 1908 – exactly a hundred years ago as I write – an old monk in Rome set out to follow in Teresa Higginson's footsteps. He was to become her first biographer. His name was Dom Adalbert, and behind him lay a chequered history.

Born Adalbert M. O'Sullivan, in Kilkenny in 1833, he had entered the Benedictine Order. He was professed at Subiaco, in the Latrium province of central Italy, some 32 miles east of Rome, where was the monastery of San Benedetto, founded by St Benedict of Nursia, and made master of novices there. He then came to England, before going back to Ireland, where he created a foundation at Leopardstown, just south of Dublin. He remained there until 1867, when the foundation failed and had to be sold. Thereafter, he occupied for four years an administrative position in the Order, before, in 1880, being appointed Superior of a foundation in New Zealand. Ten years later, this commission ended, he returned to England. The administrative part of his life having proved scarcely successful, and not sorry that it was over, he retired in 1890, determined to devote the rest of his days to writing and hagiography. He lived mostly as chaplain to the nuns at Newton Abbot, and pursued vigorous research into the lives of many persons of reputed holiness, including that of the Tuscan woman, Gemma Galgani (1878-1903). Her mystical life was in many respects similar to that of Teresa Higginson. She was constantly aware of the presence of God. She was subjected to extreme physical and psychical phenomena. She exhibited the

64. *Dom Adalbert M. O'Sullivan,*
Teresa's first biographer.

stigmata. Sometimes, too, her body bore the marks of Christ's scourging at the pillar. Blasphemous language could cause her to sweat blood. She went into visionary trances, during which she could be heard conversing with those whom she was seeing. Like Teresa, she was plagued by the Devil. Unlike Teresa, she displayed signs of diabolic possession, causing her on one occasion to spit on a crucifix. After a life of heroic suffering, borne with exemplary submission and sanctity, she died of tuberculosis at the age of twenty-five. She left a bundle of more than 230 revelatory letters, which she had addressed to her spiritual director and her confessor. She was beatified in 1933, and canonised in 1940.

Prior to a briefing which was now given to him, Father

Adalbert O'Sullivan had never so much as heard of Teresa Higginson, but, with the curious resemblance between the two women in the forefront of his mind, and having been asked by Rome to go home to England and see what tidings of Teresa he could gather, Dom Adalbert spent the next fifteen industrious years following up conscientiously, obsessively even, every clue, until he had amassed a formidable garnering of minute, well-authenticated material. Then, he sat down and wrote what he modestly subtitled "a memoir" of Teresa Higginson, Servant of God. It was published in 1924.

Dom Adalbert died in 1930, at the age of ninety-six. He was said to be at that time the oldest monk in the Benedictine Order.

Uncrooked, the long arm of coincidence not infrequently flexes in the literary life; while Dom Adalbert was putting the finishing touches to his book, Lady Anne Cecil Kerr [Lady Anne Cecil Kerr, born June 30th, 1883, died, unmarried, August 9th, 1941, was the daughter of Major General Ralph Drury Kerr, son of John William Robert Kerr, the 7th Marquess of Lothian, and Lady Anne Fitzalan-Howard.] was busily beavering away at her much more extensive volume, dealing with Teresa's life and letters.

Actually, Father O'Sullivan had, in the course of his questing peregrinations made his way up to Edinburgh in order to see Lady Anne's mother, who had known Teresa. "How often," exclaimed that lady, "have I wondered when we should hear of her again!" She then proceeded to relay to him all that the Reverend Mother of St Catherine's Convent, who was a great friend, had confided to her of the saintly little woman who had come to stay with them. Lady Anne's mother would, on her regular visits to the convent, often bump into Teresa in the passages, and would ask for her prayers.

Lady Anne remembered: "One day Reverend Mother called my mother into the chapel. 'Look,' she said, 'you can see Miss Higginson praying.' My mother always recalled the expression on Teresa's face, completely rapt as she was in prayer, with a strange sort of glow shining round her forehead."

It was only when she was a very small child that Lady Anne Cecil Kerr herself had any contact with Teresa, and her sole memory was of a little old lady dressed in black, who used to give her holy pictures.

She said: "A little later we went to Ireland, and when we returned, Teresa had left the convent and my mother lost all trace of her. But she never forgot her or the impression of radiant sanctity which seemed to emanate from her. Meanwhile, the years had passed and, apart from a few chosen friends who cherished her memory, she had been utterly forgotten."

Teresa Helena Higginson: Servant of God: "The Spouse of the Crucified, 1844-1905, by Cecil Kerr, was brought out by the London publishers, Sands, in 1927, the same publishers who, three years before, had issued the Reverend A.M. O'Sullivan, O.S.B.'s *Teresa Higginson: The Servant of God: School Teacher, 1845-1905: A Memoir* – which, incidentally, wrongly assigned her birth to the year 1845.

Kerr's critical reception was mixed, but an edition published later in French translation reviewed in *Nouvelle Revue Théologique*, November, 1936, p.1088, by the Louvain professor, M.C. Boúváaert, received a mauling. "The critical faculty, even the orthodoxy, of Teresa's spiritual directors was queried. A tendency to materialise and make unhealthy use of gifts spiritual and truths of faith was noted. Plagiarism from St Margaret Mary was suspected in some of the writings, and the ultimate indignity was that everything rested upon female evidence." ["Teresa Helena Higginson (1844-1905): A Bibliography." B. Plumb. *North West Catholic History. No.18. 1991.* pp.40-45.]

These were the two pioneer biographies. Six further publications must be noted. In 1934, the Reverend F.W. Kershaw, the editor of *The Harvest*, wrote, at the express invitation of the

Salford Teachers' Guild, *Teresa Helena Higginson: A Short Account of her Life and Letters*, published by Sands, London. The little 46-page pamphlet was of great value in that it provided the ordinary lay reader with a lucid explanation of mystical theology – ascesis, and thaumaturgics, Mystical Espousals and Mystical Marriage. In 1937, *Letters of Teresa Higginson*, Selected and Discussed by A Monk of St Augustine's Abbey, Ramsgate, was published, again by Sands. *Une grande Inconnue ou Les merveilles d'une simple vie*, is the title of a 94-page booklet published by Editions de 'Sagesse' Bellevue – Cagnotte (Landes), in 1953, and, in 1986, Brian Honnor was responsible for a privately printed 63-page booklet, *Appreciations of Teresa Helena Higginson: School Teacher & Mystic*. The fifth, was a 52-page booklet, *Teresa Helena Higginson: Servant of God*, Ann Pitts and Sister Mary Dolores. Sixth, and finally, there appeared, privately printed in 1987, *By God's Command: The Amazing Supernatural Life of Teresa Helena Higginson, Stigmatic. Servant of God*, Bernadette F.G. Hurndall.

It was in a letter to Miss Ann Pitts, in 1986, thanking her for the present of a copy of her and Sister Dolores' booklet, that Canon Francis J. Ripley, parish priest of the Church of St Oswald and St Edmund, at Ashton-in-Makerfield, provided a most interesting story that would seem to feature Teresa's revenant. I used often to encounter Father Ripley, as he then was, a lean, pink-faced, bespectacled leptomorph, who used to whizz round Liverpool on a bicycle, at the Liverpool branch of Burns, Oates, & Washbourne, then in Manchester Street, and a popular rendezvous in the 1930s and '40s for priests from all over the county, and from over the water – i.e. Cheshire and the Wirral – and where they could always be sure of a cup of tea and a cigarette with Mrs Derham, the manageress.

He told Miss Pitts: "Some years ago I gave a mission at the Church of the English Martyrs, in Whalley Range, Manchester.

Later, I returned to pay a visit and had a talk with Canon Murray. He said he wanted to tell me a story, because he did not wish to die without somebody else knowing it. I will tell it to you in his own words, as far as I can remember.

'I was a young priest at St Wilfred's, Hulme. One night I was just getting ready for bed about 11 o' clock when I heard a knock at the door. The housekeeper came and said that there was a sick call, a lady had come. So I asked her to find out if the sick person could receive the Blessed Sacrament. She came back and said she could, so I went to church, got the Blessed Sacrament, and the little lady was waiting for me. Without a word, she turned and led the way. I followed. After a while, I realised that I was going outside the parish, but as it was late I decided not to say anything. Eventually, after a long walk, she turned into a court, a cul-de-sac with three or four houses on each side, and two at the far end. She led me to the last house on the left-hand side, and stepped aside for me to go in. There was a sick person with the family gathered round. They left while I heard the sick person's confession. Then they returned, and I gave the invalid Holy Communion, and anointed him. I then left, and the lady went ahead of me again, never saying a word. At the end of the court was a gas-lamp, and in the light of it I read the name of the court and wrote it down in my diary. The lady led the way and eventually I found I was back in the parish, and so told her that I did not need her any more. She left me then. Next morning, I thought that it was my duty to notify the priest of the parish about the sick call. I thought it must be in the cathedral parish. I walked to the cathedral and told the parish priest there about what had happened. I took out my diary and there was the address. They said it was not in their parish. Eventually we found that it was in Failsworth, I took a cab to Failsworth and found that the address was in that parish and that they had been notified that a person had died there. Also that a priest had called, having been brought by a lady they did not know. Failsworth is several miles from Hulme. I was mystified by the whole experience. I could not possibly have been dreaming because the housekeeper had seen the lady at our door, and, there in my diary was the address of the court to which I had been called. A few moths later we had a meeting of priests addressed by Canon Snow. I told him about this incident. He asked me to describe the lady. I did, and he said at once that it was Teresa Higginson.'

About 1938, a year before my ordination, Canon Cartmel gave us a talk about Teresa. He said he found it difficult to support her cause for several reasons. One of them was that he had found in a letter of hers a statement that anybody who spoke against the cause would be punished by God. Next morning the procession was making its way into the chapel for Mass when Canon Cartmel was struck down by a mysterious pain. He could hardly move. As four worthy deacons were carrying him away, he was heard to remark: 'I have Teresa Higginson to thank for this.' He was a great friend of mine and I often used to go to see him when he became parish priest at St Mary's, Chorley. To his dying day, he maintained that that mysterious illness, which lasted about three weeks, came as a result of his telling the students about his objections to the cause of Teresa Higginson."

Over the years there has been a plenitude of workers in the Teresian vineyard. There were Mrs Helen Lonsdale's two daughters, Mrs Teresa Cottriall and Mrs Winifred Widdowson; both enormously energetic in their strivings. Most zealous assuredly was Miss Isabella Arkwright, of Ormside, 8 St Anne's Road, Aughton, Ormskirk, whose sister, Elizabeth, had, in 1902, gone as housekeeper to Canon Snow at Aughton, and remained with him until his death twenty years later. Miss Isabella met Teresa, who struck her as being "very natural, simple, homely and full of humour, with, however, a look that was very searching," on only one occasion, and they seem hardly to have conversed. But she knew personally many of Teresa's friends, and testified that "not one of them ever had the least doubt as to her sanctity." From the early 1920s until the time of her death in 1969, she was the self-appointed and most conscientious custodian and consultant in all things relating to Teresa. Described by Mrs McKeon as "forthright, prudent and kindly," other noble attributes, such as steadfast and self-effacing, might well be added. Like Teresa herself, and so many of the other witnesses in the case, she had been a teacher. On her retirement, she devoted her days to the furtherance of Teresa's Cause. She made it her business to persuade those who had known Teresa to set their testimony down on paper, and her home became The Teresa Higginson Repository, focal point for the garnering of all the material – correspondence, photographs, souvenirs, relics, and so forth – with regard to Teresa's life and activities, and a distribution centre for a literature of leaflets and pamphlets dealing with the case, which she had printed, and sent all over the world. She played a tireless, unique, and extremely significant part in the promotion of the cause for her beatification.

Kitty Deady (Sister Mary Evangelist) told Miss Arkwright that Louisa Higginson had given St Teresa's rosary beads to Margaret Murphy, who later gave them to her. Kitty lent them to Father Cobb – 'lent' them because of her vow of poverty, which meant that she could not *give* anything, as she had nothing of her own.

Miss Arkwright's cousin, Kitty Molyneux described the beads as: "mother-of-pearl 'Our Father', and carved brown wooden 'Hail Marys'." Those in Father Cobb's possession were exactly as thus described. Teresa had also a silver crucifix which had belonged to St Teresa. Kitty Deady said that it was a tubular crucifix.

The ultimate fate of the rosary seems somewhat bizarre. A Sister Mary Catherine, writing to Miss Catterall, from the Convent of Mary, Burngreave Road, Sheffield, on October 6th, 1930, reports: " Mrs Oxton – the Oxtons are Percy's marriage kin [Note: this is John Percy Jones, the son of William and Mary Ann *née* Higginson.] – gave Teresa's red beads to a gentleman – a Catholic at Neston – on condition he procured her a licence for a beer-shop, so they were sold for a licence – still, a Catholic has them."

Elizabeth Arkwright was Canon Snow's housekeeper for more than twenty years. Isabella wrote:

"In the year 1929, on Ascension Day, a public visit was being made to Clitheroe. It was on this particular day, while we, my sister and I, were having breakfast, that my sister, who was of a lively disposition, said to me very seriously and without looking up, 'I had a lovely dream last night.' I felt that it was in connection with Teresa in some way or other. I asked her what it was, and this is what she recounted to me.

'I dreamt Teresa came to me last night, but she was as real to me as you sitting there.' 'What did she do?' I asked. My sister replied, 'She embraced me and kissed me, and said, "Oh! I *am* glad to see you." Thinking this was in the wrong order, I said, 'You mean you were glad to see Teresa.' 'No,' she answered, 'Teresa said she was glad to see me.' I thought there was but one place where my sister could see Teresa. I then asked her, 'Were you not afraid when you felt her so real?' 'Oh no,' she answered, 'I was intensely happy, but when she went away I felt the whole world had gone to pieces.'

During the following days my sister seemed to be present in body only, but not in mind. On the Tuesday night following Ascension Day, I came in from an official ceremony. We knelt down, as was our custom, to say the rosary and other prayers which we said in common. At the end, I heard my sister say quietly, 'Agonising Heart of Jesus, have pity on the dying.' This she repeated three times. Now this was not a prayer we said together. On rising, I teased her and said, 'You were well away, were you not?' but I received no answer. She then very abruptly retired to her room. The following morning I found her dead in bed – six days after Teresa's 'visit.'

I discovered later that she had put all her papers etc. in order on the Monday before her death. From the morning of her 'dream' to the day she died, I got 'flashes' of the most beautiful smell of flowers, which seemed to pervade the surrounding air. In the afternoon of the day before her death, I was standing before my class when the air around me became permeated with the same fragrance. That same evening on returning home I got the beautiful smell on entering the living room. I called to my sister to come and inhale it as I was doing, but she did not come. When giving an account to me of Teresa's visit, my sister called it a dream, but to a friend she said, 'I have seen Teresa Higginson, she was exquisite.'"

After Miss Arkwright's death, the keepers of the flame were Tony and Gladys Moreton, whose Aughton Street home, in Ormskirk, was rapidly transformed into an overflowing archival centre.

One by one, inexorably, the deaths and exits were punctuating the onflow of the years. Canon John Constant Mussely, aged 68, in 1910. Canon Alfred Snow, aged 77, in 1922. Margaret Murphy, aged 74, in 1925. Louisa Agnes Higginson, aged 80, in 1927. Mary (Minnie) Catterall, aged 75, in 1934. She had ended her teaching career as headmistress of Holy Cross School, in Liverpool, and had retired to Wigan. Kitty Deady, aged 63, in 1938. Alfred Leo Garnett, aged 77, in 1940. Helen Lonsdale, aged 73, in 1940. Susan Ryland, aged 88, in 1941. Lady Anne Cecil Kerr, aged 58, in 1941. William Lonsdale, aged 87, in 1953. Isabella Arkwright, aged 86, in 1969. Nurse Agnes Casey, aged 91, in 1963. Tony Moreton, aged 82, in 2004.

65. Anthony and Gladys Moreton, loyal workers in the Cause, tending Teresa's grave.

Frances Jane (Fanny) Higginson died, aged seventy, on February 16th, 1916. She is buried at Neston, in the same grave as Louisa and John Percy Jones.

The Reverend Father John David Ryan, parish priest of St Winefride's, Neston, in whose churchyard Louisa Higginson was laid to rest, on December 7th, 1927, in a grave beside that of Teresa, wrote a tribute to her life and work in the *Mount Pleasant College magazine*. Louisa had been a student there in 1867-1868. After referring to her "sublime humility, alluring simplicity, and her Christ-like charity," he had this to say of her: "She died as she lived, poor in all this world's goods, but rich in the goods of heaven. Between school hours, after the school was closed for the day, she was a ministering angel among the poor, visiting, cooking their

66. Miss Isabella Arkwright of Ormskirk.
The Great Promoter of Teresa's cause for
more than forty years.

meals, cleaning their rooms, feeding and comforting and cheering them. This testimony reminds us of a remark made by Sister Mary Joseph, more than twenty years ago when someone spoke to her of the sanctity of the late Teresa Higginson. Sister said: 'I did not know Teresa, but I do know that Louisa is a saint.'"

Father Ryan had, as a matter of fact, originally been antagonistic to Teresa Higginson and her Cause, and annoyed when people came to her grave. He had regarded her as an hysterical woman, until ... one evening he had walked out of the presbytery and, happening to look at the back of the little school-house where Teresa used to live, clearly saw before his astonished eyes, floating over the entrance door, a chalice. It seemed to hover there for a few seconds, then disappeared. He was positive that it was a sign from Heaven to tell him that he was wrong about Teresa, and thereafter became her most enthusiastic devotee.

With the retirement of Louisa from teaching, the Higginson family's occupation, of nigh on forty years, of St Winefride's Cottage, the school-house at Neston, had come to an end. By 1927, she was living at No.26 Claremount Road, Wallasey, and it was from there that, on March 20th, 1927, she wrote the following slightly curious letter to Lady Anne Cecil Kerr.

> Dear Miss Cecil.
> Received Memoir on Friday. I am grateful. It must have taken up a great amount of your time. So many things told in it that never happened to Teresa. She must have imagined it. I always pray for you and your eldest brother – and shall be able to do so now as I am getting stronger and shall be able to hear daily Mass again.
> It does not take long to reach America. I shall pray fervently and often. Kind regards to her Ladyship and gratitude from
> Your sincere well-wisher,
> Louisa Higginson.

That Louisa's days were moving towards their close in rather threadbare mode seems suggested by a letter written by her on June 21st, 1927, from Wallasey, and headed "St Aloysius", to Sister Gertrude, at The Convent of Notre Dame, Clapham Common, London, S.W.4.

She writes: "You will think that I have forgotten you, but on Sunday, when I usually write, I have been so busy in the church. We have such beautiful services here. Now I can only attend the morning ones. I am too tired to go out after dinner – I always feel so tired now. ... I was before 'The Enquiry' last week (Corpus Christi). I arrived at the Archbishop's about

10.30 a.m. Dr O'Brien met me with his motor at the Liverpool Landing Stage. I never should have found it, although I always thought I knew Liverpool well. Bishop Dobson, Dr McCurdy and Father Finnessey held it. I only had to answer questions. I was very weary. I had an interview with His Grace. He came and sat with me while having a cup of tea and chatted quite homely. I arrived home about three o'clock. He went with me to the [Landing] Stage in a lovely motor, accompanied by Father Finnesey. Everyone was most kind. Miss Catterall was over this afternoon. We go out to a confectioner's and have tea and a long chat. Pray for her, she is the next to go before the 'Enquiry' and she seems very nervous. She is very kind to me. I am becoming terrible blind. I cannot see with either set of spectacles. I will get Father Fisher to write me a note and go here to the Central Hospital, where an eye specialist attends on certain days and only charges £1 or 10/- for all (testing and specs). I paid over £3 at the last time, but he was only an optician. A gentleman at Neston gave me the fee. I don't think Teresa was more than twice at Notre Dame. What tales are out. Thanksgiving every evening in the *Daily Post* and *Echo*, and I am told the grave is strewn with petitions. I think I am the only one who prays for her."

Louisa died on December 5th, 1927. She was eighty years of age.

In 1933, Our Lady was alleged to have appeared in a vision at Onkerzele, a village in the East Flanders region of Belgium, and asked for a pilgrimage to be made in honour of the Sacred Head. This was, in fact, the culmination of a series of miraculous appearances of the Virgin Mary which were reported from Belgium. The first of these Marian apparitions occurred in 1932 at the village of Beauraing, This vision – similar to that vouchsafed to 14-year-old Bernadette Soubirous in February, 1858, at the rock cave of Massabielle, beside the river Gave de

*67. Miss Elizabeth Arkwright, Isabella's
sister and Canon Snow's housekeeper
at St Mary's Church, Aughton.*

Pau, near Lourdes, in south west France – was seen in an artificial grotto to Our Lady of Lourdes, on November 29th, 1932. Then, between January 15th and March 2nd, 1933, an 11-year-old girl, Mariette Beco, had eight visions of the Virgin Mary at the village of Banneux. Finally, following the appearance of Our Lady at Onkerzele, the requested pilgrimage took place – on the day that had been prophesied by Teresa Higginson as the future feast day of the Sacred Head, and some 15,000 persons are said to have visited Onkerzele. Nine years later, on March 25th, 1942, during the German Occupation, Cardinal van Roey, Primate of Belgium, announced that, so far as the apparitions of Beauraing and Banneux were concerned, the Church's investigation was still in process under the aegis of the

68, 69. Louisa and Fanny share a burial place together with John Percy Jones in St Winefride's churchyard, Neston.

respectively responsible regional bishops, but the half dozen or so other manifestations, including those at Onkerzele, had been officially excluded.

The year 1989 saw what was surely a silly season disclosure – of the exhumation, fifty years before, of the body of Teresa Higginson at Neston churchyard. The divulger of this piece of esoterica was a Fairfield, Liverpool, resident, Edward Murphy, aged eighty-two. At the time of Teresa's alleged premature resurrection, Mr Murphy, like his father before him, was employed by a Liverpool firm of funeral directors, of Pembroke Place. Mr Murphy had not himself been actually involved in the proceedings – "It was on the list for 9 a.m. at Neston. I took it for granted that it was for Teresa Higginson, there was so much talk

about her at the time and so many pamphlets going around. I've never had any reason since to doubt that it was for her, and it's all as clear in my mind as if it were only last week." The exhumation enquiry was being handled by the firm's director, Joseph Maguire, and the Liverpool solicitor, John Taggart, but Murphy's information had come from the two workmen who went on the job with them, not from Maguire or Taggart. "About 2 p.m., the workmen came into the yard and I said to them, 'Is it finished then?' They said no, they'd come back for a new coffin. They said the original coffin had partially rotted at the foot and some water had got in. But they said the body was in 'perfect condition', and they were very astonished at this. I asked them next day how the enquiry went, and they said it finished about

70. Canon Snow.

5 p.m. The names of those on the enquiry and all the particulars were put in sealed bottles and placed back in the new coffin for when it was opened up again. They mentioned Mr Maguire and Mr Taggart being present and also a Devil's Advocate, but there could have been others."

Mr Murphy did not think that the workmen actually saw the body, or witnessed the enquiry, but picked up their information from those present. He guessed that the enquiry itself must have been held nearby, probably in the church or hall. The Maguire firm apparently dealt with a lot of church business. Mr Maguire had a brother who was a priest and a sister who was a nun. He himself was in the Knights of St Columbus, as indeed was Murphy, and Maguire often gave him Catholic Truth Society

*71. Miss Minnie Catterall in the
time of her maturity.*

pamphlets. "That's why," said Murphy, "I was very surprised he never ever mentioned anything to me about the exhumation and in those days you kept your place and didn't ask the boss questions. I fact, there was an air of apathy about the whole thing which I could never understand, as if they'd done something they shouldn't have. That was the last I heard about it, but no one ever told me to keep quiet about it."

Enquiry at the Home Office, whose permission would have been necessary for the carrying out of an exhumation, has yielded no confirmation that it gave any such authorisation. Virginia Bowes, a professional historian and a founder member of the North West Catholic History Society, who had lived in the Neston parish of St Winefride's since childhood, said that she

72. Onkerzele. The chapel at the site of the Marian vision of 1933.

had never heard mention of any event of that kind, neither could she find any reference in parish records to its having taken place. She commented: "I think one can safely say that nothing like that could have been hidden in this parish. Anything unusual would have been spotted. Even in the Neston of the 1920s, there was a sizeable population, and the parish was alive from six o'clock in the morning with workmen on their bikes. I just wonder whether people have got confused with another incident that occurred on a date after 1906 in the graveyard and quite near where Teresa Higginson is buried. A young Spanish man from Raby[35] died of tuberculosis and was buried in a lead coffin. It was taken up a year or so later by his relatives for re-burial in Spain. But the coffin was never opened."

344

Another suggested possibility is that Teresa Higginson's identity is being substituted for that of a nun in Upton, whose body, it is said, was exhumed about the same time.

Invited by Mrs Gladys Moreton to sign a declaration as to the authenticity of his statement, Edward Murphy declined.

Teresa's name was back in the public arena again following the death, in 1999, of Susan Ryland's great-nephew, Father Gordon Dick, at the age of ninety-two, for it was she who had prophesied his vocation to the priesthood. An ailing child, Gordon Dick was brought up by his grandmother in Liverpool, where the air was thought to be better than that of the industrial midlands which had been his birthplace. In his teens, he developed an inexplicable overnight desire to become a priest, but at the time the seminaries were over full with candidates, and he was turned down by them all as being, at the age of twenty, too old, and, additionally, too delicate in health. He persisted, however, and thanks to his great-aunt, Sister Barbara, was finally accepted by the Order of the Sacred Heart of Betharram, whose mother house was at Betharram, near Lourdes, where he studied for three years before being ordained on July 9th, 1939, by the Patriarch of Jerusalem. During his sixty years as a priest, he spent twenty-one of them as an army chaplain. He was still working, unofficially, at the age of eighty-two for the Liverpool parish of St Cecilia's, Tuebrook. As the only priest in the family, he was convinced that he had fulfilled Teresa's prophecy, and he used to pray to her and visit her grave at Neston.

And finally, all those who have a genuine interest in Teresa Higginson, who desire to delve more deeply into her theology, to discover the details of her very personal thoughts, what she believed, and what she had to say, owe an immense debt of gratitude to Michael Hutchings, who undertook the daunting task of copying, sorting out, arranging in date sequence, and having bound up in twelve volumes, the collected letters of Teresa Higginson – which, in conjunction with other amassed material concerning her life and mission, amount to approximately 6000 pages – a set of which, in the year 2000, he deposited in the British Library. Many of the original letters are still preserved at the Benedictine Abbey of St Augustine, at Ramsgate, in Kent.

A veritable treasure trove for the convinced and sceptic alike.

NOTE
35 A Cheshire village 2 miles north east of Neston station.

16

DILATA

For reasons which the reader of this book will well appreciate, for Teresa Higginson the brambled path to Rome has been neither straight nor free of stumbling-stones. Her Cause had been taken thither by the Archdiocese of Liverpool in the early 1930s. The preliminary work of collecting the testimonies of witnesses was carried out by the Liverpool Diocesan Tribunal, instituting the informative process, and one of the first to be summoned before that body as a major witness was, the former Nurse Agnes Casey, who had since become Sister Mary Francis, and was resident in the Poor Clare Covent, at Lynton, in Devonshire.

"One morning before 9 a.m.," she recounted, "the parlour bell rang, and our extern sister said to the portress that six priests had just arrived and wished to speak to me, so the sister came up and told our dear Reverend Mother Guardian Angel, who was Abbess then. She died in 1942, and it was some years before her death that these priests paid me this honourable visit. Well, dear Reverend Mother came down with me to the parlour, but Monsignor O'Brien, who was the Vice-Postulator of the Cause of Teresa Helena Higginson, kindly asked Reverend Mother to withdraw, as they wished to speak to me alone, so poor Reverend Mother bowed in silence and went away.

Then, Monsignor O'Brien put the Holy Bible before me and told me to take it in my hands and make a most solemn oath that what I said with regard to the Servant of God, Teresa Higginson, was the truth. You see, when anyone is giving their testimony of anyone who may eventually be raised to the altars, how very

73. Monsignor John O'Brien, centre of the front row, Vice-Postulator of the Cause of Teresa Higginson.

careful one has to be not to be governed in any way by mere natural enthusiasm, only to say the exact truth. You can imagine it was a very solemn ordeal for me, but I am sure holy Teresa was praying for me, for I felt very calm, and stood my guard (as we say) in spite of the Devil's advocate being there trying to trip me up at every moment. But I seemed to ignore his presence and thought only of the work before me.

Next to the Devil's advocate was a Doctor of Divinity, who was very kind to me, then Monsignor O'Brien, who was ever so fatherly, then three other priests, most of them writing down what I said. After this ordeal, which lasted for four hours, was over, I said to Monsignor O'Brien, I was so anxious not to make any mistake that I was afraid I may have said *less* than more, and

74. *Margaret Murphy getting on in years.*

he replied, 'My dear child, you have done very well indeed, and I am quite satisfied. So don't worry, but if anything should occur to you after we have gone, something you may have forgotten, just write it down and send it to me.' So I did, and often wrote to him as time went on.

Well now, before I left the parlour Monsignor O'Brien and all the priests put me under a most solemn obedience not to say one word to our dear Reverend Mother, or to any member of our community, or to anyone, which included, of course, any priest or religious elsewhere, and I promised absolute obedience, but you can understand what this silence cost me, not to say one word to our dear Reverend Mother of what had been said during this long interview, but our dear Lord gave me the grace to obey."

Margaret Murphy gave her evidence in Liverpool. She delivered it with diffident sincerity. A friend verified that Margaret had said several times that she had seen Teresa receiving Holy Communion miraculously. She had said, too, that when Teresa was going without food and drink, she had seen tea actually disappearing from her cup. Margaret went to Teresa's funeral, and they offered to open the coffin for her so that she could take a last look at her well-loved friend, but she thanked them and declined. She always felt, she said, that Teresa had given her life so that the mortally sick Kitty Deady might live. After Teresa's death, Margaret used to see her in dreams that were vivid and real and always betokened the imminent arrival of crosses to be borne. In the end, she asked Teresa not to come again. "I will not come until your last illness," replied Teresa. She kept her word. It was, according to Margaret, after a last dream of Teresa that she succumbed to her final illness. Throughout the years, she kept a photograph of Teresa – a smiling image of her taken in the garden at Chudleigh, holding a spray of flowers – on the mantelpiece. A priest who visited her in her old age commiserated with her on the long hours of enforced idleness she had to endure. She smiled brightly, and, turning to Teresa's photograph, told him, "I talk to her and she talks to me." When, in 1925, Margaret died, a friend of hers loyally carried out her last wishes, burning all the letters which she had received from Teresa and a lock of her hair. This irrevocably destructive rearguard action was dictated by reasons of reverence and fear that such treasured items might fall into the wrong hands.

On March 1st, 1932, Monsignor O'Brien wrote to a nun of his acquaintance, who was an ardent admirer of Teresa's: "No one could be more disappointed than I am at the slowness with which we are moving. But in such a matter as this, progress must of necessity be slow. It is slow and sure, however, and I know that you will be glad to hear that there are as you are aware some 700 letters, and since the Benedictines, whose property they are, are unwilling that the originals should be sent to Rome, it is consequently necessary that the Congregation of Rites should have undoubted proof that the type-written copies correspond in every detail with the originals.

The last time I was in Rome, I obtained permission to confide the work of comparing the copies with the originals to the Faithful Companion Sisters, who, after being put upon verily, set diligently to work, and are working still. As soon as they have finished their tedious work, then we shall hold the last meeting and make arrangements for the evidence of the witnesses and the documents pertaining to the Cause to be taken to Rome. As Postulator, I have succeeded in getting one of the Canons of S. Maria in Lata who has the advantage of being well acquainted with English, so you must pray more than ever, and get others to pray also. God in His own good time will see that His humble handmaid is glorified on earth as well as in heaven. We must faithfully do our part and then confidently leave the rest in His hands. Now that you know exactly how the Cause of holy Teresa stands, you will be able to dispel any rumours you may hear to the effect that the Cause is making no progress. It is exactly the contrary that is true."

In *The Cathedral Record* in August, 1932, the Right Reverend Monsignor John O'Brien reported the remarkable cure of Miss Jane Theresa Gore of Hollybrook, 18 Allerton Drive, Mossley Hill, Liverpool. "Miss Gore, who had attained her sixtieth year, had been suffering from weakness in the throat ever since she was eighteen. As a consequence, she had never been able to swallow with ease. It was only in 1929, however, that the malady with which she had been afflicted during all those years finally came to a head. She now began to be alarmed by the severe pains which she frequently had in her neck.

351

Being at this time Matron in the School of the Augustinean Sisters, at Haywards Heath, in Sussex, she consulted the house doctor, and, at his recommendation, she went to see a specialist who used to attend the Cottage Hospital near at hand. After a careful examination, he declared that he was sorry to have to inform her that she had a malignant cancer in the throat, and that a difficult and delicate operation was absolutely necessary.

And so, on the very next day, she journeyed to London, where she saw another specialist. Acting on his advice, she first of all underwent an operation on the trachea, the principal air passage from the larynx to the bronchial tubes. After three weeks had elapsed, she had a second operation for the removal of two cancerous growths in the neck. Although she experienced great relief, there now began, post-operatively, a continuous and most offensive discharge from the left and exterior side of the throat.

In this pitiable state she remained from April, 1929, until August in the following year. In January, 1931, she went into a nursing home in Rodney Street, Liverpool. There, with the object of obtaining relief in her breathing, which was again becoming more and more difficult, she had a piece of bone, about half an inch long, taken from her throat. After a week, she went back home, and there remained until the April of 1931, suffering night and day, the discharge being simply terrible. She had no alternative but to return to the hospital in London, where she was operated upon again. The specialist, the doctors and nurses did all they could for her; but to do anything more than to give her a little relief was beyond their power.

After a while, she went home once more, and it was not long before she began to suffer more than ever, especially when the discharge happened to stop, as it sometimes did. On these occasions her face became very red and inflamed, and swelled out to an incredible extent. So desperate was her state, that she could scarcely open her lips to take nourishment, or even to

352

speak. It was then, when to all human appearance there was no hope, that she resolved to make a pilgrimage to Neston, and to pray for nine days at the tomb of Teresa Higginson. This resolution she faithfully carried out. But even up to the morning of the ninth day, there was no visible improvement in her state. Rather, on the contrary, the disease seemed to have made further progress. The discharge from the suppurating tissue was excessive: so much so that the three thicknesses of lint and the four of gauze, which were wrapped round her neck, were literally saturated with blood and pus.

It was Sunday morning, and Miss Gore was due to leave Neston on the following day. Full of confidence she knelt once more at the foot of the grave. Wonderful to relate, that very day the discharge stopped and all her pain ceased. The following morning, which was the tenth of August, the neck was perfectly healed and quite dry. On the 17th August, she called on the specialist under whose care she had been. After a careful examination of the inside and outside of her neck, he assured her that she was cured."

A previous equally dramatic cure was reported in July, 1924. Sister Julie, of the Sisters of Notre Dame, at Mount Pleasant Convent, in Liverpool, had experienced acute pain in her right jaw for years before the cancer showed itself. She had great difficulty in opening her mouth, even to take food, and the pain was excruciating. The doctors were unable to give her relief or to diagnose the malady. At length she was put under one of the best surgeons in London, Mr Rowntree. He was deeply interested in the case and he did all that human power could do to alleviate the suffering. At length the cancer became an open wound, and the poor invalid could no longer receive Our Lord in Holy Communion. By this time she was back in Liverpool at Mount Pleasant. Mr Rowntree paid a visit to Liverpool to give a lecture for the University. He went out of his way to see Sister Julie and give her relief. He found a bone was giving her great trouble, and Sister gave an account in a letter she wrote on July 12th, 1924.

"The allusion about the bone is interesting ... Mr Rowntree says, 'Get it away immediately.' Dr B. said 'Let it come away of itself.' In my dilemma I appealed to Teresa Higginson for help. On my return from Formby, [a resort of Lancashire, 7 miles south west of Southport. The nuns very probably had a house there at that time.] Sister Adrian (a nursing sister) found it impossible to plug the wound without causing me to shriek with pain. At last I said I would prefer to sit up all night rather than have a plug inserted. Sister wept in sympathy and said that for weeks she approached the ordeal with a sickening fear; but she prayed to Teresa saying, 'If you get that bone away without blood-shedding (the bleeding was the great danger) I will believe you are a saint.' Last Tuesday night I never closed my eyes in sleep, and in the early dawn I desperately determined to detach it from the dressing. I probed and felt something hard, and emboldened by Mr Rowntree's letter, probed again and got hold of the bone; but could not move it; prayed and tried a half rotation 9 times and finally a huge lump of what looked like coralline rock with all its angles and more came away in the gauze dressing. I had expected something different [so] that I feared I had done mischief. So after Mass I sent for the nurse, saying 'What is this?' She fell straight on her knees thanking God and Teresa. Then she added, 'But this is only half out.' My heart sank. So I begged her to remove the plug, and there *on it* was the other portion, much broader but not so long.

If you write to Louisa [Higginson], tell her I shall, later. Everyone is aghast, and devotion to Teresa has increased. Sister A. has disinfected it and carries it about like a jewel in a casket, getting loads of sympathy from my friends. Tell the bone episode to any of the Sisters, it will increase devotion to Teresa."

*75. Sister Albania of Mount Pleasant
Training College, Liverpool.*

Dr Geldard, the editor of *The Cathedral Record*, announced in that magazine in March, 1934, that the Diocesan Processes in the Cause of the Servant of God Teresa Higginson – which is to say, the collection of testimonies and their committal to paper, and, presumably, the conclusion of the verification of the accuracy of the copies of Teresa's letters – having been completed some time ago, all had been deposited with the Sacred Congregation of Rites by the Vice-Postulator of the Cause, Monsignor John O'Brien, on December 7th, 1933. Monsignor Fillipo Sordini had been appointed the new Postulator of the Cause in Rome.

An address on Teresa Higginson was delivered by the Very Reverend Monsignor Adamson to the Liverpool Catholic Teachers' Association at Mount Pleasant Convent on October 25th, 1935.

Monsignor Adamson, whom I knew well, had, with Canon McCurdy, whom I also knew and who was Devil's advocate in the Teresa Higginson Cause, charge of the souls in the parish of St Clare's, Arundel Avenue, Sefton Park, Liverpool. Sister Albania I also knew. She played an important part at Mount Pleasant, had known in life, and was very devoted to the memory of, Teresa.

How appropriate it seemed, said the Monsignor, that they should be assembled that night at Mount Pleasant, the *alma mater* of so many of those whose vocation it had been to teach. Not only that, but it was here that Teresa herself had often been a visitor, it was here that she sat the examination that gained her her teacher's certificate, it was from here that she went forth on her first teaching mission to Bootle, and it was from here that she received the commission to depart upon her last, to Chudleigh. She spent a great part of her life in and around the archdiocese of Liverpool, at St Helens, Wigan, Bootle, Sabden, Ecceleshall, Osbaldeston, Newchurch, Clitheroe, at Neston on the Wirral, and in Liverpool itself. Indeed, it was in a house – above a little shop – at the top of Mount Pleasant, within a hundred yards of where they were now, that she had at one time lived. It was, he said, obvious why they should take up Teresa's Cause. What a Cause to work for, the beatification and canonisation, the recognition of the heroic virtues and the raising to the altars for public veneration of one we might say of themselves. She was one of their calling. She was a teacher. She taught in the same schools as some of them, and walked the same streets. Unquestionably, she was one of them. But, they must not, he said, expect to see their efforts crowned with success within a few months. Moreover, in addition to the delay unavoidable in the formal process, they must not expect to be entirely free from irritations and vexations at home. They would have criticism, plenty of it, as every good cause has. Much of it they would be able to ignore. On the other hand, a kindly offer to explain difficulties to their critics might often convert them to their cause. The fact that the authorities of the archdiocese had officially supported the Cause and had already forwarded it to Rome for examination was sufficient to justify belief in her sanctity. One of the chief reasons why Teresa was being continually denounced was the existence in her life of extraordinary manifestations and extraordinary happenings. These things do not happen to ordinary people, say the critics, therefore Teresa was a liar, a fraud, or at least she was deceived, even perhaps of unsound mind. We know, moreover, from our reading of the lives of the saints that God has in the past done wonderful things to them and by them, and that He sometimes uses His creatures to manifest His supernatural powers. Let your efforts be supported by constant and fervent prayer, that Teresa Higginson, the Liverpool teacher, whose Cause you have now in hand, may, in the not too distant future, be raised to the altars of the Church and acclaimed by teachers throughout the world as one of their heavenly patrons.

The delay of which Monsignor Adamson had warned persisted throughout 1936 and 1937. At last, on February 21st, 1938, a letter from Rome was written to Monsignor O'Brien:

You must have been expecting for some time news of me or rather of the Cause we have at heart – Teresa Higginson. As a matter of fact I have not written to you for the past six months. Since it was necessary just to have the approbation of the writings of the Servant of God and the Decree – *Procedi Potest ad ulteriora*. I presented myself on several occasions to the Congregation in order to obtain information about the said decree, and behold, last Friday unexpectedly I received the following note from His Excellency Monsignor Carinci, Secretary of the Congregation:

Mi reco a donare significazione alla P.V. Rev. ma alla che
Introduzione della Causa Serva di Dio Teresa Helena Higginson,
a stato posto dal Sant Uffizio il NON EXPEDIRE. *Tanto Le*
communico per sua intelligenze e norma, etc.

[Translation: It is my duty to inform you Very Reverend Father
that the Holy Office has apposed the NON EXPEDIRE
(Not Expedient) to the introduction of the Cause of
the Servant of God, Teresa Helena Higginson.
I communicate this to you for your information and
manner of procedure, etc.]

This morning I called on Monsignor the Secretary to beg for
his explanation and advice. I know of course that the Holy
Office never publishes the facts which have influenced its
decisions. On that subject I did not expect any information
from Monsignor Carinci, but he himself began to explain
that it was not the Congregation of Rites which had
pronounced the NON EXPEDIRE, and that one must be clear on
that point. Had the Holy Office discovered anything against
the Servant of God – e.g. by reason of heresy or moral
disorder, it would have been pronounced against the
introduction of the Cause its REPONATUR, and then that
would have ended it completely, but it has pronounced its
NON EXPEDIRE, and that means two things.
Firstly, that it has found in the writings a reason apart from
the person of the Servant of God. At once I answered that I
had already thought of the propaganda which Teresa had
exercised of the Devotion to the Sacred Head of Our Lord.
"Exactly," answered Monsignor the Secretary, "we have had
other cases where the Holy Office has pronounced the NON
EXPEDIRE because the Servant of God promoted the Devotion
to the Arms, the Feet of Our Lord, or some other new form of

358

devotion not yet introduced into the cultus of the Church." Secondly, it means that in itself a further procedure has been postponed *ad tempus, in non perpetuum,* for instance, a striking miracle could easily cause the Holy Office to revoke its NON EXPEDIRE. Consequently, the Cause is not lost, only its progress has been stopped for the time being or for an indefinite period. This being so, I asked Monsignor Carinci if I should continue, nevertheless, the translation of the Acts of the Diocessa in process, and his answer was"No, you must stop the translation in order not to incur expenses which might prove useless."

I sincerely regret that the Cause should have come to this. If the Devotion to the Sacred Head had been just a private devotion of the Servant of God I do not think they would have pronounced the NON EXPEDIRE, but she promoted and recommended this Devotion, and that is going too far. I beg of you Monsignor to be so good as to acquaint His Grace the Archbishop of Liverpool, our principal, on this matter.

It had taken the Sacred College nearly five years to come to a decision.

Not everybody was disappointed. Certainly Lady Catherine Ashburnham, of Ashburnham, Surrey, would not have been. She had written in a letter published in *The Tablet* of January 29th, 1938: "I gather that the presence of pathological conditions and doubtful phenomena is by no means inconsistent with heroic virtue. That may well be so, but the doubt which arises in such a case as that of Teresa Higginson is: whether apart from the abnormal phenomena, the repute for sanctity would ever have arisen. Surely there must be many good teachers and religious who have risen to a high standard of virtue, but who have not attracted attention. The thought that Teresa Higginson, a pious woman no doubt, but exhibiting every symptom of neurotic disorder, should be presented to the world as the nearest approach to the ideal of sanctity which England has produced in six hundred years, fills me with dismay, more especially when I contemplate the ridicule with which the news will be greeted by the enemies of the Church in England, and the consequent explanations and justifications we shall be obliged to offer."

Disgruntled too, was Mary Cahill, a teacher, who, according to Dame Lucy, otherwise Sister Mary Lucy, at St Mary's Abbey, Woolmer Hill, Haslemere was very anti-Teresian, and who, in January, 1951, wrote from No. 4 The Precincts, Canterbury: "Did I tell you my connection with the proposed introduction of [Teresa Higginson's] Cause? Thirty or more years ago I heard faint rumours of her, wrote to *The Universe* asking for information, and as a result had letters from five people who had known, lived with and taught with her. These repelled me in many ways. I kept the letters and when Lady Cecil Kerr appealed for any information, I sent these letters on to her. She copied and returned them, and then when her *Life* appeared I was horrified at the use she had made of them. I took the trouble to go through the book marking the places where extracts from my letters were given. She used all the parts that were in any way in favour of Teresa, and left out all, the most part, which was in any way unfavourable. A year or so later, I read an article in *The Tablet* criticising non-Catholic dishonesty in a life of Luther, so I wrote saying Catholics were guilty of the same kind of literary dishonesty. As a result, I was asked to allow the use of my letter in an article. I agreed and it led to a long and angry correspondence in *The Tablet*. Perhaps you remember it? I have all the letters and correspondence put away somewhere, so if Mother Abbess and Mother Prioress would like to study it all I could send it along and they can have a battle royal."

Sister Mary Lucy commented in her letter to Miss Arkwright, in which she enclosed the Mary Cahill screed: "It is true, I know a good many people who are against her [Teresa] –

but then most of the great saints had wicked things said against them, and plenty of propaganda. I asked one person what turned her against Teresa Higginson, and she said that somebody said she was supposed not to have eaten any food, lived on the Blessed Sacrament, and there was found in her suit-case bread and sandwiches. 'Oh,' I said. 'Did *you* see them?' 'Oh, no, but I was told all was a make up.' I told her one could not go by what they see, but the thing was – Did *she* eat them – that must be proved. Food found in a suit-case might mean many things. God's time has not come for Teresa Higginson. Wait for the atomic bomb, then, when *one* whole nation is destroyed her words of 54 years ago will be true and many more things."

Father Francis Ripley well remembered "the day the information came from Rome telling us that it was not expedient for the Cause to proceed. I went to see Canon McCurdy, who had been the Devil's advocate. Archbishop Downey was requested to withdraw certain beautiful pictures of Our Lord with a prayer to the Sacred Head of Jesus."

A very fine reproduction of Guido Reni's *"Ecce Homo"*, the original of which is in the National Gallery, that had been sent to St Winefride's as a thanksgiving offering to Teresa by Count de Remirez de Arallano, a Spanish nobleman living in London, was also expediently spirited away from the place where it had hung in the church.

Eleven years after the promulgation of the NON EXPEDIRE verdict, an unidentified correspondent writes from Rome, on February 22nd, 1949, to an unidentified cleric, but very likely Monsignor O'Brien:

"Latest, definite, and more cheering news just arrived from Rome. It is from a Consultor of the Congregation of Rites and is quite official. This is what he says: 'The Cause is DILATA (put back). This forms *no* insurmountable obstacle. An objection was raised by the Holy Office to her [Teresa's] devotion to the Sacred

Head. This could be got over by showing that she was in good faith, showed the right deference for authority, etc. What is required is an *expert postulator*, one who really knows the way to go about things and has plenty of drive. I am confident that a really "alive" postulator could get the Cause going again. The only thing is to get Archbishop Downey or some other bishop to appoint a good postulator.' There you are. It is at least more encouraging than before, and this really is official. I hope something can be done."

Another three and a half decades on, Mrs Teresa Cottriall, Helen Lonsdale's daughter, wrote, from 53 Larkfield Lane, Southport, to the Archbishop of Liverpool, the Right Reverend Derek Worlock. She was concerned as to the disposal of the accumulation of relics and documents which had been bequeathed to her and her sister by Miss Arkwright. Included among them was Teresa's Franciscan Tertiary habit, which had, however, already been promised to the nuns at St Catherine's Convent, Edinburgh.

Archbishop Worlock replied on April 11th, 1985: "As I understand it, when the Cause was first presented at Rome, the information concerning the teaching of Teresa Higginson and her various papers, etc. were examined and it was decided by Rome that the matter should not be proceeded with. Unless, as seems unlikely, Rome decrees otherwise, the matter has to be left there, though the papers are held in the Archdiocesan Archives. Accordingly, it would seem best to me that those belongings of which you speak should likewise be deposited either with the Archdiocesan authorities at the Curial Offices in Brownlow Hill, or, should you so wish, with Bishop Gray, in Birkenhead. Perhaps you would like to think this over."

{Note: A Father Skeehan was sent to assess the relics. He spent very little time in examining them, and pronounced them to be of only "cosmetic value."]

Mrs Kathleen Bence, a worker for the Cause, wrote from Thornton Court, Willaston Road, Thornton Hough, Wirral, on March 25th, 1987, to the Right Reverend Joseph Gray, Bishop of Shrewsbury:

My Lord,

Some years ago, the Cause for the Beatification of Teresa Helena Higginson was halted in Rome. There are many people around the world who have a great devotion to her and who are pressing for the Cause to be reopened. Tony and Gladys Moreton have been very active in keeping the devotion alive. During many discussions with Tony and Gladys recently, we have considered the possibility of forming a committee in order to further the Cause. Before embarking on this venture we would need your approval and blessing. In view of the active interest in the Cause, we would like to make an appointment with you to discuss the possibilities of pursuing the same and would be grateful if you could inform us of a date that would be convenient to yourself.

Six months went by in silence. On September 8th, 1987, Bishop Gray replied. "Since I am not aware of any of the details of the process or the reasons why it was discontinued, I am not in any position at this point in time to give approval for its resumption by the formation of a committee. If someone can provide me with a brief history of what has happened to date, then I will have it studied and give advice as to possible procedure."

Bishop Gray retired in 1995. He is buried in St Winefride's churchyard, Neston, not far from Teresa Higginson's grave. This was his wish. He never, however, lent his official approval to any efforts towards the reopening of her Cause.

In July, 1987, and in August, 1990, letters concerning Teresa Higginson were addressed to the Sovereign Pontiff by Sister

Mary Loreto, of the College of Higher Education, Southampton, and Mr and Mrs Anthony Moreton, respectively. They received polite formal acknowledgment.

As recently as in March, 2005, Gladys Moreton received from the Right Reverend Brian M. Noble, Bishop of Shrewsbury a letter stating that, although he understood her commitment to the Cause of Teresa Higginson, he did not as yet "feel there is a sufficiently well developed Cause to consider putting forward to Rome. Undoubtedly, there are a number of people deeply convinced of her sanctity and very keen to see this recognised officially by the Church. However, my understanding of the way such matters move forward is that there should be a very considerable ground-swell of interest before making official representation to Rome. Having said that, please do send on to me further information that you regard as relevant to moving things forward."

And there, for the present at any rate, the story ends.

EPILOGEMENA

QUO?

Whither, indeed. As of the Year of Our Lord Two Thousand and Ten how stands the long fought Cause of Teresa Helena Higginson? In limbo, I suppose, must be the most truthful answer. Precisely seventy-two years ago, Rome put it neatly aside on the shelf.

And yet the irony is that a spontaneous devotion to Teresa Higginson has arisen, and continues unabated, in the five continents of the world. Letters bearing testimony to the conviction of her sanctity and petitioning for her beatification have been received from all parts of Great Britain and Ireland, France, Germany, Italy, Holland, Belgium, Malta, the U.S.A., Canada, the West Indies, Brazil, India, China, Burma, Borneo, South Africa, Uganda, and New Zealand.

They have christened her, out of sentiment, "The Maid of the Mersey who sleeps by the Dee" ... but do not too readily hasten to mock sentiment, it is so often love's struggle to clothe feelings in the flesh of words. The universality of Teresa Higginson is impressive. She could make herself truly at home in city, town, school, bees-waxed-clean convent, and the lowliest poverty-stenching hovel. Silent of foot, she trod the pathways of adversity, grasping the hands of those she came upon in need of aid. On aching knees, she begged grace and solace for the sorrow-stricken, the pain-wracked, and the irredeemable poor. Her record commands respect, demands devotion. Catholic instinct can usually be relied upon to distinguish genuine sanctity from that which is false, and the spontaneous widespread conviction of the sanctity of Teresa Higginson on the part of thousands of different race and temperament cannot prudently be ignored.

All in God's good time, is the answer of the Faithful, and heaven and eternity lie all about us. Eternity, like infinity, is a difficult concept to grasp with a finite mind. Permit me to provide a cogent adumbration. Imagine a vast mountain twice the size of Everest. Every hundred years a small bird comes to that mountain, pecks out and carries off a grain of it in its beak. When the little bird has levelled the mountain, not even the first day of eternity will have elapsed.

But, the Church warns, in all cases which concern mysticism, stigmatisation, and ecstasy, proceed with the utmost caution, for there is a false mysticism as well as a true one. "Especially since the Great War there has been a dangerous current which draws multitudes both in Europe and America towards the false mysticism which manifests itself in the occult sciences and spiritism. There have been, notably since the 18th century, indiscreet and unbalanced minds abnormally attracted through pride and curiosity to the extraordinary. They have been ambitious to climb higher than others and be distinguished from others in the spiritual life. They are lacking in humility in their refusal to admit that there are ways which are reserved by God for the few. In spite of the Church's advice many have remained obstinate and have become lamentable victims of their own presumption and their pride." [Dr Geldard. "Teresa Helena Higginson". *The Cathedral Record*, March, 1934.]

It must be reiterated that in its appraisal of heroic sanctity, the Church takes no cognisance of the exhibition by the candidate of supernatural phenomena, such as the presentation of stigmata, ecstasies, skirmishes with the Devil, levitation and bilocation; or such personal idiosyncrasies as inedia, asomnia, xenoglossia, or, for that matter, patent hieromania. These are

366

regarded as extraneous, *de trop*. There is the possibility of the existence of a kind of dualism; that in some cases of genuinely extreme sanctity the preternatural phenomena are the by-products, the adjuncts, of the personality; that they are produced out of the mind and persona of the holy one. They do not set feet on the *via beatitatis*. The Church's judgment is based solely upon the demonstrable fact of the heroic exercise of the heroic virtues of faith, hope, and charity, by the Servant of God. Certain it is that, throughout a life of strenuous sacrifice, Teresa Higginson displayed possession of the heroic virtues in abundance. And it has indeed been confirmed that there was no insurmountable obstacle to the Cause.

From the lay point of view, however, what, as I asked at the beginning, are we to make of Teresa Higginson? Her piety does not seem to be in doubt. Hosts of witnesses from all stages of her life testify unreservedly to it. Apply the old Biblical test – "By their fruits ye shall know them" (St Matthew 7. 20) – then she was surely seeded from the Tree of Truth and Grace, for the fruits of her life yielded nothing but good, and one finds a quite extraordinary number of those who came into close contact with her, were influenced by her example, entering religious orders.

Did the very particular treatment accorded her by her parents, consequent upon their early belief that Teresa was a 'special' child, perhaps pre-condition her, make her perform what she would regard as a pre-destined rôle? Of unsoundness of mind, there is absolutely no evidence, neither in her nor familialy. She must, therefore, remain a fascinating enigma: perhaps a thaumaturge of unknown lineage, perhaps a saint within the religious meaning of the act. I simply do not know; albeit I have my leanings. How say you?

BIBLIOGRAPHY

Anonymous. *Life of Teresa Higginson: The Teacher Mystic.* Orphans' Press, Rochdale, 1927.

Anonymous. *Message of Our Lord to Teresa Higginson.* Privately printed, N.D.

Anonymous. *Une grande Inconnue ou Les merveilles d'une simple vie. Teresa Higginson (1844-1905).* Editions de 'Sagesse' Bellevue – Cagnotte (Landes), 1953.

Browne, S.J., Rev. Henry. *The Cause of Teresa Higginson.* Reprinted from the *Buckfast Abbey Chronicle*, N.D.

Catterall, Minnie. *Teresa Higginson: M. Catterall's Narrative.* W. Watson & Co., Ltd., 135 Corporation Street, Preston, 1936.

Heimann, Mary. " Higginson, Teresa Helena (1844-1905), Roman Catholic Schoolteacher and Mystic."*Oxford Dictionary of National Biography.* Oxford University Press, 2004-7.

Hocht, Johannes Maria. *Die Wahrheit uber die belgischen Muttergottes: Erscheinungen und heilungen unter Berucksichtigung der visionen von drei Deutschen bargestellt im Anschluss an eine wallsahrtnach Beauraing.* Matthias Grunewald, Berlag, Wiesbaden, c. 1934.

Honnor, Brian. *Appreciations of Teresa Helena Higginson:School-Teacher & Mystic.* Privately printed, 1986.

Hurndall, Bernadette F.G. *By God's Command: The Amazing Supernatural Life of Teresa Helena Higginson. Stigmatic. Servant of God.* Privately printed, 1987.

Kerr, Lady Cecil. *Teresa Helena Higginson.* The Catholic Truth Society of Ireland, 1933.

Kerr, Cecil. *Teresa Helena Higginson: Servant of God. "The Spouse of the Crucified" 1844-1905.* Sands, London, 1927.

Kerr, Cecil. *Teresa Helena Higginson, School Teacher and Mystic 1844-1905. Abridged from the larger Life, with 8 illustrations.* Sands, London, 1928.

Kershaw, Rev. F.W. *Teresa Helena Higginson: A Short Account of Her Life and Letters.* Sands, London. N.D. Privately republished by Tony and Gladys Moreton, 1999.

Lonsdale, Helen, (*née* Ellen Nicholson). *Teresa Higginson: A Personal Account.* N.D. Privately printed. Issued by the Magazine Committee of St Mary's and St John's, Wigan. March, 1984.

Louismet, O.S.B., Dom Savinien, Monk of Buckfast Abbey. *The Devotion to the Sacred Head*. Printed in the same pamphlet as the Rev. Henry Browne, S.J.'s article on "The Cause of Teresa Higginson."

Monk of St Augustine's Abbey, Ramsgate, A. *Letters of Teresa Higginson: Selected and Discussed*. Sands, London, 1937.

O'Maolain, Michael. *Teresa Helena Higginson: A Talk*. 4-page printed sheet. N.D. (Text of a Radio Eirin broadcast).

O'Sullivan, O.S.B., Rev. A.M. *Teresa Higginson: Servant of God: School Teacher. 1845-1905. A Memoir*. Sands, London, 1924.

Pitts, Ann. & Dolores, Sister Mary. *Teresa Helena Higginson: Servant of God*. Privately printed, N.D. *c.* 1986.

Plumb, B. 'Teresa Helena Higginson, (1844-1905): A Bibliography." *North West Catholic History*, Vol.18 (1991).

Poor Clare Colettine, (who nursed her in her last illness.) A. [Agnes Casey] *The Last Days of Teresa Helena Higginson*. The Repository, St Anne's Road, Ormskirk, 1938.

Thurston, Rev. Herbert. 'The Case of Teresa Higginson". *Catholic Medical Guardian*. July, 1937.

Thurston, Rev. Herbert. "Hagiography Past and Present". *The Tablet*, Nov. 20,1937.

Whittington-Egan, Richard. 'The Devil in Bootle", in *Liverpool Colonnade*. Philip Son & Nephew, Liverpool, 1955.

OTHER WORKS WHICH REFER TO TERESA HIGGINSON

Hole, Christina. *Haunted England: A Survey of English Ghost-Lore*. Batsford, London, 1941.

Summers, Montague. *The Supernatural Omnibus*. Gollancz, London, 1949.

Thurston, S.J., Rev. Herbert. *The Physical Phenomena of Mysticism*. Edited by J.H. Crehan, S.J. Burns Oates, London, 1951.

Wilson, Ian. *The Bleeding Mind. An Investigation into the Mysterious Phenomenon of Stigmata*. Weidenfeld & Nicolson, London, 1988.

INDEX

Acta Apostolicæ Sedis. 315

Adamson, Very Reverend
Monsignor. 296, 355-357

Adrian, Sister. 354

Africa. 186, 271, 323, 365

Albania, Sister. 321, *355*, 356

Allerton Drive, Liverpool. 351

Alphonsus of the Sacred Heart,
Sister Mary. 298

America 277, 337, 366

American Order of the Sisters of the
Blessed Sacrament. 242

Annales de Dermatologie. 69

Apocalypse, The. 270, 283

*Appreciations of Teresa Helena
Higginson: School Teacher &
Mystic*. 329

Archdiocesan Archives, Liverpool.
362

Ariel Street, Liverpool. 10, 11, 14,
106, 107, 132, 133, 143,

Arkwright, Elizabeth. *81*, 273, 333,
334, *339*

Arkwright, Isabella. 57, 60, 62, 80-
82, 87, 206, 294, 296, 331-334,
360, 362, *336*

Arkwright, Reverend Father
William. 81

Arundel Avenue, Liverpool. 356

Ashburnham, Lady Catherine. 359

Ashburnham, Surrey. 359

Ashworth, (*née* Woodward), Mrs.
Margaret. 57, 60

Assisi. 104, 139, 160, 196, 200, 229,
321

Aughton, Lancashire. 59, 93, *95*, 118,
131, *133*, 142, 189, 331, *334*

Aughton Street, Ormskirk,
Lancashire. 334

Augustinean Sisters, Haywards
Heath, Sussex, School of the.
352

Bâle. 200

Bamber, Mrs. 90

Banks, Mrs. 137, 138

Banks, Mrs. John, 273

Banneux, Belgium. 339

Baptist, Sister Mary. 300

Barbara, Sister Mary Saint (formerly
Susan Ryland). *51*, 72

Barberi, Blessed Dominic. 21, 39, 46

Batley, Yorkshire. 72

Beauraing, Belgium. 338, 339

Beco, Mariette. 339

Beckingham, Nottinghamshire. 20

Beggan, Reverend Father (later
Canon) Michael. 143

Belgaum, India. 81

Belgaum Jesuit College. 82

Belgium. 87, 198, 199, 200, 291, 338,
339, 365

Bence, Kathleen. 363

370

Benedictine Abbey of St Augustine, Ramsgate, Kent, The. 119, 329, 346

Benedictines, The. 325, 327

Bengal, Bay of. 203

Bernard, Mother. 298

Betharram, France. 345

Billé, Abbé. 204, 205

Bilocation. 84, 129, 161, 176, 202, 270, 271, 273, 277, 278, 296, 313, 318, 319, 323, 366

Birkenhead. 143, 362

Birmingham, Birchall Street, Deritend. 79

Birmingham, Geelong Place, Bridge Lane. 79

Birmingham, Moseley Street. 79

Birmingham, Temple Street. 78

Bishop Goss School, Liverpool. 57, 147

Blackburn, Lancashire. 145

Blackburn, Edward. 93, *95*

Blackburn, Mrs. Margaret. 92, 93, 247

Blacklock, Margaret. 223

Bois d'Haine, Hainault. 53

Bologna. 200

Bolton, Miss. 152

Bond, Mrs. 210, 230

Bootle. 10, 11, 15, *41, 42* 44, 58, 59, 87, 88, 90, 93, *105, 106*, 107, *108*, 111, 114, 115, 132, 135, 137, 143, 145, 147, 243, 247-249, 261, 262, 312, 314, 317, 356

Bootle, Keble Road. 93, 247

Borneo. 365

Bossuet, Jacques-Bénigne. 320, 324

Boúváaert, M.C. 328

Bowness, Mary. 17, *19*

Boyle, M. 243

Bramley, Mrs. 79, 80

Bramley, Reverend Father. 82

Brazil. 365

British Library, The. 346

Brittany. 184

Brompton Oratory, London. 196

Brownlow Hill, Liverpool. 362

Bruges. 198, 199

Burma. 365

Burnley, Lancashire. 85

Burns, Oates, & Washbourne. 329

Butler, Clara. 79

Butler's *Lives of the Saints*. 323

By God's Command: The Amazing Supernatural Life of Teresa Helena Higginson. (Hurndall). 68, 136, 329

Cagnotte. 242, 329

Cahill, Mary. 360

Calais. 200

Callaghan, Catherine. 252

Cammack, S.J., Reverend Father J.S. 315

Campana, Canon E. 307, 309

Campbell of Skerrington, Lord. 299

Canada. 365

Canoness of the Convent of the Holy Sepulchre. 184

Canterbury, The Precincts. 360

Carinci, His Excellency Monsignor. 357-359

Carlist Rising, The. 59

Carmarthen. 42

Carmelite Convent (at Gillingham, Dorsetshire), The. 198, 206

Caravaggio. 163

Carter, Mrs. 88

Cartmel, Canon. 331

Casey, Agnes. 220-223, 225-232, 234-236, 253, 321, 334, 347

Cathedral, Exeter, The. 209

Cathedral of Christ the King, Liverpool Catholic Metropolitan. 203

Cathedral Record, The. 351, 355, 366

Catherine, Sister. 177

Catherine, Sister Mary. 333

Catholic History of England. 211

Catholic Medical Guardian, The. 260, 279, 280

Catholic Times, The. 134

Catholic Truth Society of Ireland. The. 260, 342

Catterall, Kate. 11, 14, 109, 110, 250, 251, 313

Catterall, May (Minnie). 11, 12, 14, 85, 86, 93, 94, 107, 108, 109, 111, 133, 138, 142, 147, 148, 149, 150, 151, 313, 333, 334, 338, 343

Central Station, Liverpool. 198

Ceoli, Sister Florida. 164

Chelmsford. 184

Cheltenham, South Australia. 60

Chestnut Street, Liverpool. 203

Cheviot Hills. 193

China. 365

Chisnall Brothers, undertakers. 273

Chiswick. 282

Christmas, Grace. 145

Chudleigh, Devonshire. 205, 207, 209, 213, 215, 216, 217, 218, 219, 220, 222, 223, 226, 234, 241, 253, 282, 294, 296, 297, 320, 321, 350, 356

Churchill Street, Princes Park, Liverpool. 189, 190, 200, 204

Clacton-on-Sea. 174, 183, 184

Claremount Road, Wallasey. 337

Clifford, Lord. 207, 208, 209, 211, 217, 220, 221, 224, 228, 238, 253, 217

Clifford, Lady. 210, 211, 212, 217, 238

Clitheroe, Lancashire. 74, 77, 81, 82, 83, 84, 90, 152, 153, 154, 156, 166, 167, 173, 188, 333, 356

Cobb, Reverend Father. 332

College of Higher Education, Southampton. 364

Cologne. 250

Cook & Townsend, Liverpool. 137

Corvo, Baron (see Rolfe, Frederick). 20

Cottam, Miss. 80, 81

Cottini, Alfonsina. 163

Cottriall, Mrs Teresa. (née Lonsdale) 331, 362

Cowlam, Eliza. 97, 113

Cowlam, Fanny. 35

Cullen, Miss. 248, 251, 252

Curé d'Ars, Jean-Marie Baptiste Vianney. 44, 263

Curial Offices, The Liverpool. 362

Daily Post, The Liverpool. 338

Dalkeith. 174, 284, 288, 296, 301

Daly, Canon Joseph. 144

Dauvergne, Dr. 69

Dawson, Reverend Father. 223, 253, 254

Dawson, Elizabeth. 84, 90, 152, 154, 180

Damien, Reverend Father Joseph. 278, 290, 291, 296

De Arallano, Count de Remirez. 361

De Barry, Mr. 184

De Barry, Mrs. 184

De la Colombière, Reverend Father Claude. 125

De la Taille, S.J., Reverend Father Maurice. 142, 316

De Sales, Reverend Mother. 299, 301

De Vere, Beauclerk, S.J., Reverend Father Sidney. 20

De Vito, Maria. 164

Deady, Katherine. *180, 181,* 182, 235, 277, 332, 334, 350

Dee, River. 365

Del Val, Cardinal Merry. 296, 297

Dennett, Canon W. 273

Derham, Mrs. 329

Devil, The. 10, 12-14, 16, 37, 71, 96-100, 102, 103, *106, 108,* 112, 113, 114, 117, 130, 132, 142, 152, 170, 172, 184, 229, 261, 263, 278, 281, 314, 321, 326, 366

Devil's Advocate, The. 303, 316, 342, 348, 356, 361

Devonshire. 205, 213, 240, 347

Dick, Reverend Father Gordon. 345

Dickens, Charles. 113

Dieppe. 195, 200

Dillon, Lord. 17

Diocesan Commission to the Sacred Congregation of Rites, Rome. 302, 303, 315, 320

Discours sur l'histoire universelle. 324

Dobson, Bishop. 338

Dodo, Blessed. 160, 161

Dolan, Pat. 77

Dolores, Sister Mary. 329

Donna, Father Snow's dog. 167

Donnellan, Gertie. 249

Donnellan, Winifred. 248

Donnelly, Agnes. 57, 135, 245, 254

Donnelly, Jane (*née* Wood). 58, 245, 257

Donnelly, Mr. J.J. 58, 245, 246

Dowsett, Reverebd Father H. 207-209, 211-213, 215-220, 222, 224, 225, 227, 232, 233, 235, 238, 253, 321

Downey, Archbishop of Liverpool, The Right Reverend Dr. Richard. 302, 361, 362

Dublin. 17, 19, 325

Dunbar, East Lothian. 193

Ecce Homo. 361

Eccleshall, Staffordshire. 145-147

Edge Hill, Liverpool. 51

Edinburgh. 166, 167, *168, 169,* 172, 174, 175, 177, 180, 182, 183, 185, 195, 200, 206, 230, 247, 248, 252, 278, 282, 284, 295, 296, 298, 301, 324, 327, 362

Edinburgh, Cheyne Street. 174

Edinburgh, Lauriston Gardens. 166, 167, *168*

Eliot, George. 20

Emmerich, Anne Catherine. 281

Encyclopædia of Psychic Science (Fodor). 270

England's Lost Eden: Adventures in a Victorian Utopia. (Hoare). 166

English Martyrs, Whalley Range, Manchester, Church of the. 329

Eskbank. 174

Europe. 146, 366

Evangelist, Sister Mary. (Formermerly Katherine Deady). *181,* 187, 332

Everest, Mount. 366

Exchange Railway Station, Liverpool. 71

Exeter. 209

Faber, Reverend Father Frederick William. 21, 35, 39

Failsworth, Manchester. 330, 331

Fairfield, Dr. Josephine Letitia Denny. 259, 282, 305, 307, 310, 313, 317, 324

Faithful Companion Sisters, The. 351

Featherstone, Miss. 22, 31

Fenouil, Célestine. 69

Finnessey, Reverend Father. 338

Fisher, Reverend Father. 115, 338

Fitzalan-Howard, Lady Anne. 39, 327

Fleck, Elizabeth. 193, 195, *197*, 198, 206, 227

Fleck, Mary. 195

Florence, Italy. 196, 200, 214

Flynn, Joanna. 14, 107, 130, 135, 136, 141-143

Fodor, Nandor. 270

Ford Cemetery, Liverpool. 207

Formby, Lancashire. 354

France. 44, 125, 242, 339, 365

Francis, Sister Mary. 229, 321, 347

Franciscan, Tertiary Order of. 139, 195, 196, 198, 223, 241, 362

Franciscans, The. 139, 157

Fraser, Rector of Scots College, Rome, Monsignor. 195

Gainsborough, Lincolnshire. 20, 31

Garnett, Alfred Leo. 114, *191*, 203-205, *214*. *215*, 254, 255, 256, 334

Garnett, Annie. 188, 189, 192, 203, 255

Garnett, Margaret. 188, 189, *190*, 198, 203, 207

Garnett, S.J., Reverend Father Henry Joseph. 189

Gateacre, Liverpool. 39

Gave de Pau, River. 338

Geldard, Dr. 355, 366

Genoa. 195, 200

Germany. 161, 276, 307, 365

Gertrude, Sister. 337

Gethsemane, The Garden of. 160

Ghosts and Poltergeists. (Thurston). 262

Gillingham, Dorsetshire. 198, 206

Girling, Mary Ann. 161

Gladstone, William Ewart. 11

Glasgow. 249

Gore, Jane Theresa. 351, 353

Gosforth, Miss. 22

Grassendale, Liverpool. 128

Grassmarket, Edinburgh, The. 298

Grau, Reverend Father. 247, 249, 250

Gray, Bishop of Shrewsbury, The Right Reverend John. 362, 363

Great Britain. 365

Great War, (World War One), The. 176, 246, 249, 366

Guardian, Reverend Mother. 347

Guélin, Mère. 242

Gun Powder Plot, The. 189

"Hagiography: Past and Present." 304, 305

Hainault, Belgium. 53

Hall, O.S.B., Reverend Father John Placid. 128, 129, 151

Hall Street, Liverpool. 40

Hallifax, Joseph. 79

Hallifax, Frederick Fothergill. 77, 78. 79

Hallifax, Frederick William. 77, 78, *237*, 240

Hardwick, Reverend J.C. 259, 260

Hart, Dr. 67

Hart, Miss. 297

Hartley, Jesse. 11

Harvest, The. 259, 328

Hascha, Frisia. 160

Haslemere. 360

Haunted England. (Hole). 145

Her Benny. (Hocking). 88

Heythrop College, Chipping Norton, Oxfordshire. 315

Higginson, Clara Elizabeth. 21, 53

Higginson, John Edward. 21, 30

Higginson, Louisa Agnes. 21, 334

Higginson, Mary Ann. 20, 78, 333

Higginson, Mary Bowness. 17, *19*

Higginson, Robert Francis. 17, *18*

Higginson, (Junior) Robert Francis. 20

Higginon, William Bowness. 21

High Court of Justice, Edinburgh. 174

Hoare, Philip. 166

Hocking, Silas. 88

Hole, Christina. 145

Holland. 365

Holy Child of Jesus, Order of the. 59

Holy Cross School, Liverpool. *109*, 334

Holy Office, The. 319, 358. 359, 361

Holywell, North Wales. 20, 104

Home Office. 343

Hounslow. 72

Horne Street, Everton, Liverpool. 40, 77

Humphrey, S.J., Reverend Father. 301

Hurndall, Bernadette F.G. 68, 136, 329

Hutchings, Michael. 345

Hyde Park, London, Speakers' Corner. 242

Imbert-Goubeyre, Dr. A. 163

India. 81, 183, 365

Infirmary, Mill Road, Liverpool, The. 206

Ireland. 19, 20, 57, 151, 181, 260, 298, 325, 328, 365

Italy. 166, 325, 365

Ja-am-pu-da. 271-273, 323

Jesuits, The. 17, 18, 74, 82, 189, 260, 315

John Paul II, Pope. 163

Jones, Blanche. 78

Jones, Clara. 78

Jones, John. 78

Jones, John Percy. 78, 206, *129*, 333, 335, *340*

Jones, Mary Ann (*née* Higginson). 20, 78, 333

Jones, Minnie Matida. 78, *129*

Jones, William Henry. 78, 79

Joseph, Sister Mary. 336

Julie, Sister. 353, 354

Jumbo, Canon Snow's dog. 142, *133*

K., Elizabeth. 161

Keating, Archbishop of Liverpool, The Right Reverend Frederick William. 273, 302

Kelly, Mary. 137

Kelly, Canon Thomas S. 312, 313

Kerr, Reverend Father. 289, 291, 292

Kerr, Lady Anne, (*née* Fitzalan-Howard). 39, 327

Kerr, Lady Anne Cecil. 39, 44, 45, 46, 47, 50, 57, 61, 123, 132, 149, 177, 180, 196, 204, 210, 217, 240, 241, 260, 261, 278, 282, 301, 304, 305, 311, 314, 318, 321, 327, 328, 334, 337, 360

Kerr, John William Robert, 7th Marquess of Lothian. 39, 327

Kerr, Major General Ralph Drury. 39, 327

Kershaw, Reverend Father F.W. 328

Kilkenny. 325

King, Jessie. 174, 175

Knight, Bishop of Shrewsbury, The Right Reverend Edmund. 125

Knights of St Columbus. 342

Konnersreuth. 163

Landing Stage, Liverpool, The. 338

Larkfield Lane, Southport, Lancashire. 362

Lateau, Louise. 53, 54, 162, 163, 199, 281

La Stigmatisation, l'ecstase divine, les miracles de Lourdes, réponse aux libres penseurs. (Imbert-Goubeyre). 163

Lauriston Gardens, Edinburgh. 166, 167, 168

Lauriston Street, Edinburgh. 298

Lawfield Tower, Dalkeith. 284

Lazzari, Domenica. 281

Lea, S.J., Reverend Father W. 76, 79, 82, 87, 286, 291

Lechler, Dr. Alfred. 161

Leith, S.J., Reverend Father Forbes. 173, 183, 193, 194

Lennon, D.D., Reverend Father James. 46, 49, 104

Leo XIII, Pope. 196

Leopardstown. 325

Lescher, Sister Mary Philip. 42

Letters of Teresa Higginson. Selected and Discussed by a Monk of St Augustine's Abbey. 329

Linlithgow. 174, 301

Liscard, Cheshire. 41, 74

Liverpool Catholic Teachers' Association. 355

Liverpool Diocesan Tribunal. 347

Liverpool Echo. 338

Llanarth. 72

London. 39, 79, 166, 184, 195, 196, 220, 242, 279, 282, 305, 316, 328, 329, 337, 362, 353, 361

London, Bayswater. 184

Lonsdale, Helen. 92, 93, 247, 249, 31, 334, 362

Lonsdale, William. 93, 95, 334

Looe, Cornwall. 184

Loreto. 200

Loreto, Sister Mary. 363, 364

Lothian Street, Edinburgh. 299, 301

Loughglynn House, Roscommon. 17

Lourdes. 52, 163, 296, 339, 345

Lowergate, Clitheroe. 152, 154, 156, 167

Lucerne. 196, 200, 214

Lucy, Dame. (Sister Mary Lucy). 360

Lucy, Sister Mary. 360

Lugano Seminary. 307

Lunn, Reverend Father. 310

Luther, Martin. 360

Luzzatto, Sergio. 163

Lydiate, Lancashire. 139, 173, 198

Lynch, Reverend Father. 73

Lynton, Devonshire. 347

Lyster, George. 11

Macmanus, T. 142

Macpherson, Mr. 177

Macpherson, Mrs. 177

McCurdy, Canon. 338, 356, 361

McKeon, Mrs. Margaret. 298, 301, 332

McLellan, Reverend Father. 254

McLoughlin, B. 244

McNabb, Reverend Father Vincent. 242

McVey, Mrs. Bridget (née McCluskey). 284, 292, 294-297

Maguire, Joseph. 341, 342

Malta. 282, 365

Manchester. 39, 58, 74, 77, 180, 183, 260, 282, 329

Manchester Street, Liverpool. 329

Manosque, Basses Alpes. 69

Marasco, Georges. 277

Marino, Latium. 195

Martindale, S.J. Reverend Father C.C. 316

Mary, Convent of, Sheffield. 333

Mary, Sister. 287

Massabielle, Rock Cave of. 338

Mersey, The River. 10, 41

Milan. 196, 200

Mill on the Floss, The. (Elliot) 20

Mill Road Hospital, Liverpool. 202, 203, 206

Minerva Hotel, Rome. 195

Miraculous Communion. 85, 150, 152, 171

Modern Churchman, The. 259

Molloy, Mrs. 273

Molyneux, Nellie. 59

Montfort. 184

Month, The. 277, 316

Mordan Street, Liverpool. 110

Moreton, Anthony. 334, *335*, 363, 364

Moreton, Gladys. 334, *335*, 345, 363, 364

Mossley Hill, Liverpool. 351

Mount Pleasant College Magazine. 335

Mount Pleasant, Liverpool. 203, *204*, 207, 247, 248, 353, *355*, 356

Mount Street, London. 316

Mrazek, Berthe. 277

Murphy, Edward. 340-343, 345

Murphy, Margaret. 86, 148, 149, 150, *179*, 181, 182, 235, 240, 277, 332, 334, *349*. 350

Murray, Canon. 330

Mussely, Reverend Father (later Canon) John Constant. 86, 97, 148, 149, 150, 166, *178*, *179*, 180, 181, 277, 278, 334

Mystical Marriage. 154, *156*, 164, 165, 169, 171, 177, 242, 322, 329

Mystic Espousal. 69, 159, 164, 322, 329

National Gallery, The. 361

Naughton, Reverend Father J.B. 21

Neston, Cheshire. 8, 77, 87, 92, 104, 105, 107, 116, 117, 120, *129*, *134*, *136*, 138, 143, 144, *145*, *146*, 147, 174, 180, 183, 186, 207, 213, 217-219, 226, 226, 238, 239, 241, 250, 251, 255, 278, 333, 335, 337, 338, *340*, 390, 343, 344, 345, 346, 353, 356, 363

Neston Railway Station. 346

Neumann, Theresa. 163, 281

Newcastle upon Tyne. 72

Newchurch, Lancashire. 147, 148, 149, 150, 152, 166, 356

New Hall. 185

Newman, Cardinal John Henry. 21, 39

Newton Abbot. 21, 39

Newton-le-Willows, Lancashire. 40

New Zealand. 325, 365

Nicholson, Edwin. 88

Nicholson, Ellen or Helen. 85, 89, 90, *91*, *92*, 93, 94, 95, 106, 116, 135, 134, 147, 149, 150, 206, 247, 249, 250, 331, 334, 362

Nicholson, Mary. 88-91, 109

Nicholson, Robert. 89

Nixon, John. 83

Noble, Bishop of Shrewsbury, The Right Reverend Brian M. 364

Noble, Mr. and Mrs. 79-82

North West Catholic History. 328

Norton Bridge Railway Station. 146

Notable British Trials series. 259

Notes on the Life of Teresa Higginson (Canon Snow). 49, 70

Notre Dame, Clapham Common, London, Convent of. 337, 338

Nouvelle Révue Théologique. 316

Oberammergau. 113

Oblates of St Charles. 184

O'Brien, Monsignor John. 61, 294, 295, 317, 338, 347, *348*, 349, 350, 351, 355, 357, 361

O'Carroll, Reverend Father R. 20

O'Hanlon, Mary Agnes. 38

Onkerzele, Belgium. 338, 339, 340, *344*

Ormskirk, Lancashire. 57, 93, 131, 206, 273, 269, 331, 334, *336*

O'Reilly, Bishop of Liverpool. The Right Reverend Bernard. 115, 126, 128, 130, 183

Orrell, Sarah Ann. 153

Orrell, Lancashire. 47

Osbaldeston, Lancashire. 145, 147, 356

O'Sullivan, O.S.B., Reverend Father Adalbert M. 114, 119, 282, 325, *326*, 327, 328

Other Christ: Padre Pio and 19th Century Italy, The. (Luzzatto). 166

Our Lady, Lydiate, Church of. 139

Our Lady and St Joseph's School, Seacombe, Cheshire. 73

Our Lady of Light and St Osyth, Church of. 184

Our Lady of Light, Spouse of the Holy Ghost. 183

Our Lady of Selkirk. 195

Our Lady's Church, Great Mersey Street, Liverpool. 151

Oxford Street, London. 197

Oxton, Mrs. 333

Padua. 196, 200, 270

Paisley. 246, 247

Pantasaph. 104

Paris. 72, 195, 200

Patriarch of Jerusalem, The. 345

Patriarch of Venice, The. 196

Pearson, Thomas. 175

Pendle Hill, Lancashire. 74, *81*

Perry, Sister Mary Aloysius. 33, 35

Philippa, Mother. (formerly Nellie Molyneux). 59

Physical Phenomena of Mysticism, The. (Thurston). 69, 160, 281

Pio, Padre. 161, 163, 166

Pisa. 200

Pitter, S.J., Reverend Father. 177

Pitts, Ann. 329

Pius X, Pope. 196

Pius XI, Pope. 263

Plumb, B. 328

Poole Road, Liscard, Cheshire. 41, 53

Poor Clare Convent, Lynton, Devonshire. 347

Pope, Joseph. 202, 203

Postulator of the Cause in Rome (Monsignor Sordini), The. 355

Powell, Reverend Father Edward. 22, 29, 39, 42-45, 70, 71, 86-88, 91, 92, 96, 97, *98*, 101, *102*, 103-105, 107, 109, 110, 111, 115, 119, 123, 124, 126-133, 137-139, 143, 154, 166, 173, 183, 186, 198, 200, 201, 264, 271, 273, 276, 278, 279, 282, 286, 313, 314, 322-324

Preston, Lancashire. 17, 90

Princes Park, Liverpool. 189

Process, The Diocesan. 302, 317, 355

Pugin, Augustus Welby. 31

Queen Street, Newton Abbot. 222

Quest for Corvo, The. 20

Quick, Mrs. 81

Raby, Cheshire. 344

Ramsgate, Kent. 119, 329, 346

Ratcliffe. 273

Rawtenstall, Lancashire. 147, 181

Raymond Buildings, Gray's Inn, London. 305

Reni, Guido. 361

Ripley, Reverend Father (later Canon) Francis J. 329, 361

Roberts, Elizabeth. 11, 13, 107, 109

Robin Hood's Cave, Nottingham. 36

Rodney Street, Liverpool. 352

Rolfe, Frederick William Serafino Austin Lewis Mary. (Baron Corvo). 20

Rome. 8, 17, 18, 39, 44, 61, 195, 196, 200, 242, 302, 303, 305, 312, 320, 325, 327, 347, 351, 355, 357, 361-365

Rosary Beads of St Teresa, The. 59, 60, 332, 333

Roscommon. 17, 20

Roskell, The Right Reverend Richard. 21, 31, 38, 39, 177

Rouen. 200

Roughead, William. 175

Rowntree, Mr. 353, 354

Royal Humane Society, The. 223

Ruff, Teresa's dog. 218, 229

Ryan, Reverend Father John David. 335, 336

Ryland, Elizabeth. 51

Ryland, James. 51

Ryland, Susan (later Sister Mary St Barbara). 46, 50, *51*, 53, 54, 55, 60, 64-66, 70, 72, 73, 77, 82, 84, 100, 101, 103, 104, 123, 280, 304, 311, 334, 345

St Alban's School, Liscard, Cheshire. 41

St Alexander's Church, Bootle. 42, 44, 88, *93*, *96*, *97*, 107, 108, 121, 130, 131, 137, 139, 246, 261, 312

St Alexander's School, Bootle. 15, 42, 44, 58, 87, 107, 110, 135, 147, 243, 244, 245, 248, 251

St Aloysius Church, Wallasey, Cheshire. 337

St Alphonsus de Liguori. 270

St Ambrose. 196, 270

St Andrew's Convent, Eskbank, near Edinburgh. 174

St Anne's Passionist Retreat, Sutton, St Helens. 39

St Anne's School, the Cowgate, Edinburgh. 298

St Anthony of Padua. 270

St Benedict of Nursia. 325

St Catherine of Ricci. 164

St Catherine of Siena. 164, 259, 279

St Cecilia's Church, Tuebrook, Liverpool. 345

St Charles. 184, 196

St Clare. 196

St Clare's Church, Arundel Avenue, Liverpool. 365

St Clement. 270

St Colette. 164

St Cuthbert's College, Ushaw, Durham. 49

St David's Church, Dalkeith. 284

St David's School, Dalkeith. 284, 294, 301

St Edward's College, St Domingo Road, Everton, Liverpool. 43, 115

St Francis' Church, Edinburgh. 298

St Francis de Sales Church, Walton, Liverpool. 127, 138, 143

St Francis of Assisi. 104, 139, 160, 161, 195, 196, 236

St Gemma Galgani. 263, 280

St Gotthard, The. 196

St Helens, Lancashire. 39, 40, 45, 76, 356

St Ignatius' School, Edinburgh. 252, 301

St John. 38, 44, 54, 124, 152, 164, 171, 231, 283, 316, 319

St John, Mrs. 184

St John's Road, Bootle. 42, 88

St Katharine Drexel. 242

St Margaret Mary Alcoque. 125, 135

St Mary's Abbey, Woolmer Hill, Haslemere, Surrey. 360

St Mary's Church, Aughton, Lancashire. 93, 131, *133*, 142, *339*

St Mary's Church, Chorley, Lancashire. 331

St Mary's Infant School, Wigan. 47, 44, *47*, *50*, 57, 71, 73, 99, 103, 111

St Mary's Mixed School, Sabden, Lancashire. 74, *75*, *76*

St Mary's School, Edinburgh. 298, 301

St Matthew. 367

St Michael. 282

St Michael and St John the Evangelist's Church, Clitheroe. 152, *153*

St Mirren's. 246

St Oswald and St Edmund's Church, Ashton-in-Makerfield, Lancashire. 329

St Patrick's Church, Manchester. 39, 180

St Patrick's Church, South Gray's Close, Edinburgh. 174

St Peter's School, Newchurch, Lancashire. 147

St Philip's Church, Birmingham. 78

St Severus. 270

St Sylvester's Church, Silvester Street, Liverpool. 151

St Teresa of Avila. 20, 164

St Thomas Aquinas. 265

St Veronica Giuliani. 164

St Walburga, Church of. 199

St Wilfred's Church, Hulme, Manchester. 330

St Winefride's Church, Holywell. 20, 104

St Winefride's Cottage, the schoolhouse, Little Neston. 8, 87, 120, *134*, *145*, *146*, 239, 335, *340*, 343, 361, 363

Sabden, Lancashire. 74, *75*, *76*, *78*, 79, 80, *81*, 82-84, 87, 120, 313, 356

'Sacerdos'. 259

Sacred College, Rome, The. 359

380

Sacred Congregation of Rites, The. 302, 303, 355

Sacred Head, Devotion to the. 86, 87, 104, 118, 120-122, 124, 126-128, 139, 147, 158, 167, 179, 184, 185, 186, 201, 240, 251, 260, 261, 264-268, 283, 287, 288, 300, 301, 319, 322, 323, 368, 339, 358, 359, 361

Sacred Heart Church, Lauriston, Edinburgh. 301

Sacred Heart of Betharram, Order of the. 345

Sagesse. 204, 242, 329

Salford Teachers' Guild. 329

San Damiano, Covent of. 196

Santa Maria in Lata. 351

Scala Santa, The. 196

Scots College, Rome. 195

Seacombe, Cheshire. 73

Sefton Park, Liverpool. 356

Selkirk. 173, 183, 193, 195, 301

Servants of Jesus-Wisdom. 242

Shrewsbury. 39, 125, 363, 364

Shuttleworth, Miss. 136

Silly Billy. 192

Sisters of Charity, Beacon Lane, Everton, Liverpool, Convent of the. 41

Sisters of Charity, Selly Park, Birmingham, Convent of St Paul of the Cross. 72

Sisters of Mercy, Derby Road, Nottingham, Convent of the. 22, 31

Sisters of Mercy, St Catherine's Convent, Lauriston Gardens, Edinburgh. 166, 187

Sisters of Notre Dame, Mount Pleasant, Liverpool, Convent of the. 141, 353

Skeehan, Reverend Father. 362

Smith, Miss. (shopkeeper). 141

Smith, Reverend Father. 28, 29, 39

Smith, Mrs. Marie Farron. 295

Smith, Reverend Father Thomas. 127, 128, 138, 143

Smith, William H. 194, 195-196

Snow, Reverend Father (later Canon) Alfred. 22, 27, 30, 34, 49, 58, 59, 62, 70, 84, 86, 93, 102, 114, 118, 119, 123, 124, 127, 129, 131, 133, 137-140, 142, 143, 147, 148, 150, 152, 165-167, 169-171, 173, 177, 183, 185, 187-190, 198, 199, 201, 205, 207, 209, 211-213, 217, 219, 225, 227, 228, 232-235, 243, 273, 280, 288, 292, 312, 314, 321-323, 331, 333, 334, 339, 342

Society for Psychical Research, The. 259

Sordini, Monsignor Fillipo. 355

Soubirous, Bernadette. 338

South Africa. 365

Southampton. 364

Southport, Lancashire. 80, 354, 362

Spain. 59, 287, 344

Spanaciani, Sister Mary. 164

Spencer, Reverend Father Ignatius. 45, 46, 167

Statt, Mrs. Caroline. 222, 223

Stigmata. 16, 53, 54, 63, 67, 103, 160, 161, 163, 171, 285-287, 294, 324, 326, 366

Stockbridge, Edinburgh. 174

Stone, Staffordshire. 21, 39, 146

Stonehaven, Aberdeenshire. 254

Stonyhurst. 17, 126

Stourbridge, Worcestershire. 72

Strowbridge, Tom. 253

Subiaco. 325

Summers, Montague. 145

Supernatural Omnibus, The. 145

Sutton, St Helens, Lancashire. 39, 45

Tablet, The. 258, 302, 304, 305, 307, 308, 310, 312, 313, 315-318, 320, 323, 359, 360

Taggart, John. 341, 342

Teignmouth, Devonshire. 223, 226, 227, 233, 253, 282

Teresa Lonsdale, Aunt. 247

Teresa Helena Higginson. (Catholic Truth Society pamphlet – Kerr). 260, 318

"Teresa Helena Higginson (1844-1905): A Bibliography." 328

Teresa Helena Higginson: A Short Account of Her Life and Letters. (Kershaw). 329

Teresa Helena Higginson: Servant of God. (Pitts & Dolores). 329

Teresa Helena Higginson: Servant of God. "The Spouse of the Crucified." 1844-1905. (Kerr). 328

Teresa Higginson: The Servant of God: School Teacher, 1845-1905: A Memoir. (O'Sullivan). 328

Thompson, Reverend Father Bernard. 239

Thornton Hough, Wirral. 363

Thurston, S.J., Reverend Herbert. 69, 160, 260, 262-264, 271, 277, 279-281, 308, 310, 317-319, 323

Tilberry, Ellen. 20

Trelawney, Cornwall. 184

Trelawney, Sir Henry. 184

Trent Port, Nottinghamshire. 20

Tresidder, Dr. William E. 221, 226

Trial of Peter Barnes and Others. (I.R.A. Coventry explosion). 259

Trial of John Thomas Straffen. 259

Tunstall, Reverend Father E. 147

Turin. 200

Turret, Keble Road, Bootle, The. 247

Uganda. 365

Ugbrooke. 253, 254

Ullathorne, O.S.B., Bishop of Birmingham, The Right Reverent William. 125

Ulverston, Lancashire. 17

Une grande Inconnue ou Les merveilles d'une simple vie. 329

United States of America. 277, 337, 365, 366

The Universe. 360

University of Lierpool. 353

Upper Warwick Street, Liverpool. 189

Upton, The Wirral, Cheshire. 345

Ushaw. 39, 49, 62, 104

Van Roey, Cardinal. 339

Vaughan, Cardinal Herbert Alfred. 184, 186

Venice. 196, 200

Vice-Postulator, A. 318-320, 347, 348, 355

Walburga, Mother Mary. 37

Wallasey, Cheshire. 74, 337

Walshe, Dr. (later Sir) Francis Martin Rouse. 258, 302, 320, 322

Walton, Liverpool 127, 138, 143

Warlomont, Dr. M. 163

Weld, S.J., Monsignor Alfred. 126, 127

Wells, Reverend Father Thomas. 49, 50, 52, 53, 55, 61-64, 66, 67, 70, 71, 73, 84, 99-101, 103, 123

West, Rebecca. 282

West Derby Union Board of Guardians. 206

West Indies. 282, 365

West Port, Edinburgh. 298

West Rasen, Lincolnshire. 35, 113

Whaley Bridge, Derbyshire. 36

Whalley Railway Station. 84

What Father Cuthbert Knew, (Christmas). 145

Whiteside, Archbishop of Liverpool, The Right Reverend Thomas. 183

Widdowson, Mrs. Winifred (*née* Lonsdale). 331

Wigan. 10, 47, 50, 51, 68, 71, 73, 98, 101, 111, 120, 123, 249, 286, 304, 313, 334, 356

Wilberforce, Reverend Father Arthur Henry Bertram. 118, 126, 146, 264, 282

Willaston Road, Thornton Hough, Wirral. 363

Wirral, The. 8, 329, 356, 363

Woodward, Margaret. 47, 53, 55, 57, 60, 63, 64, 66, 67, 100, 120

Woolmer Hill, Haslemere, Surrey. 360

Workhouse, The Liverpool. 203, 206, 255

Worlock, Archbishop of Liverpool, The Right Reverend Derek. 362

Wutz, Dr. 163

Xavier, Sister Mary. (formerly Eliza Cowlam). 97

Zug, Switzerland. 200

Zurich. 200

RICHARD WHITTINGTON-EGAN was born in Liverpool in 1924. He originally read medicine and was to qualify for the Bar, but his career was interrupted by the Second World War, in which he served with the army in France, Switzerland, Germany, Austria and Italy.

He spent 30 years as a journalist and critic on Fleet Street and contributed articles and reviews to many of Britain's leading newspapers and periodicals. He has also been a frequent broadcaster and made many appearances on television.

Richard is a director of Britain's oldest monthly magazine, *Contemporary Review*, founded in 1866. The author of over 25 books, he has published widely on criminous and medico-legal matters and is an acknowledged world authority on Jack the Ripper.